P9-ECW-612

THOUGHTS
AND ADVENTURES

THOUGHTS
AND ADVENTURES

by
THE RT. HON.
WINSTON S. CHURCHILL
O.M., C.H., M.P.

ODHAMS PRESS LIMITED
LONG ACRE, LONDON

First Published November, 1932
First Published by Odhams Press Ltd. 1947
Reprinted 1948, 1949

MADE AND PRINTED IN GREAT BRITAIN
BY JOHN GARDNER (PRINTERS) LIMITED, LITHERLAND, LIVERPOOL, 20
S.149.3R.T.

CONTENTS

CONTENTS

PUBLISHER'S NOTE TO NEW EDITION

THE reminiscences and reflections which make up this volume are a selection of the articles that Mr. Churchill wrote for publication in newspapers and periodicals between 1924 and 1931, and the text for this edition is that used for the first publication in volume form in 1932.

Although largely exhibiting Mr. Churchill in a rather lighter vein than usual, few of these papers are wholly unshadowed by war, whether by the smoke of the actual cannonade or by the lowering cloud upon the horizon ahead, and many pages will be found to have acquired a different emphasis for readers today. In particular they will not need Mr. Churchill's exhortation, contained in his Preface, to treat seriously the two articles SHALL WE ALL COMMIT SUICIDE? and FIFTY YEARS HENCE. His dismal forebodings of a bomb no bigger than an orange, which might blast a township at a stroke, no longer need justification; nor has the danger become less remote that mankind may become enslaved to the soulless mechanisms it has begotten.

September, 1947.

THE WORKS OF
WINSTON SPENCER CHURCHILL

The following is a list of all the works of Winston Spencer Churchill that have been issued in volume form.

The Story of the Malakand Field Force, 1898; The River War, 1899; Savrola, 1900; London to Ladysmith via Pretoria, 1900; Ian Hamilton's March, 1900; Lord Randolph Churchill, 1906; My African Journey, 1908; Liberalism and the Social Problem, 1909; The World Crisis, 1923-31; My Early Life, 1930; India, 1931; Thoughts and Adventures, 1932; Marlborough, 1933-38; Great Contemporaries, 1937; Arms and the Covenant, 1938; Step by Step, 1939; Into Battle, 1941; The Unrelenting Struggle, 1942; The End of the Beginning, 1943; Onwards to Victory, 1944; The Dawn of Liberation, 1945; Victory, 1946; Secret Session Speeches, 1946; The Sinews of Peace, 1948; The Second World War (Vol. I, The Gathering Storm), 1948; Painting as a Pastime, 1948.

PREFACE TO ORIGINAL EDITION

THE reading of these pages has brought home to me with even more than usual clearness the extreme diversity of event and atmosphere through which a man of my generation, now in its twelfth lustre, has passed and is passing. First the 'settled state of order,' as we now see it bright and diminished in the *camera obscura* of memory, full of colour and action, but on so small a scale that such a trifle as Sidney Street stood out as a peak of adventure and sensation: then the incomparable tragedy of the War: now confusion, uncertainty and peril, the powers of light and darkness perhaps in counterpoise, with Satan and Michael doubtfully reviewing their battalions, and the world, for all we can tell, heading for the cross-roads which may lead to the two alternative Infernos I have tried to adumbrate in *Shall we all Commit Suicide?* and *Fifty Years Hence*: has there ever in history been an epoch of such pith and moment?

Many of these papers touch on the lighter side of grave affairs, but I should be sorry if on this account my two nightmares were taken merely as the amusing speculations of a dilettante Cassandra; for they are offered in deadly earnest as a warning of what may easily come to pass if Civilization cannot take itself in hand and turn its back on those Cities of Destruction and Enslavement to which Science holds the keys.

Meantime the pleasures of life are luckily still with us, and in giving thanks for some of those which have a special appeal to me I have brought my book to a happy ending.

> *Le monde est vieux, dit-on: je le crois; cependant*
> *Il le faut amuser encor comme un enfant.*

WINSTON S. CHURCHILL.

CHARTWELL,
September, 1932.

A SECOND CHOICE

I F I had to live my life over again in the same surroundings, no doubt I should have the same perplexities and hesitations; no doubt I should have my same sense of proportion, my same guiding lights, my same onward thrust, my same limitations. And if these came in contact with the same external facts, why should I not run as the result along exactly the same grooves? Of course if the externals are varied, if accident and chance flow out through new uncharted channels, I shall vary accordingly. But then I should not be living my life over again, I should be living another life in a world whose structure and history would to a large extent diverge from this one.

If, for instance, when I went to Monte Carlo and staked my money on red, as I usually do, having a preference for the optimistic side of things, and the whirling ivory ball had fallen into a red slot in the roulette wheel instead of falling, as it nearly always did on these occasions, into a black slot, I might have made a lot of money. If I had invested this money twenty years ago in plots of land on the lake shore at Chicago and had never gone to Monte Carlo any more, I might be a multi-millionaire. On the other hand, if fired by my good luck I had continued to gamble, I might have become an habitué of the tables, and should now be one of those melancholy shadows we see creeping in the evening around the gaming and so-called pleasure resorts of Europe. Clearly two processes are at work, the first dictating where the ivory ball is to come to rest and the second what reaction it is to produce in me. If both these are to vary, their interplay becomes too intricate for us even to catch one glimpse of what might have been! Therefore let us suppose that the march of events and its freaks and accidents remain as we now know them and that all that happens is that I have another choice.

But now I must ask an important question: Do I have my new choice *with my present knowledge* of what has actually happened? Or am I to have nothing better in health, character, knowledge and faith to guide me next time than I had before? If the latter, our argument comes very quickly to a dead end. If the same choice and the same environment were at any given moment to be repeated, and I were the same person, I should infallibly take the same step. If, for instance, I were the sort of person who would spin a coin to settle whether he should take a journey, or buy a house, or open a lawsuit, or join a government, and the coin in fact came down tails up as it had before, I should certainly act as I did then.

If, then, there is to be any reality in the new choice offered to me to live my life over again, I must have foreknowledge. I must carry back with me to this new starting-point the whole picture and story of the world and of my own part in it, as I now know them. Then surely I shall know what to make for and what to avoid; then surely I shall be able to choose my path with certainty. I shall have success in all my dealings. Thus armed I shall be able to guide others and, indeed, guide the human race away from the follies in which they wallow, away from the errors to which they are slaves, away from the endless tribulations in which they plunge themselves.

But wait a minute. All that I was offered was one choice, to live my life over again. I take back with me to that moment all that I know to-day. But once I have exercised my choice my present picture of existing world's history and all my own life-story is out of date, or rather it will never happen. Of course if I use my foreknowledge only in some trifling matter, that will not make much appreciable difference in the currents of cause and effect. But it will nevertheless make immediately a different world around me.

I might, for instance, without altering the economy of the universe, use my foreknowledge to back the winner of the

Derby at the first moment that I began to live my life over again. But my foreknowledge would give me no assurance about the next Derby. True that in the life of the world as it has worked out, I know the name of the horse which won. But now something new has happened. I have won such an enormous stake that several important bookmakers have defaulted. One of their richest clients was ruined in the crash. In despair he jumped into a pond. The client happened to be the owner of the horse that was going to win the Derby next year. His untimely death of course disqualified his horse. Under our silly rules it was struck out of the race, and I, proceeding to Epsom next year with all my foreknowledge, found myself the most ignorant man on the Downs about what was going to happen. I was so cluttered up with all my recollections of the way the other horses had run in the world as it would have been, that I made the most foolish speculations about what would now happen in the new world which my supernatural intuition had made. Thus we may say that if one had the chance to live one's life over again foreknowledge would, in important decisions, be only fully effective once. Thereafter I should be dealing with a continually diverging skein of consequence which would increasingly affect my immediate environment.

If these thoughts are true about small personal matters, consider how much more potent and how final would be a new choice with foreknowledge upon some great or decisive issue. When my armoured train was thrown off the rails by the Boers in the South African War and I had to try to clear the line under fire, I was obliged to keep getting in and out of the cab of the engine which was our sole motive power. I therefore took off my Mauser pistol, which got in my way. But for this I should forty minutes later have fired two or three shots at twenty yards at a mounted burgher named Botha, who summoned me to surrender. If I had killed him on that day, November 15, 1899, the history of South Africa would certainly have been different and almost certainly would have been less fortunate. This was the Botha who

3

afterward became Commander-in-Chief of the Boers and later Prime Minister of the South African Union. But for his authority and vigour the South African rebellion which broke out at the beginning of the Great War might never have been nipped in the bud. In this case the Australian and New Zealand army corps then sailing in convoy across the Indian Ocean would have been deflected from Cairo to the Cape. All preparations to divert the convoy at Colombo had actually been made. Instead of guarding the Suez Canal it would have fought with the Boer insurgents. By such events both the Australian and South African points of view would have been profoundly altered. Moreover, unless the Anzacs had been available in Egypt by the end of 1914 there would have been no nucleus of an army to attack the Gallipoli Peninsula in the spring, and all that tremendous story would have worked out quite differently. Perhaps it would have been better, perhaps it would have been worse. Imagination bifurcates and loses itself along the ever-multiplying paths of the labyrinth.

But at the moment when I was climbing in and out of the cab of that railway engine in Natal it was a thoughtless and unwise act on my part to lay aside the pistol upon which my chances of escape from a situation in which I was deeply compromised might in fact in a very short time depend. No use to say, 'But if you had known with your foreknowledge that he was not going to shoot you, and that the Boers would treat you kindly and that Botha would become a great man who would unite South Africa more strongly with the British crown, you need not have fired at him.' That is not conclusive. Many other things would have been happening simultaneously. If I had kept my pistol I should have been slower getting in and out of the engine, and I might have been hit by some bullet which as it was missed me by an inch or two, and Botha, galloping forward in hot pursuit of the fugitives from the wreck of the train, might have met—not me with my foreknowledge—but some private soldier with a rifle, who would have shot him dead, while I myself, sent with the wounded into the unhealthy Intombi Spruit hospital at

Ladysmith, should probably have died of enteric fever.

If we look back on our past life we shall see that one of its most usual experiences is that we have been helped by our mistakes and injured by our most sagacious decisions. I suppose if I had to relive my life I ought to eschew the habit of smoking. Look at all the money I have wasted on tobacco. Think of it all invested and mounting up at compound interest year after year. I remember my father in his most sparkling mood, his eye gleaming through the haze of his cigarette, saying, 'Why begin? If you want to have an eye that is true, and a hand that does not quiver, if you want never to ask yourself a question as you ride at a fence, don't smoke.'

But consider! How can I tell that the soothing influence of tobacco upon my nervous system may not have enabled me to comport myself with calm and with courtesy in some awkward personal encounter or negotiation, or carried me serenely through some critical hours of anxious waiting? How can I tell that my temper would have been as sweet or my companionship as agreeable if I had abjured from my youth the goddess Nicotine? Now that I think of it, if I had not turned back to get that matchbox which I left behind in my dug-out in Flanders, might I not just have walked into the shell which pitched so harmlessly a hundred yards ahead?

So far as my own personal course has been concerned, I have mostly acted in politics as I felt I wanted to act. When I have desired to do or say anything and have refrained therefrom through prudence, slothfulness or being dissuaded by others, I have always felt ashamed of myself at the time; though sometimes afterwards I saw that it was lucky for me I was checked. I do not see how it would have been possible for me in the mood I was in after the South African War to have worked enthusiastically with the Conservative party in the mood they were in at that time. Even apart from the Free Trade quarrel, I was in full reaction against the war and they in full exploitation in the political sphere of the so-called victory. Thus when the Protection issue was raised

I was already disposed to view all their actions in the most critical light. The flood tides of a new generation long pent-up flowed forward with the breaking of the dikes upon the low-lying country. Of course it is a lamentable thing to leave the party which you have been brought up in from a child, and where nearly all your friends and kinsmen are. Still, I am sure that in those days I acted in accordance with my deepest feeling and with all that recklessness in so doing which belongs to youth and is indeed the glory of youth and its most formidable quality.

When the Great War broke out and I started with the enormous prestige of having prepared the fleet in spite of so much opposition and of having it ready according to the science of those days, almost to a single ship, at the fateful hour, I made the singular mistake of being as much interested in the military as in the naval operations. Thus, without prejudice to my Admiralty work, I was led into taking minor military responsibilities upon my shoulders which exposed me to all those deadly risks on a small scale that await those in high stations who come too closely in contact with action in detail.

I ought, for instance, never to have gone to Antwerp. I ought to have remained in London and endeavoured to force the Cabinet and Lord Kitchener to take more effective action than they did, while I all the time sat in my position of great authority with all the precautions which shield great authority from rough mischance. Instead, I passed four or five vivid days amid the shells, excitement and tragedy of the defence of Antwerp. I soon became so deeply involved in the local event that I had in common decency to offer to the Government my resignation of my office as First Lord of the Admiralty in order to see things through on the spot. Lucky indeed it was for me that my offer was not accepted, for I should only have been involved in the command of a situation which locally at any rate had already been rendered hopeless by the general course of the War. In all great business very large errors are excused or even unperceived, but in definite and local matters small mistakes are punished out of all proportion. I might well have lost all the esteem I gained by the mobilization and readiness of the fleet, through getting mixed up in the firing-lines at Antwerp. Those who are charged with the direction of supreme affairs must sit on the mountain-tops of control; they must never descend into the valleys of direct physical and personal action.

It seems clear now that when Lord Kitchener went back upon his undertaking to send the 29th Division to reinforce the army gathering in Egypt for the Dardanelles expedition and delayed it for nearly three weeks, I should have been prudent then to have broken off the naval attack. It would have been quite easy to do so, and all arrangements were made upon that basis. I did not do it, and from that moment I became accountable for an operation the vital control of which had passed to other hands. The fortunes of the great enterprise which I had set on foot were henceforward to be decided by other people. But I was to bear the whole burden in the event of miscarriage. Undoubtedly I might have obtained a far larger measure of influence upon the general course of the War if I had detached myself in the Admiralty from all special responsibility and made the ships sail away once the troops were fatally delayed. However, it must not be forgotten that the land attack upon the Gallipoli Peninsula, costly and unsuccessful as it was, played a great part in bringing Italy into the War in the nick of time, kept Bulgaria in awed suspense through the summer of 1915, and before it was finished broke the heart of the Turkish army.

Sometimes our mistakes and errors turn to great good fortune. When the Conservatives suddenly plunged into Protection in 1923, a dozen Liberal constituencies pressed me to be their candidate. And clearly Manchester was for every reason the battle-ground on which I should have fought. A seat was offered me there, which, as it happened, I should in all probability have won. Instead, through some obscure complex I chose to go off and fight against a Socialist in Leicester, where, being also attacked by the Conservatives,

I was of course defeated. On learning of these two results in such sharp contrast, I could have kicked myself. Yet as it turned out, it was the very fact that I was out of Parliament, free from all attachment and entanglement in any particular constituency, that enabled me to make an independent and unbiased judgment of the situation when the Liberals most unwisely and wrongly put the Socialist minority government for the first time into power, thus sealing their own doom.

Thus I found myself free a few months later to champion the anti-Socialist cause in the Westminster by-election, and so regained for a time at least the good will of all those strong Conservative elements, some of whose deepest feelings I share and can at critical moments express, although they have never liked or trusted me. But for my erroneous judgment in the General Election of 1923 I should have never have regained contact with the great party into which I was born and from which I had been severed by so many years of bitter quarrel.

When I survey in the light of these reflections the scene of my past life as a whole, I have no doubt that I do not wish to live it over again. Happy, vivid and full of interest as it has been, I do not seek to tread again the toilsome and dangerous path. Not even an opportunity of making a different set of mistakes and experiencing a different series of adventures and successes would lure me. How can I tell that the good fortune which has up to the present attended me with fair constancy would not be lacking at some critical moment in another chain of causation?

Let us be contented with what has happened to us and thankful for all we have been spared. Let us accept the natural order in which we move. Let us reconcile ourselves to the mysterious rhythm of our destinies, such as they must be in this world of space and time. Let us treasure our joys but not bewail our sorrows. The glory of light cannot exist without its shadows. Life is a whole, and good and ill must be accepted together. The journey has been enjoyable and well worth making—once.

CARTOONS AND CARTOONISTS

I ALWAYS loved cartoons. At my private school at Brighton there were three or four volumes of cartoons from *Punch*, and on Sundays we were allowed to study them. This was a very good way of learning history, or at any rate of learning something. Here, week after week, all the salient events of the world were portrayed in caricature, sometimes grave and sometimes gay. The responsibility of Sir John Tenniel and other famous cartoonists must be very great. Many are the youthful eyes that have rested upon their designs, and many the lifelong impressions formed thereby. I got an entirely erroneous conception of Julius Cæsar from this source.

Mr. Gladstone was frequently portrayed as Julius Cæsar, an august being crowned with myrtle, entitled to the greatest respect, a sort of glorified headmaster. We knew he was Prime Minister and the cleverest man in the country; a man of virtue, correctitude, and impeccability, the sort of man who was always telling you what you had done wrong, and never had to form up and be told what he had done wrong himself; the sort of man who made the rules and enforced them and never had to break them. He was venerable, majestic, formidable, benevolent. So that was what Julius Cæsar was like, a good, great, splendid man! It was quite a surprise to me in later years to learn that Julius Cæsar was the caucus manager of a political party in Rome, that his private life was a scandal, printable only in a learned tongue; that he was a wicked adventurer; that he had absolutely nothing in him that any respectable Victorian could tolerate. This was a shock!

Then there were the cartoons, as one turned the pages over, which showed wars breaking into the political stream.

They seemed to stand out so vividly. Here you saw 'England's Vigil Before the Crimea,' Britannia down on her knees praying in a church with an unsheathed sword in her hand, about to get up and give hell to somebody. There were other cartoons about the Crimea which seemed to indicate that the war had not all been on this high level. In fact, there appeared to be exposures of Government incompetence and horrible neglect of the wounded. We saw Florence Nightingale with a lamp, and a large fleet of ships with funnels and cannons all launched only after the war was over. Thus the Crimean War.

Then came the mutiny in India, and a lovely cartoon of the British Lion's vengeance on the Bengal Tiger. A great fierce lion leaping downwards through the air, and the caitiff tiger crouching sideways, most ill-placed to receive the impact!

Then came the Franco-Prussian War, beginning with a cartoon of King William as the guest of Napoleon III. singing: 'I'm a young man from the country, but you can't come over me.' Then we saw real European war between the greatest nations, shells bursting into pieces visible as they separated, and with a bang you could almost hear. France defeated—a woman, beautiful and terrific in distress, resisting sword in hand amid the explosions a blond and apparently irresistible Germania. Golly! How I sympathized with France!

And then, over the page, France prostrate but still with her broken sword in hand, and the German woman (not nearly so good-looking, in fact rather fat, but stronger than ever) standing over her, also sword in hand, saying: 'And for my security you shall cede me these fortresses.' To which the prostrate France replied: 'Not an inch of our territory, not a stone of our fortresses!' How could I not champion France? All the English boys who grew up then had this idea somewhere in their minds and pictured France ill-treated, beaten down, unchivalrously used by a sort of suet-dumpling Germany, uncommonly efficient and punctual, and with that very sharp sword. All of them got the notion that it would be a fine thing and only fair if some day this same broken, trampled France stood up and had her revenge upon the dumpling lady. Presently, when in later volumes and later years I saw the most famous of all cartoons—Tenniel's 'Dropping the Pilot'—and that silly young German Emperor getting rid of Bismarck, it seemed as if France might some day have her chance.

Here, too, I gained my first great interest in the American Civil War. First of all, Mr. Punch was against the South, and we had a picture of a fierce young woman, Miss Carolina, about to whip a naked slave, a sort of Uncle Tom, with a kind of scourge which, not being yet myself removed out of the zone of such possibilities, I regarded as undoubtedly severe. I was all for the slave. Then later on the Yankees came on the scene. There was a whole regiment of them running away from a place called Bull Run; their muskets, with bayonets fixed, were on their shoulders as they doubled in fours, and their noses were long and red. They ran very fast, and the signpost pointed to Canada. The legend was 'I'se gwine to take Canada.' So Mr. Punch had turned against the North; and apparently there was a row between the North and England too. However, the war went on, and there was a picture of North and South, two savage, haggard men in shirts and breeches, grappling and stabbing each other with knives as they reeled into an abyss called Bankruptcy. Finally, I seem to remember a picture of Lincoln's tomb, and Britannia, very sad, laying a wreath upon the cold marble, rather like the one we used to see on Mr. Gladstone-Cæsar's brow.

It was with these impressions in mind that one read the history books. They have great power indeed, the cartoonists. All the antagonisms of nations and of individuals are displayed in their harshest terms; and children, poring in wonderment at them, take it for granted that these were the real moves on the great chess-board of life. But anyhow, whatever children get or got from the dead pages of *Punch*, cartoons are the regular food on which the grown-up children of to-day

11

SIR JOHN TENNIEL.

THE AMERICAN CIVIL WAR

are fed and nourished. On these very often they form their views of public men and public affairs; on these very often they vote. Luckily, however, if you have enough on all sides and on every question, they lose their potency, and things do not work out so badly as one might expect.

But how, reader—gentle reader, as the Victorians used to say—would you like to be cartooned yourself? How would you like to feel that millions of people saw you always in the most ridiculous situations, or portrayed as every kind of wretched animal, or with a nose on your face like a wart, when really your nose is quite a serviceable and presentable member? How would you like to feel that millions of people think of you like that?—that shocking object, that contemptible being, that wretched tatterdemalion, a proper target for public hatred and derision! Fancy having that process going on every week, often every day, over the whole of your life; and all your fellow-countrymen and friends and family seeing you thus held up to mockery and shame!

Would it not worry you? After all, you cannot go round and say to all the spectators: 'This cartoon is not true; it is not correct; it is not fair. My nose is not like that; my hat is not so small; look at it; see, you can put it on your own fat head. Is it not big enough?' Or, 'I was not in a ridiculous position on this question. I acted from high motives and on solid arguments. Read my speech of the twenty-sixth of January three years ago. There are five pages of it in Hansard; that will show you where I stand. And I did not get the worst of it. On the contrary, in the long run justice was done, and I triumphed.' Oh, no, you can't do that. You never can catch up. You can never correct these first impressions. All these new generations growing up will only know that you have a bloated appearance and a wart of a nose, and have always been scored-off. How would you like that, gentle reader?

But it is not so bad as you would expect. Just as eels are supposed to get used to skinning, so politicians get used to being caricatured. In fact, by a strange trait in human nature they even get to like it. If we must confess it, they are quite offended and downcast when the cartoons stop. They wonder what has gone wrong, they wonder what they have done amiss. They fear old age and obsolescence are creeping upon them. They murmur: 'We are not mauled and maltreated as we used to be. The great days are ended.'

My father, Lord Randolph Churchill, was over five feet nine and a half inches—quite a passable stature—but because he was depicted in conflict with Mr. Gladstone, he was always represented as a midget, a midget with enormous moustaches, and great fierce, bulbous eyes. The first recipe for caricaturing Lord Randolph Churchill was to take a bulldog or a pugdog and you could not go far wrong. After that you put this head on the body of a mannikin, and against it you drew this magnificent Gladstone, dressed like the disreputable Julius Cæsar (as I have now found him out to be). To this day I get letters from old people asking how tall my father really was. 'Is it really true he was more than five feet high? We had a bet about it at our club last night. Perhaps you wouldn't mind telling us if it was so. It was agreed your answer should settle it.' So I suppose that long after I have passed beyond the pencils of cartoonists my son will have to write and answer letters, saying that my nose was not like a wart, and my hats were well fitted by one of the best hatters in London.

Here is a cartoon by Poy. I was sent out to Cairo as Colonial Secretary to settle the fortunes of Palestine and Mesopotamia. I had no sooner got to Cairo than the political situation in London, which had seemed halycon calm, broke up into a cyclone. Mr. Bonar Law's health and spirits collapsed and he resigned. I had taken my paint-box to Cairo, and while the Conference was working under my guidance I made some lovely pictures of the Pyramids. Of course, I was neglected in all the rearrangements which took place in London. Lord Northcliffe was delighted with this cartoon. He sent me the original. He was particularly pleased with the little Arab newsvendor. He thought it splendid. He roared with merriment as he pointed its beauties out to me. I accepted the gift with a stock grin. Of course, it was only a joke, but there was quite enough truth in it for it to be more funny to others than to oneself!

Low is the greatest of our modern cartoonists. The greatest because of the vividness of his political conceptions, and because he possesses what few cartoonists have—a grand technique of draughtsmanship. He has all the knowledge and flair of the late Sir Frederick Carruthers-Gould. But Gould only drew with great difficulty. Low is a master of black and white; he is the Charlie Chaplin of caricature, and tragedy and comedy are the same to him. Low is at once made and hampered by his upbringing. He is a little pre-War Australian radical. When he was growing to years of discretion, the best

POY.

IMAGINE BEING CAUGHT LIKE THIS!
While Mr. Churchill was painting the Pyramids, a Cabinet crisis
had broken out in England.

way of getting a laugh was to gibe at the established order of things, and especially at the British Empire. Here was the British Empire emerging into conscious existence fanned by the quiet loyalty of hundreds of millions of faithful people under every sky and climate. To jeer at its fatted soul was the

15

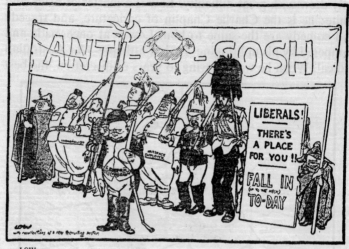

LOW.

THE RECRUITING PARADE
During the election of 1924

delight of the green-eyed young Antipodean radical. And as the Empire, etc., seemed strong enough to stand anything, the process was not only amusing and profitable; it was safe. Anyhow, this mood governed Low's outlook; and governs it to-day. There he is, with his little tyke and his Joan Bull and her baby, deriding regularly everything that is of importance to our self-preservation.

Now look at his cartoon dealing with the election of 1924. There is not a figure in it that is not instinct with maliciously-perceived truth. Really it is a masterpiece. When it appeared in the *Star* I was so tickled with it that I wrote and offered to purchase it. So they sent it me as a handsome gift. I showed it to Lord Birkenhead. He had not seen it before. I said cheerfully: 'What a wonderful caricaturist! He gets you to a nicety. It's astonishing how like you are to your cartoons.' F. E. took up the picture, all beautifully framed, and gazed at it pensively, rather a solemn look coming over the grave and charming lines of his face, and handed it back to me with

16

the remark: 'You seem to be the only one who's flattered.'
I thought this very good.

Afterwards he began to resent Low's cartoons of him.
Certainly the loathing and contempt which our Australian
radical put into his pencil were obvious; and when the cartoons extended to deriding the entire Smith family without
respect of age or sex, he had good grounds for complaint.
He never forgave the insults.

Next is a very recent cartoon by Low. Here he is particularly mischievous. This truly Laboucherian jester has been
engaged by Lord Beaverbrook's *Evening Standard,* supposed
to be a Conservative paper. But Low's pencil is not only not
servile, it is essentially mutinous. You cannot bridle the wild
ass of the desert, still less prohibit its natural hee-haw. Grave
issues had arisen about India. A fierce by-election was afoot
in London in which Lord Beaverbrook was greatly interested.
Low was all for a retreat in India, and for this purpose he
supposes Mr. Baldwin is on his side. He has always demanded
absolute freedom of composition, subject to an editorial right

LOW.

ON THE SPOT

The 'bumping off' of Mr. Baldwin for his Indian policy. Mr. Churchill (Cigarface) in the taxi

17

STRUBE

MR. CHURCHILL AS CHANCELLOR OF THE EXCHEQUER INTRODUCING 'THE
LITTLE MAN'—MR. JOHN BULL

to refuse the goods at their own loss. He thought: 'Nothing will do Mr. Churchill and my chief more harm and nothing will more prejudice this by-election than if I can represent the whole of the public ferment concentrated thereupon as if it were a frame-up by Chicago gangsters to bump-off the good, wise, and venerable, but rather tedious Mr. B.' I owe him no grudge. *Tout comprendre c'est tout pardonner*.

These two cartoons by Strube are very good examples of his genial spirit. His great creation of the 'Little Man' has

CAPTIVES OF THE GREAT HOWSUF K'HOMENS BEING LED BACK

A RARE FRAGMENT FROM THE
A cartoon by Poy on the resumption of

18

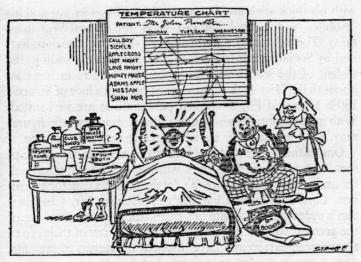

STRUBE.

DERBY FEVER—NEARING THE CRISIS

Published in 1927 after Mr. Churchill as Chancellor of the Exchequer had introduced his measure for taxing betting

become as much a reality in the popular mind as any live subject of caricature. Strube's Little Man is very different from Poy's Mr. John Citizen; but there is this in common between them: they both exhibit trials and misfortunes descending ceaselessly upon a weak and battered being. What a gulf separates these characterizations of our national type from the bluff, strong, hale, and hearty John Bull of former times,

IN CHAINS TO THE PALACE OF HOUESTMHINSTA, A.D. 1931.

'MEDES AND PERSIANS' EXHIBITION

Parliament, Jan. 1931, inspired by Exhibition

19

with his thick stick and his square-topped bowler hat and his resolute, rugged face! The change is due to post-War mentality. The exhausted nation weighed down by taxation, harried by Socialists; its trade declining, its doles expanding; the trident of the sea already gone, and the sceptre in the East about to fall! For such situations the careworn face of Strube's Little Man and Poy's haggard paterfamilias are well-suited. With a new mentality and a new outlook more cheerful figures may, we hope, soon be devised to greet returning fortune.

One of the most necessary features of a public man's equipment is some distinctive mark which everyone learns to look for and to recognize. Disraeli's forelock, Mr. Gladstone's collars, Lord Randolph Churchill's moustache, Mr. Chamberlain's eyeglass, Mr. Baldwin's pipe—these 'properties' are of the greatest value. I have never indulged in any of them, so to fill the need cartoonists have invented the legend of my hats. This arose in the following way. I was at Southport during the General Election of 1910. I went for a walk with my wife along the sands. A very tiny felt hat—I do not know where it came from—had been packed with my luggage. It lay on the hall table, and without thinking I put it on. As we came back from our walk, there was the photographer, and he took a picture. Ever since, the cartoonists and paragraphists have dwelt on my hats; how many they are; how strange and queer; and how I am always changing them, and what importance I attach to them, and so on. It is all rubbish, and it is all founded upon a single photograph. Well, if it is a help to these worthy gentlemen in their hard work, why should I complain? Indeed, I think I will convert the legend into a reality by buying myself a new hat on purpose!

The most fierce and terrible cartoonist was Louis Raemakers. The agony of the War drew from his pencil more savage expressions of hate than I have ever seen elsewhere in black and white. Certainly he was able to put into his drawings a passion of protest and scorn which no words, spoken or written, could ever convey. Max Beerbohm has also a great dramatic power. No series of cartoons is more impressive than those in which he portrays the varying relationships of France and Germany in the last hundred years. In twelve pages of drawings the history of a terrible century is laid bare so plainly that everyone can feel it, and so profoundly that even the most deeply-instructed person finds his imagination and memories stirred.

I rather enjoy commenting on these cartoonists, and putting them in their proper places. It makes me feel I am 'getting my own back.' Farewell to them—grave and gay, kind and spiteful, true and misleading. There is a great tide of good nature and comprehension in civilized mankind which sweeps to and fro and washes all the pebbles against each other, cleans the beach of seaweed, strawberry-baskets and lobster-pots. Hurrah for the tide!

CONSISTENCY IN POLITICS

No one has written more boldly on this subject than Emerson:

'Why should you keep your head over your shoulder? Why drag about this corpse of your memory, lest you contradict somewhat you have stated in this or that public place? Suppose you should contradict yourself; what then? . .

'A foolish consistency is the hobgoblin of little minds, adored by little statesmen and philosophers and divines . . .

'Speak what you think now in hard words and to-morrow speak what to-morrow thinks in hard words again, though it contradict everything you said to-day.'

These are considerable assertions, and they may well stimulate thought upon this well-worn topic. A distinction should be drawn at the outset between two kinds of politicai inconsistency. First, a Statesman in contact with the moving current of events and anxious to keep the ship on an even keel and steer a steady course may lean all his weight now on one side and now on the other. His arguments in each case when contrasted can be shown to be not only very different in character, but contradictory in spirit and opposite in direction: yet his object will throughout have remained the same. His resolves, his wishes, his outlook may have been unchanged; his methods may be verbally irreconcilable. We cannot call this inconsistency. In fact it may be claimed to be the truest consistency. The only way a man can remain consistent amid changing circumstances is to change with them while preserving the same dominating purpose. Lord Halifax on being derided as a trimmer made the celebrated reply: 'I trim as the temperate zone trims between the climate in which men are roasted and the climate in which they are frozen.'

No greater example in this field can be found than Burke. His *Thoughts on the Present Discontents*, his writings and speeches on the conciliation of America, form the main and lasting armoury of Liberal opinion throughout the English-speaking world. His *Letters on a Regicide Peace*, and *Reflections on the French Revolution*, will continue to furnish Conservatives for all time with the most formidable array of opposing weapons. On the one hand he is revealed as a foremost apostle of Liberty, on the other as the redoubtable champion of Authority. But a charge of political inconsistency applied to this great life appears a mean and petty thing. History easily discerns the reasons and forces which actuated him, and the immense changes in the problems he was facing which evoked from the same profound mind and sincere spirit these entirely contrary manifestations. His soul revolted against tyranny, whether it appeared in the aspect of a domineering Monarch and a corrupt Court and Parliamentary system, or whether, mouthing the watch-words of a non-existent liberty, it towered up against him in the dictation of a brutal mob and wicked sect. No one can read the Burke of Liberty and the Burke of Authority without feeling that here was the same man pursuing the same ends, seeking the same ideals of society and Government, and defending them from assaults, now from one extreme, now from the other. The same danger approached the same man from different directions and in different forms, and the same man turned to face it with incomparable weapons, drawn from the same armoury, used in a different quarter, but for the same purpose.

It is inevitable that frequent changes should take place in the region of action. A policy is pursued up to a certain point; it becomes evident at last that it can be carried no further. New facts arise which clearly render it obsolete; new difficulties, which make it impracticable. A new and possibly the opposite solution presents itself with overwhelming force. To abandon the old policy is often necessarily to adopt the new. It sometimes happens that the same men, the same Government, the same Party have to execute this *volte face*. It may be their duty to do so because it is the sole manner of discharging their responsibilities, or because they are the only combination strong enough to do what is needed in the new circumstances. In such a case the inconsistency is not merely verbal, but actual, and ought to be boldly avowed. In place of arguments for coercion, there must be arguments for conciliation; and these must come from the same lips as the former. But all this may be capable of reasonable and honourable explanation. Statesmen may say bluntly, 'We have failed to coerce; we have now to conciliate,' or alternatively, 'We have failed to conciliate; we have now to coerce.'

Ireland with its mysterious and sinister influence has been responsible for many changes of this kind in British politics. We see Mr. Gladstone in 1886 after five years of coercion, after the fiercest denunciation of Irish Nationalists 'marching through rapine to the disintegration of the Empire,' turn in a month to those policies of reconciliation to which the rest of his life was devoted. Mr. Gladstone in his majestic and saintly manner gave many comforting and convincing reasons for his change, and there is no doubt that his whole nature was uplifted and inspired by his new departure. But behind all the eloquence and high-sounding declamation there was a very practical reason for his change, which in private at any rate he did not conceal.

During the interval between the fall of his Government in 1885 and his resumption of power in 1886, a Conservative Government held office with the support of the Irish vote, and the people—wrongly no doubt but sincerely—thought the Conservatives were themselves meditating a solution of the Irish problem on Home Rule lines. Confronted with this supposed fact he felt it impossible for the Liberal Party to march further along the path of coercion and a denial of Irish claims. But Mr. Gladstone was wrong in his judgment of the impending Conservative action. The Conservative Party would never at that stage have been capable of a Home Rule policy. They might have coquetted with the Irish vote as a manœuvre in their fierce political battle with the Liberals; but any decided advance towards Home Rule would have split them from end to end, dethroned their leaders in such a course, and destroyed the power of the Party as a governing instrument. Mr. Gladstone gave to his opponents through this miscalculation what was virtually a twenty years' reign of power. Nevertheless the judgment of history will probably declare that Mr. Gladstone was right both in his resistance to Home Rule up to a certain point and in his espousal of it thereafter. Certainly the change which he made upon this question in 1886, for which he was so much condemned, was in every way a lesser change than that which was made by the whole Conservative Party on this same question thirty-five years later in 1921.

Apart from action in the march of events, there is an inconsistency arising from a change of mood or heart. '*Le cœur a ses raisons que la raison ne connaît pas.*' Few men avoid such changes in their lives, and few public men have been able to conceal them. Usually youth is for freedom and reform, maturity for judicious compromise, and old age for stability and repose. The normal progression is from Left to Right, and often from extreme Left to extreme Right. Mr. Gladstone's progress was by a striking exception in the opposite direction. In the immense period covered by his life he moved steadily and irresistibly from being 'the rising hope of stern unbending Tories' to become the greatest Liberal statesman of the nineteenth century. Enormous was the change of mood which this august transition represented. From the young Member of Parliament whose speech against the abolition of slavery attracted the attention of the House of Commons in 1833, from the famous Minister who supported the Confederate States against the North in the sixties, to the fiery orator who pleaded the cause of Bulgarian independence in the eighties, and the veteran Premier, the last scraps of whose matchless strength were freely offered in the nineties to the cause of Irish self-government—it was a transit almost astronomical in its scale.

It were a thankless theme to examine how far ambition to lead played its unconscious but unceasing part in such an evolution. Ideas acquire a momentum of their own. The stimulus of a vast concentration of public support is almost irresistible in its potency. The resentments engendered by the warfare of opponents, the practical responsibilities of a Party Leader—all take a hand. And in the main great numbers are at least an explanation for great changes. 'I have always marched,' said Napoleon, 'with the opinion of four or five millions of men.' To which, without risking the reproach of cynicism, we may add two other sayings: 'In a democratic country possessing representative institutions it is occasionally necessary to defer to the opinions of other people'; and, 'I am their leader; I must follow them.' The integrity of Mr. Gladstone's career is redeemed by the fact that these two last considerations played a far smaller part in his life than in those of many lesser public men whose consistency has never been impugned.

It is evident that a political leader responsible for the direction of affairs must, even if unchanging in heart or objective, give his counsel now on the one side and now on the other of many public issues. Take for instance the strength and expense of the armed forces of a country in any particular period. This depends upon no absolute or natural law. It relates simply to the circumstances of the time and to the view that a man may hold of the probability of dangers, actual or potential, which threaten his country. Would there, for instance, be any inconsistency in a British Minister urging the most extreme and rapid naval preparations in the years preceding the outbreak of the Great War with Germany, and advocating a modest establishment and strict retrenchment in the years following the destruction of the German naval power? He might think that the danger had passed and had carried away with it the need for intense preparation. He might believe that a long period of peace would follow the exhaustion of the World War, and that financial and economic recovery were more necessary to the country than continuous armed strength. He might think that the Air was taking the place of the Sea in military matters. And he might be right

26

and truly consistent both in the former and in the latter advocacy. But it would be easy to show a wide discrepancy between the sets of arguments in the two periods. Questions of this kind do not depend upon the intrinsic logic of the reasoning used on the one hand or the other, but on taking a just view of the governing facts of different periods. Such changes must, however, be considered in each particular case with regard to the personal situation of the individual. If it can be shown that he swims with the current in both cases, his titles to a true consistency must be more studiously examined than if he swims against it.

A more searching scrutiny should also be applied to changes of view in relation not to events but to systems of thought and doctrine. In modern British politics no greater contrast can be found than in comparing the Free Trade speeches of the late Mr. Joseph Chamberlain as President of the Board of Trade in the early eighties, with the Protectionist speeches which he delivered during the Tariff campaign at the beginning of the nineteenth century. Here we are dealing not with the turbulent flow of events, but with precise methods of thought. Those who read Mr. Chamberlain's Free Trade speeches will find that almost every economic argument which he used in 1904 was foreseen and countered by him in 1884. Yet the sincerity of his later views was generally accepted by friends and opponents alike. And after all, once he had come to think differently on economic subjects, was it not better that he should unhesitatingly give his country the benefit of his altered convictions? Still, it must be observed that the basis of reasoning had changed very little in the twenty years' interval, that the problem was mainly an abstract one in its character, and that it was substantially the same problem. There need be no impeachment of honesty of purpose or of a zealous and unceasing care for the public interest. But there is clearly in this case a contradiction of argument in regard to the same theory which amounts to self-stultification.

We may illustrate this distinction further. Mr. Chamberlain argued in 1884 that a tax on imports was paid by the home consumer, and in 1904 that it was paid, very largely at any rate, by the foreigner. We cannot help feeling that the reasoning processes underlying these two conclusions are fundamentally incompatible, and it is hard to understand how a man who once saw the one process so clearly should subsequently have visualized and accepted the opposite process with equal vehemence and precision. It would have been better, tactically at any rate, for Mr. Chamberlain to have relinquished the abstract argument altogether and to have relied exclusively in his advocacy upon the facts—the world facts—which were really his reasons, the importance of consolidating the British Empire by means of a Zollverein, and the necessity of rallying support for that policy among the British industrial interests and the Conservative working classes; for these considerations, in his view, over-ruled—whether or not they contradicted—the validity of his purely economic conviction.

A Statesman should always try to do what he believes is best in the long view for his country, and he should not be dissuaded from so acting by having to divorce himself from a great body of doctrine to which he formerly sincerely adhered. Those, however, who are forced to these gloomy choices must regard their situation in this respect as unlucky. The great Sir Robert Peel must certainly be looked on as falling within the sweep of this shadow. Of him Lord John Russell sourly observed:

'He has twice changed his opinion on the greatest political question of his day. Once when the Protestant Church was to be defended and the Protestant Constitution rescued from the attacks of the Roman Catholics, which it was said would ruin it, the Right Honourable Gentleman undertook to lead the defence. Again, the Corn Laws were powerfully attacked in this House and out of it. He took the lead of his Party to resist a change and to defend Protection. I think, on both occasions, he has come to a wise conclusion, and to a decision most beneficial to his country; first, when he repealed the Roman Catholic disabilities, and, secondly, when he abolished Protection. But that those who followed him—men that had committed themselves to these questions, on the faith of his political wisdom, on the faith of his sagacity, led by the great eloquence and ability he displayed in debate—that when they found he had changed his opinions and proposed measures different from those on the faith of which they had followed him—that they should exhibit warmth and resentment was not only natural, but I should have been surprised if they had not displayed it.'

This was a hard, yet not unjust, commentary upon the career of one of the most eminent and one of the noblest of our public men; for here not merely a change of view is in question, but the workaday good faith of a leader towards those who had depended upon his guidance and had not shared in his conversion.

A change of Party is usually considered a much more serious breach of consistency than a change of view. In fact as long as a man works with a Party he will rarely find himself accused of inconsistency, no matter how widely his opinions at one time on any subject can be shown to have altered. Yet Parties are subject to changes and inconsistencies not less glaring than those of individuals. How should it be otherwise in the fierce swirl of Parliamentary conflict and Electoral fortune? Change with a Party, however inconsistent, is at least defended by the power of numbers. To remain constant when a Party changes is to excite invidious challenge. Moreover, a separation from Party affects all manner of personal relations and sunders old comradeship. Still, a sincere conviction, in harmony with the needs of the time and upon a great issue, will be found to override all other factors; and it is right and in the public interest that it should. Politics is a generous profession. The motives and characters of public men, though constantly criticized, are in the end broadly and fairly judged. But, anyhow, where is Consistency to-day? The greatest Conservative majority any modern Parliament has seen is led by the creator of the Socialist party, and dutifully cheers the very Statesman who a few years ago was one of the leaders of a General Strike which he only last year tried to make again legal. A life-long Free Trader at the Board of Trade has framed and passed amid the loudest plaudits a whole-hearted Protectionist Tariff. The Government which only yesterday took office to keep the £ sterling from falling, is now supported for its exertions to keep it from rising. These astonishing tergiversations could be multiplied: but they suffice. Let us quote the charitable lines of Crabbe, in the hopes of a similar measure of indulgence:

'Minutely trace man's life; year after year,
Through all his days let all his deeds appear,
And then, though some may in that life be strange,
Yet there appears no vast nor sudden change;
The links that bind those various deeds are seen,
And no mysterious void is left between.'

PERSONAL CONTACTS

ALMOST the chief mystery of life is what makes one do things. Let the reader look back over the path he has travelled and examine searchingly and faithfully the reasons, impressions, motives, occasions which led him to this or that decisive step in his career. Sometimes he will find that people who impressed him least, influenced him most. Small people, casual remarks, and little things very often shape our lives more powerfully than the deliberate, solemn advice of great people at critical moments. Men and women as often as not address themselves to serious emergencies with resolution and with a conscious desire to choose the best way. But usually in our brief hazardous existence some trifle, some accident, some quite unexpected and irrelevant fact has laid the board in such a way as to determine the move we make. We have always to be on our guard against being thrown off our true course by chance and circumstance; and the glory of human nature lies in our seeming capacity to exercise conscious control of our own destiny. In a broad view, large principles, a good heart, high aims, a firm faith, we may find some charts and a compass for our voyage. Still, as we lean over the stern of the ship and watch the swirling eddies in our wake, the most rigid and resolute of us must feel how many currents are playing their part in the movements of the vessel that bears us onwards.

It is therefore with some reserve that I select from Memory's album a few snap-shots, thumb-nail sketches or fading daguerreotypes of people who have impressed me in the past.

The greatest and most powerful influence in my early life was of course my father. Although I had talked with him so seldom and never for a moment on equal terms, I conceived an intense admiration and affection for him; and, after his early death, for his memory. I read industriously almost every word he had ever spoken and learnt by heart large portions of his speeches. I took my politics almost unquestioningly from him. He seemed to me to have possessed in the days of his prime the key alike to popular oratory and political action. Although Lord Randolph Churchill lived and died a loyal Tory, he was in fact during the whole of his political life, and especially during its finest phase after he had left office for ever, a liberal-minded man. He saw no reason why the old glories of Church and State, of King and country, should not be reconciled with modern democracy; or why the masses of working people should not become the chief defenders of those ancient institutions by which their liberties and progress had been achieved. It is this union of past and present, of tradition and progress, this golden chain, never yet broken, because no undue strain is placed upon it, that has constituted the peculiar merit and sovereign quality of English national life. When I became most closely acquainted with his thought and theme, he was already dead.

. . . .

When I first went to the United States in 1895, I was a subaltern of cavalry. I was met on the quay by Mr. Bourke Cockran, a great friend of my American relations, who had most kindly undertaken to look after me during my stay in the city. I must record the strong impression which this remarkable man made upon my untutored mind. I have never seen his like, or in some respects his equal. With his enormous head, gleaming eyes and flexible countenance, he looked uncommonly like the portraits of Charles James Fox. It was not my fortune to hear any of his orations, but his conversation, in point, in pith, in rotundity, in antithesis, and in comprehension, exceeded anything I have ever heard.

Originally a Democrat and a Tammany Tiger, he was affronted by Mr. Bryan's Free Silver campaign. He took sides against his party and delivered from Republican platforms a memorable series of speeches. Later on when the Currency issue was—for the time being—disposed of, he rejoined his old friends. This double transference of party loyalties naturally exposed him to much abuse. I must affirm that never during our acquaintance of twenty years did I detect any inconsistency in the general body of doctrine upon which his views were founded. All his convictions were of one piece.

In England the political opinion of men and parties grows like a tree shading its trunk with its branches, shaped or twisted by the winds, rooted according to its strains, stunted by drought or maimed by storm. In America opinions are taken from the standard text-books and platforms are made by machinery according to the exigencies of party without concern for individuals. We produce few of their clear-cut political types or clear-cut party programmes. In our affairs as in those of Nature there are always frayed edges, borderlands, compromises, anomalies. Few lines are drawn that are not smudged. Across the ocean it is all crisp and sharp. Cockran by that 'frequent recurrence to first principles' which the American constitution enjoins had evolved a complete scheme of political thought which enabled him to present a sincere and effective front in every direction according to changing circumstances. He was pacifist, individualist, democrat, capitalist, and a 'Gold-bug.' Above all he was a Free-Trader and repeatedly declared that this was the underlying doctrine by which all the others were united. Thus he was equally opposed to socialists, inflationists and protectionists, and he resisted them on all occasions. In consequence there was in his life no lack of fighting. Nor would there have been had he lived longer.

.   .   .   .

Next let me present the picture of a Treasury official of the old school, of the great days of Gladstone and Disraeli. Sir Francis Mowatt had served under both these famous Chancellors of the Exchequer, and had been private secretary for some years to Mr. Gladstone. He represented the complete triumphant Victorian view of economics and finance; strict parsimony; exact accounting; free imports whatever the rest of the world might do; suave, steady government; no wars; no flag-waving; just paying off debt and reducing taxation and keeping out of scrapes; and for the rest—for trade, industry, agriculture, social life—*laissez-faire* and *laissez-aller*. Let the Government reduce itself and its demands upon the public to a minimum; let the nation live of its own; let social and industrial organization take whatever course it pleased, subject to the law of the land and the Ten Commandments. Let the money fructify in the pockets of the people. Like Bourke Cockran he would consign to the uttermost limbo jingoes, Imperialists, bimetallists, socialists, protectionists, and their like.

Tall, spare, with a noble brow, a bright eye and strong jaws, this faithful servant of the Crown, self-effacing, but self-respecting, resolute, convinced, sure of himself, sure of his theme, dwelt modestly and frugally for nearly fifty years at or near the centre of the British governing machine. Governments, Liberal or Tory, came and went. He served them all with equal fidelity, cherishing his Gladstonian sentiment as a purely private affair. He was one of the friends I inherited from my father. He loved to talk to me about Lord Randolph's short tenure as Chancellor of the Exchequer. How quick he had been to learn the sound principles of public finance, how readily he had mown down his fair trade or protectionist wild oats, and how resolutely he had fought for public economy and reduction of armaments! What fun he was to work with and serve! What a tragedy had laid him low! Such was my introduction, and it afforded a firm basis for an affectionate friendship.

Presently I began to criticize Mr. Brodrick's Army expansion and to plead the cause of economy in Parliament. Old Mowatt, then head of the Civil Service, said a word to me now and then and put me in touch with some younger officials, afterwards themselves eminent, with whom it was very helpful to talk—not secrets, for these were never divulged, but published facts set in their true proportion and with their proper emphasis. Then came the fiscal controversy of 1903. The great Joe Chamberlain, the Radical hero of the 'eighties, the Tory hero of the hour, brought protection—a kind of watered-down protection with food taxes—once again into the political arena. An intense political crisis slowly and progressively developed. Mr. Ritchie, the blameless Chancellor of the Exchequer, was held up by Mowatt, his chief adviser, right in the forefront of the battle, and went down fighting with his free-trade colours flying. Mowatt, going far beyond the ordinary limits of a Civil Servant, making no secret of his views, courting dismissal, challenging the administration in admirable State papers, carried on the struggle himself. He armed me with facts and arguments of a general character and equipped me with a knowledge of economics, very necessary to a young man who, at twenty-eight, is called upon to take a prominent part in a national controversy.

· · · · · · · ·

My earliest years in Parliament were lived within the orbit of Lord Hugh Cecil. Here for the first time, and I am afraid almost for the last, I met a real Tory, a being out of the seventeenth century, but equipped with every modern convenience and aptitude. Oliver Wendell Holmes says somewhere that 'Youth with an ecclesiastical turn manifests its abilities exceptionally early.' Certainly this cherished son of the long-established Conservative Prime Minister leapt into the political arena accoutred with every intellectual weapon and with earnest resolve to defend causes which nobody then seemed to consider very important and few people now bother about at all. I had scarcely got into Parliament when he drew me into his vehement resistance to the Bill for allowing a man to marry his deceased wife's sister. I was myself at first sight inclined to think this might be a very excusable and often reasonable arrangement. A widower with four or five young children might often turn to his wife's sister to bring up his family. If he loved and admired his wife, it seemed natural

35

that he should find in her sister many of the traits which had enchanted him before. There would also be a groundwork of intimacy and affection. The union would be one between those of riper years. Certainly there were in fact many happy homes constructed on this basis.

But when I pointed out these considerations to Lord Hugh Cecil, he was scandalized at my ignorance of Ecclesiastical Law, and still more of the profound reasons underlying that law. The object of the Christian Church, he explained, was to enlarge the bounds of family affection to the widest possible extent without admitting within those bounds the possibility of sex disturbance. Here were noble and delightful relationships where the deceased wife's sister without fear of scandal could enter the widower's house and discharge in perfect honour over long years her duty to her beloved nephews and nieces. Dethrone the principle of prohibited degrees, and in hundreds—nay in thousands—of households the position of these devoted women, hitherto unquestioned, would become a target for comment and calumny. All this, in itself important, was only a single instance of our duty to preserve the structure of humane, enlightened, Christian society. Once the downward steps were taken, once one's moral and intellectual feet slipped upon the slope of plausible indulgence, there would be found no halting-place short of a general Paganism and Hedonism, possibly agreeable from time to time in this world of fleeting trials and choices, but fatal hereafter through measureless ages, if not indeed through eternity itself.

These arguments enforced with splendid eloquence and flame of faith induced me to assist Lord Hugh in the prolonged and successful obstruction of the Deceased Wife's Sister Bill of 1901 in the Grand Committee. After some weary weeks we convinced the supporters of the measure—or 'promoters' as, imputing their private interests, we derisively called them— that there was no limit to the arguments which could be used against their project, or at least to the energy with which these arguments could be advanced, embroidered, or indeed repeated. In the end Lord Hugh had recourse to a Parliamentary stratagem which involved him in a serious charge of casuistry. Private members' Bills are much at the mercy of time. On whether the vote could be recorded before the clock struck four depended the fate of the obnoxious measure. A majority in its favour was assured. In those days it used to take the members of the House of Commons rather more than a quarter of an hour to walk through the lobbies to record their votes. When the debate came to an end there were only eighteen minutes left. Lord Hugh *loitered in the lobby!* Accompanied by about a score of Tories, among whom to my surprise I perceived the venerable figure of Sir Michael Hicks-Beach, Chancellor of the Exchequer, he literally crawled inch by inch across the matting which led to the portals where the votes were counted. By fifteen seconds the stroke of the clock preceded the end of the division on the measure, upon which months of labour had been consumed by the partisans of either view. The Bill was in consequence dead, and the further fortunes of the cause were relegated to the chances and mischances of another year.

The Radicals and Nonconformists who, as was rudely insinuated, wished to regularize at the expense of the Church their immoral relations with their deceased wives' sisters, took a very hostile view of this manœuvre. They declared it 'shabby,' 'tricky', 'not playing the game', 'not cricket'. They howled, and would have hissed had it not been disorderly, at Lord Hugh when he at last re-entered the Chamber. He bore these manifestations with the most perfect contempt permissible to a devout person. He had broken nothing in the rules of procedure as they then were; he had merely exercised his Parliamentary rights, which certainly at that time included a full discretion as to the speed with which he should move through the lobby. If his opponents had been ignorant that such a latitude existed and had imprudently prolonged the debate and left too little time for the division, that only served them right. And what was all this talk of 'not playing cricket', when the transcendental character of the marriage tie was at stake?

37

Questioned as to how far he would carry this argument, he indicated that he would carry it as far as possible, short of violence or illegality. The Conservatives must respect the laws of Britain, or else nothing would be left standing. Dissenters would refuse to pay rates and tenants would neglect their rents. Many important secular rights would in fact be jeopardized. But all this public-school chatter about 'playing the game' was rubbish. We were not playing a game; we were discharging a solemn and indeed awful duty. We had been let loose in this world with a conscious power of choice for a brief interlude in an unending existence, and by our faith and actions we should be judged for ever.

I must admit that in the growing tolerances of the age I was ultimately induced to acquiesce in the legalizing of a man's marriage with his deceased wife's sister. But Lord Hugh Cecil's point of view, although superseded by irresistible mass movements towards an altogether easier and more indulgent state of society, is one which may crop up again some day.

．　．　．　．　．　．　．　．　．

No one can have worked as closely as I have with Mr. Lloyd George without being both impressed and influenced by him. The reputation which he has long enjoyed as a parliamentary and platform speaker has often been an exaggerated one. Extraordinary as have been his successes in public, it is in conclaves of eight or nine, or four or five, or in personal discussion man to man, that his persuasive arts reach their fullest excellence. At his best he could almost talk a bird out of a tree. An intense comprehension of the more amiable weaknesses of human nature: a sure gift of getting on the right side of a man from the beginning of a talk: a complete avoidance of anything in the nature of chop-logic reasoning: a deft touch in dealing with realities: the sudden presenting of positions hitherto unexpected, but apparently conciliatory and attractive—all these are modes and methods in which he is a natural adept. I have seen him turn a Cabinet round in less than ten minutes, and yet when the process was complete, no one could remember any particular argument to which to attribute their change of view.

He has realized acutely the truth of the adage 'A man convinced against his will, is of the same opinion still.' He never in the days when I knew him best thought of giving *himself* satisfaction by what he said. He had no partiality for fine phrases, he thought only and constantly of the effect produced upon other persons. Indeed many of those whom he had converted, honestly believed at the end that it was they who had finally converted him! Yet there was truth behind the argument and good sense, a practical view, a far-sighted outlook.

One of his most impressive faculties was the power of seeing, in moments when everyone was asking about the next step, the step after that. To use sporting terms, he was often hunting in the next field to that through which we were all galloping. Just as we had all made up our minds where to jump the fence, he would exclaim, 'Anyone can see that; but how are we going to get over the canal, or the railway line over there? See, we must make for that bridge or that level crossing, otherwise we shall be hopelessly thrown out. That means a big jump now, and not the easy one you were all thinking about.' I may say he has never hunted with hounds in his life, but had he been born to the part of a nimrod instead of to that of a wizard, foxes would have had a bad time.

Naturally such a man greatly influenced me. When I crossed the floor of the House and left the Conservative Party in 1904, it was by his side I took my seat. Thenceforward we worked together, not indeed without differences, or even quarrels, but in the main in practically continuous association, for nearly twenty years. He was the greatest master of the art of getting things done and of putting things through that I ever knew; in fact no British politician in my day has possessed half his competence as a mover of men and affairs. When the English history of the first quarter of the twentieth century is written, it will be seen that the greater part of our fortunes in peace and in war were shaped by this one man. It was he who gave to orthodox Liberalism the entirely new inflexion of an ardent social policy. All the great schemes of insurance which have entered for ever into the life of the British people, originated or flowed from him. He it was who cast our finances intently upon the line of progressive taxation of wealth as an equalizing factor in the social system. He it was who in the darkest year of the War seized the supreme power and wielded it undauntedly till overwhelming victory was won. He it was who for good or for ill settled the Irish question, or at least shifted it out of the main path of the British Empire. All these matters belong to history, and at the present time strong currents of censure or at least disapproval are running against much of his life's work. Its merits will be long disputed; but no one will challenge its magnitude.

In a way I think that sometimes I influenced him, and so to a large extent did Lord Balfour and Lord Birkenhead when they came to work with him. We were able to show him often that other side of the picture of politics, which in his youth as a radical, dissenting, Welsh nationalist leader, brought up in narrow surroundings and enforcedly-frugal conditions, he had never been called upon to think much about. The British Empire and our own island will be the losers from the fact that the political forces of the Right, the moment we escaped from the war period, repulsed him so incontinently. He was also no doubt blameworthy himself. At any rate the divorce was complete. The Carlton Club meeting in 1922 terminated so far as we now know for ever the association of this astonishing 'Doer of Things' with the orthodox or professional Imperialist forces of the Right, or Die-hards as they are sometimes called. The Conservative Party denounced and expelled the Welsh wizard and acclaimed 'Honest Mr. Baldwin.' Now it appears they are still dissatisfied with their own leader. They have for the present happily settled down, for a while, under a Socialist, a war-time Pacifist, an anti-Imperialist, and a supporter of the General Strike. But it is understood that he will not interfere with Tory policy. L. G. is taboo.

THE BATTLE OF SIDNEY STREET

On the morning of December 17, 1910, all England was startled and astonished by the accounts which filled the newspapers of an extraordinary crime. At half-past ten on the previous night a Mr. Isenstein, the owner of a fancy-goods shop in Houndsditch, became alarmed by mysterious rappings at the back of his premises. These rappings had been noticed a fortnight earlier, and the police had already made inquiries about them. But now they were louder and nearer, and evidently came from the house next door. Mr. Isenstein sent for the police. A party of six officers and constables arrived; two were posted at the rear of the premises, and the sergeant, followed by three others, went up to the door of the house whence the rapping was believed to proceed and knocked. Following the custom which, till then, had long been almost invariable in England, all the police were unarmed. The door was opened about six inches by a man.

'Have you been working here?' asked the sergeant.

No answer.

'Do you understand English? Have you anyone in the house who can speak English?'

The man closed the door all but an inch, and leaving the question unanswered, disappeared upstairs. The sergeant pushed the door open and entered a gas-lighted room. There seemed no special reason for precautions. The sergeant was only making an ordinary police inquiry, and he stood for a minute waiting. It was his last. Suddenly a door was flung open, a pistol-shot rang out, and the sergeant fell in the doorway. Another shot, this time from the dark stairway, drove the advancing police from the door; through that door a

41

man's hand with a long automatic pistol appeared, a succession of shots was fired, and in a few seconds all four constables lay dead, dying, or wounded in the street. A figure sprang from the house, firing right and left. There remained only Constable Choate, unarmed and already wounded. This officer unhesitatingly grappled with the assassin, and, in spite of being twice more shot in the body, was still holding him when he was shot again from behind by another of the criminals and fell dying from twelve separate wounds. The gang of murderers shook off the pursuit of the sixth policeman at the rear of the premises and disappeared into the darkness and movement of London by night, leaving for the moment neither trace nor clue.

The subsequent police investigation showed that a systematic burglary was being planned, not against Mr. Isenstein's premises, but against those of an adjoining jeweller, where £30,000 worth of goods was kept locked up in a safe. The brick wall between the buildings had been nearly tunnelled through, and in the tunnel were found complete and perfect burglars' outfits for forcing a safe with an acetylene flame.

At three o'clock the next morning a doctor was summoned by two women to attend a young man who gave the name of George Gardstein, and explained that he had been shot in the back by mistake with a revolver by a friend three hours before. This man, whose name was Morountzef, was the criminal who killed the police sergeant, and it appeared that in the scuffle with Constable Choate he had been pierced through the lungs and stomach by one of the bullets which had traversed the body of the heroic officer. He expired before morning, leaving behind him a Browning automatic pistol, a dagger, and a violin.

Such in brief outline was the story which the newspapers of the next few days gradually unfolded. We were clearly in the presence of a class of crime and a type of criminal which for generations had found no counterpart in England. The ruthless ferocity of the criminals, their intelligence, their unerring marksmanship, their modern weapons and equipment, all disclosed the characteristics of the Russian Anarchist. It was ascertained in the days that followed that the murderers belonged to a small colony of about twenty Letts from Baltic Russia, who, under the leadership of an Anarchist known as 'Peter the Painter', had ensconced themselves in the heart of London. It was in fact, in the language of later years, a 'germ cell' of murder, anarchy, and revolution. These fierce beings, living, as it was said, 'just like animals', were pursuing their predatory schemes and dark conspiracies. Although they were thieves and murderers for personal ends, all their actions had also a political character. 'Peter the Painter' was one of those wild beasts who, in later years, amid the convulsions of the Great War, were to devour and ravage the Russian State and people.

Wrath and indignation at this monstrous crime were general throughout the country. The whole resources of Scotland Yard were concentrated on the pursuit of the criminals. As Home Secretary I immediately ordered the police to be provided with the best pattern of automatic pistol then procurable. The brave constables who had fallen in the discharge of their duty were accorded a public funeral, and their coffins, covered with the Union Jack, lay in St. Paul's Cathedral during a solemn memorial service attended by the dignitaries of the City of London.

There followed an interlude while all the resources of which a civilized community can dispose were directed to hunting down the criminals.

·   ·   ·   ·   ·   ·   ·

At about ten o'clock on the morning of January 3 I was in my bath, when I was surprised by an urgent knocking at the door.

'There is a message from the Home Office on the telephone absolutely immediate.'

Dripping wet and shrouded in a towel I hurried to the instrument, and received the following news:

43

'The Anarchists who murdered the police have been surrounded in a house in the East End—No. 100 Sidney Street—and are firing on the police with automatic pistols. They have shot one man and appear to have plenty of ammunition. Authority is requested to send for troops to arrest or kill them.'

I replied at once, giving the necessary permission and directing the police to use whatever force was necessary. In about twenty minutes I was at the Home Office. There I found my principal adviser, Mr. Ernley Blackwell, who told me that no further information had been received, except that the Anarchists had been effectually surrounded, but were still firing in all directions. No one knew how many Anarchists there were or what measures were going to be taken. In these circumstances I thought it my duty to see what was going on myself, and my advisers concurred in the propriety of such a step. I must, however, admit that convictions of duty were supported by a strong sense of curiosity which perhaps it would have been well to keep in check.

We started at once in a motor-car. Down the Strand, through the City towards Houndsditch, until at length at about noon we reached the point where all traffic was stopped. We got out of the car. There was a considerable crowd of angry and alarmed people, and I noticed the unusual spectacle of Metropolitan constables armed with shotguns hastily procured from a local gunsmith. The attitude of the crowd was not particularly friendly, and there were several cries of 'Oo let 'em in?' in allusion to the refusal of the Liberal Government to introduce drastic laws restricting the immigration of aliens. Just at this moment, however, a shot rang out perhaps a couple of hundred yards away, followed by another and another, until there was a regular fusillade. Accompanied by an inspector, we proceeded down the empty street, turned a corner, turned another corner, and reached a group of policemen, several of whom were armed, and a number of onlookers and journalists who had found themselves within the police cordon when it was originally closed and had been permitted to remain. Another street ran at right angles across our path. Up this street fifty or sixty yards to the left was the house (No. 100) in which the murderers had barricaded themselves. On the opposite side in front of us, police, Scots Guardsmen, and spectators were crouching behind the projecting corners of the buildings; and from both sides of the street, from the street itself, and from numerous windows, policemen and other persons were firing rifles, pistols, and shotguns with increasing frequency at the house which harboured the desperadoes. These replied every minute or two, shooting sometimes up and down the street and sometimes at their assailants in front. The bullets struck the brickwork and ricochetted hither and thither. We have since become only too familiar with scenes of this kind, and the spectacle of street fighting has long lost its novelty in Europe. But nothing of the sort had ever been seen within living memory in quiet, law-abiding, comfortable England; and from this point of view at least my journey was well repaid.

But the situation almost immediately became embarrassing. Some of the police officers were anxious to storm the building at once with their pistols. Others rightly thought it better to take more time and to avoid the almost certain loss of three or four valuable lives. It was no part of my duty to take personal control or to give executive decisions. From my chair in the Home Office I could have sent any order and it would have been immediately acted on, but it was not for me to interfere with those who were in charge on the spot. Yet, on the other hand, my position of authority, far above them all, attracted inevitably to itself direct responsibility. I saw now that I should have done much better to have remained quietly in my office. On the other hand, it was impossible to get into one's car and drive away while matters stood in such great uncertainty, and moreover were extremely interesting.

Being anxious to have a direct view of the besieged house, I now crossed the street and took shelter in the doorway of a warehouse on the opposite side. Here I found Lord Knutsford, the Chairman of the London Hospital, and together we watched the closing scenes of the drama.

Plans were now made to storm the building from several sides at once. One party, emerging from the next-door house, was to rush the front door and charge up the stairs; another party of police and soldiers would break into the second floor at the back through a window; a third, smashing-in the roof, would leap down on the assassins from above. There could be no doubt about the result of such an attack, but it certainly seemed that loss of life would be caused, not only by the fire of the Anarchists, but also from shots fired by the attackers in the confusion. My own instincts turned at once to a direct advance up the staircase behind a steel plate or shield, and search was made in the foundries of the neighbourhood for one of a suitable size. Meanwhile, however, the problem settled itself. At about half-past one a wisp of smoke curled out of the shattered upper windows of the besieged house, and in a few minutes it was plainly on fire. The conflagration gained apace, burning downwards. To the crackling of wood succeeded the roar of flames. Still the Anarchists, descending storey by storey, kept up their fire, and bullets continued to strike the brickwork of the surrounding houses and pavement.

Now occurred a curious incident, which, for the first time, made my presence on the spot useful. The ordinary functions of British life had been proceeding inflexibly to within a few feet of the danger-zone, and the postman on his rounds actually delivered his letters at the house next door. Suddenly, with a stir and a clatter, up came the fire brigade, scattering the crowds gathered on the approaches to the scene and thrusting through them until they reached the police cordon at the beginning of the danger-zone. The inspector of police forbade further progress, and the fire brigade officer declared it his duty to advance. A fire was raging, and he was bound to extinguish it. Anarchists, automatic pistols, danger-zones, nothing of this sort was mentioned in the Regulations of the London Fire Brigade. When the police officer pointed out that his men would be shot down, he replied simply that orders were orders and that he had no alternative. I now intervened to settle this dispute, at one moment quite heated. I told the fire-brigade officer on my authority as Home Secretary, that the house was to be allowed to burn down and that he was to stand by in readiness to prevent the conflagration from spreading. I then returned to my coign of vantage on the opposite side of the road.

The flames were now beginning to invade the ground floor of the doomed house. Some minutes had passed without a shot being fired by the Anarchists. No human being could live longer in the building. Everyone expected to see the Anarchists—how many there were was not known for certain—sally out, pistol in hand, into the open street. A hundred rifles, revolvers, and shotguns were levelled at the smouldering doorway. The minutes passed in intense excitement, and the flames invaded the whole ground floor. At last it became certain that these human fiends had perished. Suddenly, upon a spontaneous impulse which led everyone into the open, a detective inspector walked quickly to the door and kicked it open. I followed a few yards behind, accompanied by a police sergeant with a double-barrelled shotgun. There was nothing but smoke and flame inside the building. The firemen rushed forward into the empty street with their hoses, and behind them surged a crowd of soldiers, journalists, photographers, and spectators. It was already three o'clock, and leaving the now-dying fire to be dealt with by the fire brigade and the ruins to be searched by the police, I went home.

Besides the police inspector shot in the morning, a colour sergeant of the Guards and three civilians had been wounded by bullets, and a police sergeant struck, but not seriously injured, by a ricochet. Up to this moment no lives had been lost except those of the murderers. Alas, the day was not yet done! A falling wall injured five of the firemen, two in the most grave manner. There were found in the ruins of Sidney Street two charred bodies, one shot by a British bullet and one apparently suffocated by smoke. These were established to be the corpses of Fritz Svaars and Jacob Vogel, both members

47

of 'Peter the Painter's' Anarchist gang, and both certainly concerned in the police murders. One Browning and two Mauser pistols and six gun-metal bomb-cases were found amid the ruins, together with many cartridges.

Thus ended the battle of Sidney Street. Of 'Peter the Painter' not a trace was ever found. He vanished completely. Rumour has repeatedly claimed him as one of the Bolshevik liberators and saviours of Russia. Certainly his qualities and record would well have fitted him to take an honoured place in that noble band. But of this Rumour is alone the foundation.

Party controversy was then at its height in England, and I was much criticized in the newspapers and in Parliament for my share in this curious episode. Mr. Balfour in the House of Commons was especially sarcastic.

'We are concerned to observe,' he said in solemn tones, 'photographs in the illustrated newspapers of the Home Secretary in the danger-zone. I understand what the photographer was doing, but why the Home Secretary?'

And with this not altogether unjust reflection I may bring the story to an end.

THE GERMAN SPLENDOUR

IN the year 1906 when I was Under-Secretary of State for the Colonies I received an invitation from the German Emperor to attend as his guest the Annual Manœuvres of the German Army in Silesia. Having obtained the permission of the British Government, I set out for Breslau at the beginning of September, and was accommodated with other Imperial and official guests in the comfortable old-world 'Golden Goose' Hotel. The manœuvres were on a great scale, a whole Army Corps and one completely-mobilized division at war strength being employed. Everything was managed with the usual German efficiency, and with rigid care in matters of the smallest detail. The large number of visitors, including of course representatives of all the armies in Europe, were handled and moved with the most minute consideration of rank and etiquette, and as far as the Emperor's own guests were concerned, an element of personal hospitality was mingled with the official ceremonial and routine. The week, while brilliant and deeply interesting, was most strenuous, and except sometimes on active service, I have hardly ever been so short of sleep. Every night there was a glittering full-dress banquet, at which the Emperor—or in his absence on the manœuvre ground the Empress—presided. We went to bed shortly before midnight only to be aroused at 3 or 4 o'clock in the morning to join the special train which conveyed us to the particular point of the battlefield where the situation of the opposing armies could be studied. Here, as the first light paled the Eastern sky, we mounted our horses and, each accompanied by an officer of the German General Staff, set off wherever we liked to go. After 10 or 12 hours of riding about and watching the operations, we gathered again in the special train at

49

some new point and got back to Breslau in time to dress for the next banquet, followed by an Imperial tattoo, another brief interlude of sleep, and another 4-o'clock-in-the-morning departure. Such was the cycle of our hours.

Magnificent was the spectacle of German military and Imperial splendour so brilliantly displayed to foreign eyes. Several scenes linger in my memory which illustrated the pomp and power of the German Empire. When the Emperor, resplendent in the uniform of the White Silesian Cuirassiers, rode through the streets of Breslau at the head of a sparkling cavalcade, he was rapturously welcomed by his dutiful subjects. A large portion of the road was lined, not by troops, but by many thousands of elderly men obviously belonging to the poorer classes, all dressed punctiliously in ancient black frock-coats and tall hats. These were the old soldiers, to whom special positions of honour were accorded, and indeed they formed a striking background of sombre civic strength to the white uniforms of the Emperor and his Cuirassiers.

In the Review which preceded the manoeuvres 50,000 horse, foot and artillery marched past the Emperor and his galaxy of kings and princes. The Infantry, regiment by regiment, in line of battalion quarter columns, reminded one more of great Atlantic rollers than human formations. Clouds of cavalry, avalanches of field guns and—at that time a novelty—squadrons of motor-cars (private and military) completed the array. For five hours the immense defilade continued. Yet this was only a twentieth of the armed strength of the regular German Army before mobilization; and the same martial display could have been produced simultaneously in every province of the Empire. I thought of our tiny British Army, in which the parade of a single division and a brigade of Cavalry at Aldershot was a notable event. I watched from time to time the thoughtful, sombre visage of the French Military Attaché, who sat on his horse beside me absorbed in reflections which it would not have been difficult to plumb. The very atmosphere was pervaded by a sense of inexhaustible and exuberant manhood and deadly panoply. The glories of this world and force abounding could not present a more formidable, and even stupefying, manifestation.

On the evening of this Review the Emperor gave his dinner to the Province. Three or four hundred Silesian functionaries and notables, together with the foreign guests, in uniforms of every colour and loaded with gold lace and decorations, assembled in a spacious hall. The Emperor spoke with his usual facility and with the majesty that none could deny. The German staff officer at my side translated in a whisper sentence by sentence into excellent English. It was the year 1906, the Centenary of the Battle of Jena. 'A hundred years ago,' said William II, 'Germany was reduced to the abyss of ruin. Our armies were everywhere captured or dispersed, our fortresses taken, our Capital captured by hostile troops, the very structure of our State broken into fragments, long years of foreign domination ahead.' Only a hundred years ago! It seemed incredible that a single century, four fleeting generations, should have sufficed to raise the mighty fabric of power and wealth, energy and organization, of which we were the awe-struck witnesses. What an amazing contrast: 1806-1906! What a contrast also between the bounding fortunes of martial Germany and the slow-growing continuity of British national life, which after 900 years of immunity from foreign invasion still wore a modest and self-questioning garb. But more amazing still would have been the contrast if the curtains of the future could for a moment have been swept aside, and if that glittering throng could have perceived that scarcely ten years separated triumphant Germany from a collapse, subjugation and prostration, far more complete and lasting than any that had darkened the morrow of Jena.

The manoeuvres however for all their impressive scale of mechanism revealed many questionable features to an instructed eye. Like others in the handful of British officers, who in various capacities were watching the operations, I had carried away from the South African veldt a very lively and modern sense of what rifle bullets could do. On the effects of the fire of large numbers of guns we could only use our imagination.

51

But where the power of the magazine rifle was concerned we felt sure we possessed a practical experience denied to the leaders of these trampling hosts. We watched with astonishment the movements of dense columns of men over bare slopes, within a few hundred yards of woods along whose entrenched outskirts lines of riflemen burned blank cartridges in unceasing fusillade. As the climax of the manœuvres approached the opposing infantry masses came very close to one another. Presently we found them lying on the ground fifty yards apart in dense formation, bayonets fixed and the front ranks firing furiously. More astonishing still—on the order to charge being given, these placid phalanxes rose from the ground and still with bayonets fixed advanced *through* each other with perfect drill, and lay down dutifully on the other side toes to toes. Whatever else this might amount to, it did not form contact with reality at any point. Besides South Africa I had also vividly in my mind the Battle of Omdurman, where we had shot down quite easily, with hardly any loss, more than 11,000 Dervishes in formations much less dense, and at ranges far greater than those which were now on every side exhibited to our gaze. We had said to ourselves after Omdurman, 'This is the end of these sort of spectacles. There will never be such fools in the world again.'

Some inkling of the truth about modern fire had already begun to circulate in the German Army. As we advanced over the rolling downs, accompanying an attack delivered by a line of massed columns of infantry under the fire of at least 100 guns, and of thousands of happily harmless rifles, I noticed signs of unconcealed impatience among the German officers with whom I rode. A Princess, who in full uniform was leading her regiment, was in the easy assurance of Royal privilege indignantly 'outspoken.' 'What folly!' she exclaimed. 'It is madness. The Generals should all be dismissed.' And so on. But in the main everything passed off happily.

At the Grand Finale the Emperor led in person a charge of 30 or 40 squadrons of cavalry upon a long line of field guns in the centre of the enemy's position. We all galloped along in the greatest glee, and the surging waves of horsemen soon overwhelmed and swept through the rows of venomous-looking little cannons which presumed to confront them. 'Do you think it is all right?' we asked an Artillery Officer whose battery the Umpire had loyally adjudged to be captured. 'Certainly it is all right,' he replied. 'They are His Majesty's own guns. Why shouldn't he capture them? It is an honour for us to serve His Majesty in this manner.' But there was a twinkle in his eye.

After the bugles had sounded the 'Cease Fire' over the wide plain, the great German Staff drew together round their War Lord on the summit of a little hill behind which a crowd of green-clad soldiers speedily erected a small wooden chalet for his Military Quarters in the field. The Emperor welcomed his personal guests with that unaffected and easy grace which was habitual to him, and added so much to his charm and popularity. He talked to foreign visitors with the freedom and manner of an agreeable host at an English country-house party, while all around the stiff uniformed figures of his Generals and Aides-de-Camp stood immobile and passive, each rooted to his particular spot. 'What do you think of this beautiful Silesia?' he asked me in his facile English. 'Fine country, isn't it? Well worth fighting for, and,' he added, 'well fought over. These fields are ankle-deep in blood. There,' pointing to the town of Liegnitz, 'is where Frederick fought his battle. Down there,' he indicated a wooded valley, 'is the Katsbach stream, where we beat the French in 1813 in our war of Liberation.' I made such comments as occurred to me. 'Have you seen everything you want? I wish you to see everything perfectly freely. Tell me, is there anything you have not seen that you would like to see? Have you seen my new gun?' I said I had seen it at a certain distance. 'Oh, but you must see it close to.' Then, turning to an officer, 'Take him and show him our new gun. There is a battery over there. Show him how it works.' And with a gracious wave I was dismissed. As I left the circle I was conscious of a perceptible bristling, almost a murmur, among the military potentates who composed it.

When we arrived at the Battery an appreciable parley took place between the Emperor's Aide-de-Camp and the artillery commander. However, before the Imperial insignia every reluctance faded. The gun was displayed. Its breech was opened, and the motions of loading and firing it were gone through by the gunner. I made it evident that I did not wish to pry too closely, and after the usual heel-clicking and saluting we took our departure. There was really nothing for the German officers to worry about. The Emperor knew quite well that I was not an artillery expert, and could learn nothing from a superficial view of his field gun that was not certainly already known by the War Offices of Paris and London. But the impression which he raised in my mind that he was the private proprietor of all these vast and terrific machines, and that he relieved its grim organization with a touch of personal amiability and confidence, was not an unpleasant one.

It was three years before I saw the German Army once more. I was again the guest of the Emperor, and the manœuvres were this time at Wurzburg, in Bavaria. Many things had changed in the interval. The European outlook had sensibly darkened. The growth of the German Navy had led to the first heavy British counter-measures. The controversy between the British and German Admiralties was sharp. The gradual association of British and French interests was more pronounced. The Young Turk Revolution at Constantinople had set in motion a disturbing train of events in the southeast of Europe. I was now a Member of the Cabinet and President of the Board of Trade—'Handels-Minister' as I was described on my invitation. In 1906 the Emperor had talked to me in great animation and at some length about various Colonial questions, including particularly the native revolt in German South-West Africa. In 1909 I had only one short conversation with him. In this he avoided all military and serious matters, and confined himself to chaff about the Lloyd George Budget and various phases of British domestic politics, with which he showed himself surprisingly well acquainted. This, except for a formal leave-taking, was the last occasion on which I ever spoke to the Emperor, though it was not to be my last contact with the German Army.

The manœuvres at Wurzburg showed a great change in German military tactics. A remarkable stride had been made in modernizing their Infantry formations and adapting them to actual war conditions. The absurdities of the Silesian manœuvres were not repeated. The dense masses were rarely, if ever, seen. The Artillery was not ranged in long lines, but dotted about wherever conveniences of the ground suggested. The whole extent of the battlefield was far greater. The Cavalry were hardly at all in evidence, and then only on distant flanks. The Infantry advanced in successive skirmish lines, and machine-guns everywhere had begun to be a feature. Although these formations were still to British eyes much too dense for modern fire, they nevertheless constituted an enormous advance upon 1906. They were, I believe, substantially the formations with which the German Army five years later entered the Great War, and which were then proved to be superior in efficiency to those of their French opponents.

The next review I saw in Germany was when in 1919 I visited Cologne at the head of the Army Council, and when forty thousand British troops marched past in the solemn glitter of unchallengeable victory. But I did not expect ever to witness such a spectacle when I left Wurzburg in 1909. Indeed no fancy could have seemed more wild.

The reverberations of the Turkish Revolution were already perceptible in the centre of German military life at Wurzburg. Mahmoud Shefket Pasha, the Young-Turkish Minister of War, and Enver Bey were the principal military guests of the German Headquarters. Over both these men hung tragic fates. Shefket was soon to be murdered in Constantinople. Before Enver there stretched a road of toil, of terrorism, of crime, of disaster which was not to end until his own undaunted heart and eager frame were stilled for ever. Indeed these Wurzburg manœuvres make in my mind the picture of a Belshazzar feast. Upon how many of those who marched and cantered in that autumn sunlight had the dark angel set his seal! Violent un-

timely death, ruin and humiliation worse than death, privation, mutilation, despair to the simple soldier, the downfall of
their pride and subsistence to the chiefs: such were the fates—
could we but have read them—which brooded over thousands
and tens of thousands of these virile figures. All the Kings and
Princes of Germany, all the Generals of her Empire, clustered
round the banqueting-tables. Ten years were to see them scattered, exiled, deposed, in penury, in obloquy—the victims of
a fatal system in which they were inextricably involved. And
for the Kaiser, that bright figure, the spoilt child of fortune,
the envy of Europe—for him in the long series of heart-breaking disappointments and disillusions, of failure and undying
self-reproach, which across the devastation of Europe was to
lead him to the wood-cutter's block at Doorn—there was
surely reserved the sternest punishment of all.

One final incident remains in my mind. I made the acquaintance of Enver. I was attracted by this fine-looking young officer, whose audacious gesture had at the peril of his life swept
away the decayed regime of Abdul Hamid, and who had become in one leopard-spring the hero of the Turkish nation
and the probable master of its destinies. He evinced a desire
to talk about the Bagdad Railway, with certain aspects of
which my Department was specially concerned, and with
which question as a Minister I was of course closely acquainted. No opportunity presented itself for this conversation until
the last day of the manœuvres, when we rode together alone
for an hour amid the thunder of the closing cannonade. We
were deep in our subject, and discussing it from an angle not
entirely in accord with German views, when we noticed that
the horse of the Royal Equerry, who rode behind us, was
causing his rider continuous trouble. Four separate times did
this animal apparently escape from control, and each time its
bounds and curvets carried our attendant close up to us, either
between us or alongside, in which position after apologizing
for his clumsiness he remained until actually directed to fall
back. Over the face of the young Turkish leader, and newly-
triumphant conspirator, there played a smile of frank and per-

fect comprehension. There was no need for us to exchange suspicions.

Had it been possible for the main lines of British policy to have been more in accord with legitimate Turkish aspirations, I am sure we could have worked agreeably with Enver Bey. But all the puppets in the world tragedy were held too tightly in the grip of destiny. Events moved forward remorseless to the supreme catastrophe.

MY SPY STORY

THERE is a well-defined class of people prone to 'Spy-mania' and whose minds are peculiarly affected by anything in the nature of espionage or counter-espionage. The War was the heyday of these worthy folk in every country. No suspicions were too outrageous to be nourished, no tale too improbable to be believed, and the energies of thousands of amateur and irregular detectives reinforced at every moment and in every district the stern and unsleeping vigilance of the public authorities. There is no doubt that these voluntary activities, although they led to the discovery of innumerable mare's nests and often inflicted unmerited sufferings upon individuals, constituted on the whole an important additional element of security. Sharp eyes followed everybody's movements; long ears awaited every incautious expression in the streets, in the public conveyances, on the railways, in the theatre, in the restaurant or tavern; tireless industry unravelled to the third and fourth generation the genealogy of all who bore non-British names or who had married foreign wives. During the air-raids, when national excitement was fanned by anger and alarm, no match could be struck which was not noticed, no chink of light could escape from a carelessly-curtained window without instant complaint and swift information to the Police. Thus did whole communities protect themselves against the subtle peril which dwelt privily in their midst.

In the higher ranges of Secret Service work the actual facts in many cases were in every respect equal to the most fantastic inventions of romance or melodrama. Tangle within tangle, plot and counter-plot, ruse and treachery, cross and double-cross, true agent, false agent, double agent, gold and

steel, the bomb, the dagger and the firing party were interwoven in many a texture so intricate as to be incredible and
yet true. The Chief and the high officers of the Secret Service
revelled in these subterranean labyrinths, and amid the crash
of war pursued their task with cold and silent passion. There
has been disseminated by spontaneous efforts of the public
Press from time to time the theory that John Bull, especially
under Liberal administrations, is a simple sentimentalist,
without care or forethought, and a ready dupe of continental
craft and machinations. This too perhaps had its utility. In
fact however it is probable that, upon the whole, during the
War, the British Secret Service was more efficient and gained
greater triumphs, both in the detection of spies and in the
collection of information from the enemy, than that of any
other country, hostile, allied or neutral.

Here is my own true spy story, and the only one with
which I have ever been directly concerned.

In September, 1914, the state of our northern war harbours caused us lively anxiety. In all our Channel ports
there were anchorages secured by moles and breakwaters,
and the gates to these were closed with nets and booms
capable of resisting not only the entrance of a destroyer or
submarine but of stopping a torpedo fired through from
outside. But the Fleet had now moved to the North, and
since Rosyth was not yet completed, it used in general the
enormous anchorage of Scapa Flow in the Orkney Islands,
or alternatively Cromarty Firth a little to the southward.
Up to the outbreak of the War the only danger which had
been apprehended in these northern harbours had been an
attack by destroyers; and against these, temporary booms
and improvised batteries, rapidly called into being in the
early weeks of the War, were held to be a sufficient defence.
But now in September the fear of the submarine actually
coming into the harbours and attacking the sleeping ships
laid its pressure on every responsible mind. Once this idea
had been formed it was insistently magnified in everyone's
consciousness. Alarms were raised by night and day with-

out foundation. Periscopes that never existed were seen, and more than once the whole Grand Fleet proceeded to sea in order to find on the broad waters that assurance and safety which it had lost in those places of rest where above all it ought to have been able to feel secure. At this time therefore, while measures of netting the northern harbours with anti-submarine obstructions were being pressed forward with feverish activity, the Grand Fleet was encouraged to change its anchorages at frequent and uncertain intervals. Some-times in the North, sometimes on the East and sometimes on the West coast of Scotland the great vessels which were our safeguard and on which the issue of the whole war depended, found a series of temporary habitations. The solitary con-dition of their safety was that not one single enemy should know where they were and that they should not remain in any one place long enough for anyone to find out. We were therefore passing through a period of exceptional tension.

I had occasion to visit the Fleet in order to discuss per-sonally with the Commander-in-Chief these and other urgent problems, and one evening, in the middle of that trying September, I travelled from London in a special train with several high officers and technical authorities from the Ad-miralty. Our train pulled up at daybreak at a wayside station somewhere in the Highlands, and from here a motor trip of 50 or 60 miles would take us to the Bay on the West Coast in which the Grand Fleet was at that moment sheltering—one cannot refuse to say 'hiding'—from a danger which though exaggerated by our imaginations, was also terribly real, and potentially fatal.

We started off by motor in a clear delicious autumn morn-ing, myself, my Naval Secretary, the Director of Intelligence (now Admiral of the Fleet Sir Henry Oliver), and a Flotilla Commodore since renowned as Sir Reginald Tyrwhitt. It was a charming drive through the splendid scenery of the Scottish Highlands, and absorbed in the topics we were to discuss with the Commander-in-Chief, to which swift motion, cool air and a changing landscape were an agreeable accompaniment, we said little to one another. Suddenly the Flotilla Commodore, who was sitting in the back of the car with the Director of Intelligence, said so loud that I could hear him, 'Look, there is a searchlight on the top of that house.' 'What's that?' I said, turning round, following with my eye the gaze of the two officers. But before I could see what had struck their attention the car swung quickly round a corner and the object, whatever it was, was invisible. 'A searchlight, sir,' said the Commodore, 'is mounted on top of one of the houses over there' (pointing). A searchlight, I must explain, is a considerable apparatus of about the size of a big drum.

'Surely,' I said, 'that is unlikely in the middle of the Highlands.'

'Sir,' said the Commodore, 'I know a searchlight when I see one.'

'Well, but what could it be for, why should we have mounted one here? Do you know anything about it, Admiral?'

The Director of Intelligence knew nothing. He was sure however that it could serve no British naval purpose. On the other hand both officers were certain they had seen it.

In war-time everything that is unexplained requires to be probed, and here we were confronted with a complete mystery. We racked our brains for the rest of the journey and no one could suggest any reasonable or innocent explanation.

At last the road went winding downwards round a purple hill, and before us far below there gleamed a bay of blue water in which rode at anchor, outlined in miniature as in a plan, the twenty Dreadnoughts and Super-Dreadnoughts on which the command of the seas depended. Around them and darting about between them were many scores of small craft. The vessels themselves were painted for the first time in the queer mottled fashion which marked the early beginnings of the science of *Camouflage*. The whole scene bursting thus suddenly upon the eye and with all its immense significance filling the mind, was one which I shall never forget. Not a house, not a building of any kind disfigured the splendid hills and cliffs that ran down on either side to ocean water. Yet gathered together in this solitude and narrow compass was the floating steel city with its thirty or forty thousand inhabitants upon whose strength, loyalty, courage and devotion our lives and freedom, and as we may perhaps assert still the freedom of the world, from minute to minute depended. Last night not a vessel had been there; to-morrow morning perhaps the bay would again be empty; but to-day the vital and all-powerful instrument of the world war was reposing on its bosom.

'What would the German Emperor give,' I said to my companions, 'to see this?'

'He would have to get the news back,' said the Commodore, 'if he was to do any good with it.' 'And then,' added the Admiral, who was a man of facts and figures, 'it would take about forty-eight hours before anything could get at us.' 'But,' I persisted, drawn on by the sombre current of reflection, 'suppose a submarine flotilla were lurking about behind some of the islands and suppose a Zeppelin came over and saw the Fleet, couldn't she tell them and lay them on at once?' 'By day,' was the reply, 'she would be seen and we should put to sea, by night she would probably not see the Fleet. The whole coast is full of bays.'

'Suppose there was a spy on shore who signalled to the Zeppelin, and that the Zeppelin without coming near the bay signalled to the submarines,' I persevered. 'Suppose, for instance, sir,' responded the Admiral, 'someone had a *searchlight . . .*'

Then we went on board the *Iron Duke*, and all the morning we were locked in conference on the many grave matters which had to be discussed with Sir John Jellicoe and his Admirals, nor was it until we lunched on board the Flagship that anything like ordinary conversation was possible. Then someone started the topic of the searchlight forty miles inland on the top of what looked like a shooting-lodge in the middle of a deer-forest.

'We have seen a very suspicious thing this morning,' I

said only half seriously to the Commander-in-Chief. 'What do you think of it yourself?'

'Whereabouts was it?'

My companions explained the general position. The Commander-in-Chief paused and reflected before he answered, then he said, 'There might be something in it. We have heard several bad rumours about that place.' He mentioned the name of the shooting estate. 'It is said that there are a number of foreigners there. We have had a report that an aeroplane had an accident there before the War, and also that one has been seen in the neighbourhood since, which we were not able to trace. Anyhow,' he added, 'what do they want a searchlight for?'

I said to the Director of Intelligence, 'You are a properly-constituted authority under the Defence of the Realm Act, are you not?' 'You mean, sir,' he replied, 'that we might go and look them up ourselves on the way back.' 'If we have half an hour to spare,' I answered, 'we might just as well find out what the searchlight is wanted for.'

It was dark when our conferences were finished, but before leaving we requisitioned four pistols from the armoury of the *Iron Duke* and put them under the seat of the car. As we swept along through the night I could not help thinking perhaps we might fall into a hornet's nest. If the sinister hypothesis was justified, if the searchlight was an enemy signal and a Scotch shooting-lodge a nest of desperate German spies, we might receive the sort of welcome the police had had at Houndsditch. However, suspicion and curiosity went hand in hand, and the excitement of adventure spurred them both.

'We are quite close here now, sir,' said the Commodore, directing the driver to reduce speed, 'the entrance gate is in this clump of trees. I marked it myself this morning.'

'We had better get out,' I said, 'and walk up, and the chauffeur can report if anything goes wrong.' Accordingly with our pistols in our pockets we marched up the drive, and after a couple of hundred yards arrived at the entrance of a good-sized stone house at one end of which there stood a tall square tower. We rang the front-door bell. It was duly answered by a portly respectable butler. My three companions were in naval uniform, and the butler seemed startled at such a visit.

'Whose house is this?' we asked. The name was given. 'Is your master at home?' 'Yes, sir,' he said, 'he is at dinner with the house-party.' 'Tell him that some officers from the Admiralty wish to see him at once.'

The butler departed and we pushed into the hall.

There was a pause, and presently the dining-room door opened and a clatter of conversation suddenly stilled, and out came a ruddy grey-headed gentleman who, as we thought with some perturbation, inquired, 'What can I do for you?'

'Have you got a searchlight on the top of your tower?' asked the Admiral.

I must interpolate here that I was still sceptical about the existence of the searchlight. If there were a searchlight, if that fact were established, I could not think of any alternative but treason. I was therefore startled at the admission which followed.

'Yes, we have a searchlight on the tower.'

'When did you put it up?'

'Some time ago, two or three years ago, I think.'

'What did you put it up for?'

'To what do I owe the honour of this visit?' countered the host, 'and what right have you to put me these questions?'

'We have every right,' replied Admiral Oliver. 'I am the Director of Naval Intelligence, and I possess full authority under the law to enquire into any suspicious circumstances. Will you kindly explain at once what you use this searchlight for?'

'Ah,' said the host, peering at me, 'I recognize you, Mr. Winston Churchill.' 'The question is,' I replied, 'what do you use your searchlight for?'

There was a strained silence, and then the old gentleman replied, 'We use it to locate the game on the hill-sides. From the tower we can see several of the beats, and the searchlight gleams on the eyes of the deer, and shows us where they are lying, so we know where to send the stalkers in the morning. And,' he added, warming to his subject, 'we can tell deer from cattle by the searchlight, as the glint of the eyes of the cattle is white and that of the deer has a greenish tint.' This farrago of improbabilities and impossibilities confirmed my deepest suspicions, and I think those of my companions. At any rate we made no comment upon them.

'We wish to see the searchlight,' I said. 'We wish you to show it to us yourself.'

'Certainly,' replied our unwilling host. 'You will have to climb up the spiral staircase of the tower.'

'You go ahead,' we answered.

He opened a door leading out of the hall and disclosed the first steps of a stone staircase. We made a military disposition to guard against foul play. The Naval Secretary remained at the bottom of the stairs, and the Admiral, the Commodore and I followed the old gentleman up their winding course. At any rate we had a hostage, we had a stronghold and, outside the gate, we had a connecting link with unlimited reinforcements.

It was a high tower, and the stairs corkscrewed several times; at length, however, we reached the top and emerged on a fairly broad square platform with low battlements. There in the middle, sure enough, was the searchlight. It was a 24-inch medium Destroyer instrument, bolted strongly into the roof. It was, as far as we could see, quite capable of being used.

'Do you expect us to believe this story of yours,' I asked the old gentleman, 'that you use this searchlight to pick up game on distant hill-sides and that you can tell deer from cattle by the glint in their eyes?'

'Well, it is quite true, whatever you think.'

'You will have to give these explanations to the proper

authorities. For the present we are going to dismantle your searchlight so that it cannot be used.'

'You can do what you choose,' he replied, evidently very indignant.

'We are going to,' I said, and we proceeded accordingly.

Then we descended the stairs, bearing with us various parts of the mechanism, and after sullen adieux we joined our motor-car outside the entrance gate.

.   .   .   .

I have told this story exactly as it happened; but the most extraordinary part in my opinion is yet to come. There was nothing in it at all. The most searching investigations of the local and central authorities discovered no grounds for the slightest suspicion. The searchlight had been erected four years before and had apparently been used at that date for sweeping the hill-sides. It had not been used, according to overwhelming testimony, since the War began. It was not in fact capable of being used at the moment when we examined it. The owner of the house was a gentleman of high reputation and undoubted patriotism. He was entertaining a party of thoroughly respectable people. There were no foreigners in the house or on the estate. No confirmation could be obtained of the rumour which we had heard on the *Iron Duke* of an aeroplane accident on the estate before the War or of an unaccountable aeroplane having been seen in the neighbourhood. There was nothing in fact, except the searchlight on the castle tower and the unreasonable explanation given for its presence there.

Although the owner of the castle may have experienced a natural anger at this sudden nocturnal call and the suspicions which it implied, he could at least solace himself by the reflection that grounds far less disquieting had consigned many other persons during the war period to far greater inconvenience; and for myself I say without hesitation that in similar circumstances I should do the same again.

WITH THE GRENADIERS

WHEN the British Government determined to abandon the campaign at the Dardanelles and all the hopes that had been placed upon it, and when the evacuation of Gallipoli was impending, I thought it necessary to quit their counsels and betook myself to the armies. I had asked to be allowed to join my Yeomanry Regiment, at that time serving in the French theatre and quartered in rest billets not far from Boulogne. As the crowd of officers and men returning from leave was streaming off the steamer in the French port, I heard my name called out by the Military Landing Officer and was told that the Commander-in-Chief, Sir John French, had sent a car to take me at once to his headquarters. Sir John had been hostile to me in South Africa, but for many years we had been friends. We had faced the vicissitudes of pre-war years together; we had collaborated closely in all the work of preparation for the movement of the Expeditionary Force to France in the event of war; and in the early critical months I had been thrown constantly into the most intimate relations with him. The fast staff car soon carried me to the Chateau of Blondecque near St. Omer, where his headquarters lay. We dined together almost alone, and talked long on the war situation on the same footing as if I had still been First Lord of the Admiralty, responsible for carrying his armies across the Channel in the feverish hours of August, 1914.

It was not until the next morning that he said to me, 'What would you like to do?'

I said that I would do whatever I was told.

He said, 'My power is no longer what it was. I am, as it were, riding at single anchor. But it still counts for something. Will you take a Brigade?'

I answered that of course I should be proud to do so, but that before I could undertake any such responsibility, I must learn first-hand the special conditions of trench warfare.

I must explain to the reader that, having been trained professionally for about five years as a soldier, and having prior to the Great War seen as much actual fighting as almost any of the Colonels and Generals in the British Army, I had certain credentials which were accepted in military circles. I was not a Regular, but neither was I a civilian volunteer. I fell in that intermediate category described as 'the Dug-outs'. However presumptuous it may have been, I did not feel incapable of discharging the duties in question, provided I had a month or two in the line to measure the novel conditions of the Great War for myself.

The Commander-in-Chief said that this was quite right and that he would attach me for instruction to any Division I liked. I said that the Guards was the best school of all. He thereupon invited Lord Cavan, who commanded the Guards Division, to come and see him a few days later; and after a pleasant conversation I found myself duly posted to this famous unit.

The Guards were then holding the line in front of Merville. It was the depth of winter, and this part of the front was fairly active.

'I will send you,' said Lord Cavan, 'to one of the best Colonels I have. You will learn more from —— than from anyone else. His battalion goes into the line to-morrow. If you come and lunch with me at La Gorgue at one o'clock, you will be in plenty of time.'

Accordingly the next day, having packed what I thought was a very modest kit, I repaired to the headquarters of the Guards Division and was most kindly welcomed by its gallant Commander. As soon as a frugal lunch was over, the General took me himself in his car to the Grenadier battalion I was to join as a major under instruction previous to higher appointment. The Companies had already begun their march to the trenches, and the Colonel, the Adjutant and the Battalion staff were on the point of setting out. There were salutes and smiles and clickings of heels. A few friendly commonplaces were exchanged between the Divisional General and the Battalion officers; and then His Lordship got into his car and drove off, leaving me very like a new boy at school in charge of the Headmaster, the monitors and the senior scholars. We were to ride on and overtake the Battalion a mile or so ahead of us. My new host had considerately provided a pony; and jogging along we soon caught up the marching troops and reined our horses into a walk among them. It was a dull November afternoon, and an icy drizzle fell over the darkening plain. As we approached the line, the red flashes of the guns stabbed the sombre landscape on either side of the road, to the sound of an intermittent cannonade. We paced onwards for about half an hour without a word being spoken on either side.

Then the Colonel: 'I think I ought to tell you that we were not at all consulted in the matter of your coming to join us.'

I replied respectfully that I had had no idea myself which battalion I was to be sent to, but that I dared say it would be all right. Anyhow we must make the best of it.

There was another prolonged silence.

Then the Adjutant: 'I am afraid we have had to cut down your kit rather, Major. There are no communication trenches here. We are doing all our reliefs over the top. The men have little more than what they stand up in. We have found a servant for you, who is carrying a spare pair of socks and your shaving gear. We have had to leave the rest behind.'

I said that was quite all right and that I was sure I should be very comfortable.

We continued to progress in the same sombre silence. Presently the landscape began to change. The shell-holes in the neighbouring fields became more numerous and the road broken and littered with débris. The inhabited country was left behind. The scattered houses changed to ruins. The leafless trees were scarred and split and around them grass and weeds grew tall and rank. Night descended, and no sound was heard but the crunch of marching feet and the occasional bang of an adjacent gun.

At length there was a halt. Orderlies advanced to take our horses. From this point we must proceed on foot. The four Companies quitted the road and moved slowly off in various directions into the darkness across the two miles of sopping fields beyond which an occasional Véry light, rising bright and blue, betokened the position of the line.

The headquarters of the Battalion were established in a pulverized ruin called Ebenezer Farm. Enough brickwork remained to afford some protection from shells and bullets, but not enough to make an enemy suppose it was a likely abode of men. Behind these crumbling walls a small sandbag structure with three or four compartments served as the Colonel's headquarters. A charcoal fire added the unusual element of warmth. It had taken us nearly three hours to reach this place, and it was, I suppose, about half-past six by the clock. The Colonel and the Adjutant were busy getting the Battalion into the line and receiving reports as to how the relief of the Coldstreamers we were replacing was proceeding. When all this was over, we had some food and strong tea with condensed milk. There was a little general conversation during this meal. But his subordinates evidently stood in the gravest awe of their Commanding Officer, and very few remarks were made except on topics which he himself initiated. At about eight o'clock a dead Grenadier was brought in and laid out in the ruined farm-house for burial next day. The Second-in-Command asked me where I would sleep. There was a signal office in the Battalion Headquarters, or there was a dug-out 200 yards away. The signal office was about eight feet square occupied by four busy Morse signallers, and was stifling hot. Having surveyed it, I said I should like to see the dug-out. Accordingly we walked out into the sleet and through the dripping grass. The dug-out was very difficult to find, and it was apparently considered dangerous to show the flash of an electric torch. However, after a quarter of an hour we found it. It was a sort of pit four feet deep, containing about one foot of water. I thanked the Second-in-Command for the trouble he had taken in finding me this resting place, and said that on the whole I thought I should do better in the signal office. We talked a little about 'trench feet,' then the prevailing malady, and he explained to me the organization of the 'sockatorium,' a dug-out in the trenches where wet socks were continually being dried and returned to their owners. The bullets, skimming over the front line, whistled drearily as we walked back to Ebenezer Farm. Such was my welcome in the Grenadier Guards.

It will always be a source of pride to me that I succeeded in making myself perfectly at home with these men and formed friendships which I enjoy to-day. It took about forty-eight hours to wear through their natural prejudice against 'politicians' of all kinds, but particularly of the non-Conservative brands. Knowing the professional Army as I did and having led a variegated life, I was infinitely amused at the elaborate pains they took to put me in my place and to make me realize that nothing counted at the front except military rank and behaviour. The weather remained atrociously cold, but the Colonel gradually and appreciably thawed. He took immense pains to explain to me every detail of the economy and discipline of his battalion. I asked if I might accompany him on the rounds which he made to the trenches once each day and once each night. He accepted the suggestion, and thereafter we slid or splashed or plodded together through snow or mud—for the weather alternated cruelly—across the bullet-swept fields and in and amid the labyrinth of trenches. Sometimes when there were a good many bullets he became quite genial.

'Always ask me anything you want to know. It is my duty to give you all information.'

'It is very good of you, Sir.'

'I am quite willing to do it.'

'Thank you very much, Sir.'

The *splat* in air of four or five bullets, greeting us as we

71

tramped up Sign Post Lane (which, as everybody knows, is close to the village of Neuve Chapelle), led me to observe, 'They're all high.'

'I hope so,' said the Colonel.

We used to tramp about like this for two or three hours at a time each day and night; and bit by bit he forgot that I was a 'politician' and that he 'had not been consulted in the matter of my coming to his battalion.'

When we went out of the line for a short period of rest, there was a general relaxation of the intensely strenuous life of discipline which the Guards invariably preserved when in actual contact with the enemy; and before ten days were past from the time I made my first incursion into the Colonel's Mess, I might as well have been an absolutely blameless Regular officer who had never strayed from the strict professional path. When the Second-in-Command went home on leave, I was invited temporarily to undertake his duties. This was certainly one of the greatest honours I had ever received. The offer emboldened me to make a suggestion to the Colonel. I said that I thought I should learn of the conditions in the trenches better if I lived with the Companies actually in the line instead of at the Battalion Headquarters. The Colonel considered this a praiseworthy suggestion, and made arrangements accordingly. I must confess to the reader that I was prompted by what many will think a somewhat inadequate motive. Battalion Headquarters when in the line was strictly 'dry.' Nothing but the strong tea with the condensed milk, a very unpleasant beverage, ever appeared there. The Companies' messes in the trenches were, however, allowed more latitude. And as I have always believed in the moderate and regular use of alcohol, especially under conditions of winter war, I gladly moved my handful of belongings from Ebenezer Farm to a Company in the line. I had known one of the Company officers, Edward Grigg, for some years before the War, and was sure of the most cordial welcome which the circumstances of the time would admit.

I wish I could convey to the reader the admiration which

I felt and feel for these magnificent Grenadiers. Although there was no battle or serious action, yet the front was very lively. Cannonade and fusillade were unceasing. The weather changed from hard frost to soaking rain, and back again to frost, with spiteful rapidity. No one was ever dry or warm. The trenches taken over from the Indian Corps were in the worst condition: the parapets in many places not bullet-proof; the ditches undrained; the wire lamentably defective. The troops had to work night after night on the enemy's side of the trenches strengthening their parapets and wire, and a steady trickle of casualties flowed painfully back to the hospitals, while the graveyard of Ebenezer Farm still grew. The officers helped the men in their labours, walked about in No Man's Land, or sat on the parapets for hours at a time while the work was proceeding and the bullets whined and whistled through the night. Every morning the trenches were well sprinkled with shell, and many requests—not all of which could be granted—went back to headquarters for retaliation. Still the spirit of the Battalion was such that even a stranger and a visitor caught something of their indomitable good temper and felt the support of their inflexible discipline.

. . . .

The longer one lives, the more one realizes that everything depends upon chance, and the harder it is to believe that this omnipotent factor in human affairs arises simply from the blind interplay of events. Chance, Fortune, Luck, Destiny, Fate, Providence seem to me only different ways of expressing the same thing, to wit, that a man's own contribution to his life story is continually dominated by an external superior power. If anyone will look back over the course of even ten years' experience, he will see what tiny incidents, utterly unimportant in themselves, have in fact governed the whole of his fortunes and career. This is true of ordinary life. But in war, which is an intense form of life, Chance casts aside all veils and disguises and presents herself nakedly from moment to moment as the direct arbiter over all persons and events. Starting out in the morning you leave your matches behind you. Before you have gone a hundred yards, you return to get them and thus miss the shell which arrived for your express benefit from ten miles away, and are no doubt shocked to find how nearly you missed the appointed rendezvous. You stay behind an extra half-minute to pay some civility to a foreign officer who has unexpectedly presented himself; another man takes your place in walking up the communication trench. Crash! He is no more. You may walk to the right or to the left of a particular tree, and it makes the difference whether you rise to command an Army Corps or are sent home crippled or paralysed for life. You are walking up a duckboard track; in front of you a shell is falling at half-minute intervals; you think it fool-hardy to walk straight along the track, especially as you notice that you will reach the danger-point almost on the tick of time; you deflect fifty yards to the left; but the gun is traversing at the same time, and meets you with a grim smile in the midst of your precautions.

We must remember La Fontaine:

> 'On rencontre sa destinée
> Souvent par des chemins qu'on prend pour l'éviter.'

The ancient Egyptians carried their reverence for a corpse to a height never paralleled in history. Their supreme desire was to preserve the pitiful remains of earthly life in solitude and dignity for ever. They quarried their tombs deep in the living rock. Shaft led into gallery, and gallery opened into shaft. To these devices of secrecy the embalmers added their wonderful art. Never was so great an effort made by human beings to achieve such a particular object. It procured exactly the opposite result. As it turned out, it was the only conceivable manner in which they could have achieved the opposite result. Four thousand years afterwards the bodies of their kings and princes are dragged from their hiding-places to be exposed to vulgar and unsympathetic gaze in the halls of the

Boulak Museum. They just managed by infinite effort, sacrifice and skill to achieve the one thing above all others they wished to avoid. These observations tempt me to relate a very trifling experience which happened to me in the days when I dwelt with the Grenadiers.

. . . .

One afternoon when I had been about a week in the line with the Company, I sat myself down in our tiny sand-bagged shelter to write some letters home. On this part of the front the water was so near the surface that we were defended by breastworks rather than trenches. In consequence there were no dug-outs in the ordinary sense. Slight sand-bag structures with a sheet of corrugated iron and one layer of sandbags for a roof formed our only protection. The morning shelling had stopped, and custom led to the belief that we should have a quiet interval. I got out my writing-pad and stylo and was soon absorbed in a letter. I had written for perhaps a quarter of an hour when an Orderly presented himself at the entrance to the shelter, and saluting with Guardsman-like smartness, handed me a field telegram:

'The Corps Commander wishes to see Major Churchill at four o'clock at Merville. A car will be waiting at the Rouge Croix cross-roads at 3.15.'

I had known General —— personally for a good many years. But it was rather unusual to bring an officer out of the line, and I wondered what this summons could mean. I did not much like the prospect of trapesing across three miles of muddy fields, the greater part under the observation of the enemy by daylight, and then toiling back all the way in the evening. However, the order brooked no question, and in a rather sulky mood I put away my unfinished letter, arrayed myself in my trappings, and prepared to set out on my trudge. The two tall Grenadiers who acted as our servants were busy tidying-up the shelter.

75

'You must take your man with you,' said the Company Commander, 'to carry your coat. It is always better not to be alone, and he knows the way back in the dark.'

Accordingly in a few minutes we set out towards Rouge Croix. We had scarcely got 200 yards from the trenches when I heard the shriek of approaching shells, and looking round I saw four or five projectiles bursting over the trenches we had left. The firing continued for about a quarter of an hour, and then ceased. I thought no more of the matter, and toiled and sweated my way through the slush towards Rouge Croix. What on earth could the General want me for? It must be something important, or he would surely not have summoned me in this way.

At last I reached the rendezvous—a shattered inn at these exceptionally unhealthy cross-roads. There was no motor-car. I waited impatiently for nearly an hour. Presently there appeared a staff officer on foot.

'Are you Major Churchill?'

I said I was.

'There was a mistake,' he said, 'about sending the car for you. It went to the wrong place, and now it is too late for you to see the General at Merville. He has already gone back to his Headquarters at Hinges. You can rejoin your unit.'

I said, 'Thank you very much. Would it be troubling you too much to let me know the nature of the business on which the General required to bring me out of the line?'

'Oh,' said the staff officer airily, 'it was nothing in particular. He thought as he was coming up this way, he would like to have a talk with you. But perhaps there will be some other opportunity.'

I was indignant; and as the staff officer was no more than a Major, I did not take any more pains to conceal my ill temper than he to conceal his indifference to it. It was now nearly dark, and I had to begin another long, sliding, slippery, splashing waddle back to the trenches. I lost my way in the dark, and it must have been nearly two hours before I got into Sign Post Lane. The cold rain descended steadily, and

76

what with perspiration (for I was wearing my entire wardrobe) and the downpour, I was quite wet through. The bullets whistled venomously down Sign Post Lane, and I was glad when at last I came into the shelter of the breastworks of the line. I had still nearly a mile to go through a labyrinth of trenches. The sedentary life of a Cabinet Minister, which I had quitted scarcely a month before, had not left me much opportunity to keep fit. Tired out and very thirsty, I put my head into the nearest Company Mess for a drink.

'Hello,' they said, 'you're in luck to-day.'

'I haven't seen much of it,' I replied. 'I've been made a fool of.' And I made some suitable remark about the impropriety of Corps Commanders indulging their sociable inclinations at the expense of their subordinates.

'Well, you're in luck all the same,' said the Grenadier officers, 'as you will see when you get back to your Company.'

I did not understand their allusions at all. Having consumed a very welcome tumbler of whisky and water, I splashed out again into the rain and mud, and ten minutes later arrived at my own Company. I had got within twenty yards of my shelter when a Sergeant, saluting, said:

'We have shifted your kit to Mr. ——'s dug-out, Sir.'

'Why?' I asked.

'Yours has been blown up, Sir.'

'Any harm done?'

'Your kit's all right, Sir, but —— was killed. Better not go in there, Sir, it's in an awful mess.'

I now began to understand the conversation in the Company Mess.

'When did it happen?' I asked.

'About five minutes after you left, Sir. A whizzbang came in through the roof and blew his head off.'

Suddenly I felt my irritation against General —— pass completely from my mind. All sense of grievance departed in a flash. As I walked to my new abode, I reflected how thoughtful it had been of him to wish to see me again, and to show courtesy to a subordinate, when he had so much responsibility on his shoulders. And then upon these quaint reflections there came the strong sensation that a hand had been stretched out to move me in the nick of time from a fatal spot. But whether it was General ——'s hand or not, I cannot tell.

'PLUGSTREET'

EVERYONE remembers the remark of the old man at the point of death: that his life had been full of troubles most of which had never happened. The following incident may serve as a personal example of this comforting reflection.

In February, 1916, I was commanding the 6th Royal Scots Fusiliers in Flanders. We had for some weeks been holding the well-known sector of the line near 'Plugstreet' (Ploegsteert) Wood and Village. The front was comparatively calm, and the battalion moved in and out of the trenches on six-day spells with only the usual experiences of local bombardments, sniping and trench raids and counter-raids. Our so-called 'rest' billets when out of the line were separated by scarcely a mile and a half of flat country from our front trenches, at this point distant about three hundred yards from those of the Germans. In this situation, living on a little more than a square mile of ground, we were destined to remain for over three months. My own headquarters when resting were only about a thousand yards away from those I occupied when we were actually holding the front. It therefore made very little difference to us whether we were in or out of the trenches, and we lost about the same number of men through shell fire.

When I had joined the army in the previous November, I had written, at the invitation of the Commander-in-Chief, a paper embodying my ideas upon new methods of attacking the enemy. This Memorandum, entitled 'Variants of the Offensive,' dealt with many secret projects in which I was deeply interested, including the scheme of using caterpillar vehicles (afterwards called 'Tanks') in large numbers by surprise and in conjunction with smoke and other devices. The importance of this paper at the date at which it was written (December 3, 1915) can best be judged from the following extract:

'3. *Caterpillars.*—The cutting of the enemy's wire and the general domination of his firing-line can be effective by engines of this character. About seventy are now nearing completion in England, and should be inspected. None should be used until all can be used at once. They should be disposed secretly along the whole attacking front two or three hundred yards apart. Ten or fifteen minutes before the assault these engines should move forward over the best line of advance open, passing through or across our trenches at prepared points. They are capable of traversing any ordinary obstacle, ditch, breastwork, or trench. They carry two or three Maxims each, and can be fitted with flame-apparatus. Nothing but a direct hit from a field-gun will stop them. On reaching the enemy's wire they turn to the left or right and run down parallel to the enemy's trench, sweeping his parapet with their fire, and crushing and cutting the barbed wire in lanes and in a slightly serpentine course. While doing this the Caterpillars will be so close to the enemy's line that they will be immune from his artillery. Through the gaps thus made the shield-bearing infantry will advance.

'*If artillery is used to cut wire the direction and imminence of the attack is proclaimed days beforehand. But by this method the assault follows the wire-cutting almost immediately, i.e. before any reinforcements can be brought up by the enemy, or any special defensive measures taken.*'

At the same time as I gave a typescript copy to the Commander-in-Chief, I had sent a duplicate to the Committee of Imperial Defence, where it was printed with all precautions of secrecy, and early in February, 1916, a proof of this vital document was forwarded to me in France, reaching me through the army post office while I was actually at my headquarters in the line. The rule against taking secret documents into the front line was strict and well-known, and as I gazed at the print in my sandbagged, half-demolished farm the feeling that the enemy was scarcely a thousand yards away

became strangely accentuated in my mind. However, we were
to go into our 'rest billets' a mile farther back at daybreak.
I would then make such revisions in the proof as were necessary, and send it in by an officer for transmission to London
through the Army Headquarters at Bailleul.

'Plugstreet' Village consisted in the main of a long row of
well-built brick houses, some of them four storeys high,
looking blankly towards the enemy across flat, soppy fields.
Up to this time, except for its church, it had been very little
injured by artillery fire. Many of the houses had holes in them,
but all were perfectly weatherproof and comfortable, and in
most windows the glass was not broken.

The IXth Scottish Division, of which my battalion formed
a part, had, however, a most energetic General in command,
who had been steadily stirring things up, and the Germans
replied to our bombardments by continual retaliation which
eventually reduced the countryside to a pockmarked wilderness scarred with shapeless ruins. My 'rest' headquarters
were in a small red-brick convent, hitherto quite intact. I had
a comfortable, well-furnished room on the ground-floor, with
a large bay-window looking straight out upon the front line
and barely out of rifle-shot of the enemy. In this window there
was a writing-table, and here, after breakfast, at about ten
o'clock on the morning of which I write, I sat myself down
and began to tackle my correspondence, which had accumulated during our spell in the trenches, and in particular to
address myself to 'Variants of the Offensive.'

I must have been working for about half an hour when
my attention was distracted by two or three shell-bursts
about 300 yards away in the field immediately beyond that
in front of our house. Farther away, up in the line and at the
corner of 'Plugstreet' Wood, little white puffs of shrapnel
showed an unwonted liveliness. I paused to watch the firing,
as if from a box at the theatre. A few minutes passed, and two
or three more shells burst with loud detonations about 200
yards away, but this time in the field directly before my eyes.
Then, after a minute or so, came another. There is no shell

more unpleasant to the experienced ear than the one which comes straight towards you and bursts short. You hear the whine growing to a whistle, ever more intense in note and pregnant with the menace of approach, and it is only when you see a cartload of earth leap into the air in front of you that you are quite sure that no harm is done. This particular shell (a 4·2) burst with a disagreeable bang the other side of the road, about 40 or 50 yards away. It occurred to me that our house (we called it 'the tall thin house') might very likely be the enemy's target, and that the next shell might quite comfortably hit the bull's-eye. At the same time more distant crashes in other parts of the village seemed to show that 'Plugstreet' was about to receive special attention at the enemy's hands.

We had no defences of any kind, but at the back of the room in which I was writing there was a small cellar below the level of the ground and with a brick roof. In this the old lady with her daughter, who had remained in the convent after the departure of the nuns, had already taken refuge, together with two of the battalion telegraphists. It seemed foolish to go on sitting with only a sheet of glass between one and the projectiles, but, on the other hand, I did not think much of the cellar. The vaulted roof looked strong but was actually only two bricks thick. The place was so crowded that there was barely room for anyone else, so I got up from my table and, passing out of the back door, went into the adjoining building, which was used as our battalion office. Here also were large windows facing the front, but there was besides a back room where at any rate two brick walls stood between me and the fire. Against field artillery a barrier of two walls is a fair defence: the first explodes the shell, the second probably stops the pieces. Here then I sat down to wait until the shelling stopped. I left all my letters and papers, as I thought, lying on the table near the window. I do not suggest my departure was hurried, but neither was it unduly delayed. It was dignified but decided.

And now 'Plugstreet' Village began to endure one of the

first of those methodical bombardments which gradually reduced it to ruins. Every minute or two came shells, some bursting on the fronts of the houses, some piercing their roofs, others exploding in the courtyards and offices behind. The shriek of the approaching projectiles, their explosions and the crash and rattle of falling brickwork, became almost continuous. My Adjutant soon joined me in our back room, and here we sat and smoked, at first not unpleasantly excited, but gradually becoming silent and sulky. From time to time tremendous explosions close at hand told us that the neighbouring buildings were struck. The soot came down the chimney in clouds, and the yard at the back, on to which we now looked, was strewn with fragments of brick and masonry. One shell burst on the face of the opposite building before our eyes, making a gaping hole. We continued to sit in our chairs, putting our faith rather doubtfully in our two brick walls. When one has been under shell fire every day for a month, one does not exaggerate these experiences. They were the commonplaces of the life of millions in those strange times.

The bombardment lasted about an hour and a half. The intervals between the shells grew longer, and presently all was silent again. My second-in-command presented himself in the highest spirits. He had been making a tour of the men's billets when the enemy began to fire on the village, and had remained a serene spectator a few hundred yards away, waiting, as he put it, 'until the rain stopped.'

Together we returned to the 'tall thin house.' As we entered by the back door a scene of devastation met our eyes. The room in which I had been writing was wrecked and shattered. Daylight streamed through a large hole in the brickwork above the bay-window. The table, the furniture, papers, objects of all kinds, had been hurled into confusion. Everything was covered with thick, fine, red brick-dust. Then, from the back of the house, appeared the old woman and her daughter, completely terrified; behind them one of the signallers, grinning.

'Oh, mon Commandant,' said the girl, 'come and look at the cellar where we were; it came into the midst of us.'

We followed: the brickwork which formed the roof of the cellar had been shattered, and there on the floor lay a long 30-lb. shell, unexploded. This shell had come through the architrave of the bay-window on a steep angle of descent, smashed through the brickwork of the little cellar, and fallen literally into the midst of these poor people crowded together, slightly injuring one of the signallers but otherwise doing no harm to anybody. One may imagine the spasm of terror of these two women when this monster arrived almost in their laps, and when of course they thought it would explode immediately. They had suffered far more than the pain of death.

Having told them they must pack up and quit their home at once, I returned into my wrecked writing-room. As the shell had not exploded, nothing was scorched or seriously damaged. Laboriously I collected my papers, kit and belongings. All needed only to be shaken free of thick fine brick-dust, and for the moment I thought nothing was missing. Still, as the letters and sheets of notepaper were gradually collected, I began to think it odd that I should not find the one paper of which I was in search and to which I attached—rightly as history has proved—extreme importance. At last everything was picked up; the soldier-servants came in and swept the room; nowhere could I find my precious document. Nothing was missing but that, and nothing mattered but that. It had gone; it had vanished completely. How and by what agency could it have been spirited away? Certainly not by the shell. If the room had been blasted by an explosion, the explanation would have been complete; but if this document alone among my papers was not found in the litter of the room, it must have been taken by someone, and by someone—observe—who comprehended its immense significance.

I now began to feel very seriously alarmed. 'Plugstreet' stood on one of the last vestiges of soil left to the Belgian people. The frontier line was but a few hundred yards away.

Our Intelligence reports had warned us of the probability of spies among the inhabitants who still remained. Suspicion filled every breast, and every possible precaution was always to be taken. My imagination began to construct half a dozen sinister explanations. Some sure agent of the enemy dwelling in our midst, realizing that I was a person whose correspondence would be of exceptional importance, watching day after day in the hopes of spying upon it, had entered the room in the confusion after the shell had struck it, had seized the paper, attracted no doubt by the words printed in red ink across it, 'This document is the property of His Majesty's Government,' and had vanished as swiftly as he came. Even now he might be making his way to some place where an enemy aeroplane could take him across the line by night. Every sort of terrifying possibility crowded in upon my mind, and no remedy of any kind suggested itself. The woman and her daughter had not seen any strangers about, but were so frightened out of their wits that they could give no assurance. The signaller had been busy with his injured comrade. We searched the house again and all in it; but not a trace! I passed the next three days in helpless anxiety. I reproached myself a thousand times with not having sent the document back by an officer the moment it had been so incontinently brought to me in the line by the military post. Why had I ever let it out of my possession for a second?

This brings me to the remark of the dying old man with which the account of this incident opens, and I may at once relieve the anxiety of the reader and clear my own character for prudence. On the third day I happened to put my hand into my right inner breast-pocket, which I hardly ever used. There I found, safe and secure, the paper I had been so feverishly seeking. Instinctively, in leaving the room over which swift peril was impending, I had picked up the one thing that mattered and put it in my pocket. Seeing it once again safely in my hand, I gave a gasp of delight and relief, and the precarious, battered abodes of 'Plugstreet' under rainy skies and bitter winds seemed as safe and comfortable as home.

THE U-BOAT WAR

THE fifth and final volume upon the Naval Operations of the War has in due course appeared. It covers the whole of the Navy's work in the last two years of the War. There it is at last. The story of all that the Navy did. But the epic that lies therein is frozen. The book is not an inspiring book. It repels not only by its mass of technical detail, but by the fact that it is the composite work of different hands. The able historian has evidently had to submit his chapters to authorities and departments; and important personages in the story have clearly applied their pruning-knives and ink-erasers with no timid hand. The result is a sort of official amalgam which seems to be neither a plain, fearless narrative nor a fair and searching analytical examination of the great disputes. Nevertheless, so grim and startling are its abundant materials, so vast and costly the tremendous engines of war moving through its pages, so deadly the issues at stake, that this carefully jumbled mass of incident and detail is a veritable treasure-house of information upon the last two most gigantic years of the naval war.

To understand the main issues of this final volume, it is necessary to bear in mind the earlier phases of the War. The years 1914 and 1915 had vindicated Admiralty strategy. The vastness of the unseen tasks performed by the Fleets was not fully appreciated in those days of stress and strain. The whole of the enemy trade had been swept off the outer seas, and all avenues of victualment and reinforcement were held for the sole use of the Allies. In April, 1915, England enjoyed a supremacy at sea the like of which had never been seen even in the days of Nelson. Security was so complete as to pass almost unnoticed. There remained to Germany in all the

oceans only a couple of fugitive cruisers, the *Dresden* lurking
stealthily beneath the glaciers of Tierra del Fuego, and the
Koenigsberg lying helpless and imprisoned in the steamy
recesses of a South African lagoon. It was accepted as a matter
of course that the seas were safe for all the Allies, and an insurance of less than one per cent. was sufficient to cover
merchant ships putting to sea in time of war unguarded and
unrestricted in every direction from every port.

The guarantee for all this marvellous immunity was the
Grand Fleet lying almost motionless in its remote northern
harbour at Scapa Flow. It ruled the seas as they have never
been ruled in our history. The whole of the War ultimately
hinged upon this silent, sedulously-guarded, and rarely visible
pivot. But for the Grand Fleet, Germany would at once have
attacked and severed all the Allied communications at sea,
and have threatened the coast of France at every point.
But for the Grand Fleet, the German cruisers and other ships
of war, ranging the Atlantic and the Channel at will, would
have accomplished in a few weeks an entire suspension of our
ocean traffic, and at once enforced that remorseless blockade
for which her U-boats were afterwards to struggle for two
bitter years, and to struggle in vain. But for the Grand Fleet
in the first phases, the whole war-structure of the Allies must
have collapsed. It was upon the seas the 'sure shield' behind
which France defended herself, and under which twenty-two
million men from first to last were finally carried or recarried
to and from the Allied fighting lines.

The strategic effect of placing the Grand Fleet at Scapa
Flow before the declaration of war had been alike complete
and instantaneous. When at the end of August, 1914, the
prestige of the Royal Navy was proved by the brilliant and
lucky dash into the Heligoland Bight, the Kaiser—all his
inferiority-complexes confirmed by the sinkings of his cruisers
on their very war parade ground—accepted the triumph of
British naval power on the surface of the seas.

The thoughts of the German Admirals, thus foiled, turned
inevitably to the submarine. Here was a wonderful and

terrible new weapon, whose power and endurance had never been tested by any country till war came. Yet it was not until February, 1915, that Germany resolved to employ this weapon against commerce, and von Pohl was allowed to proclaim the first German blockade of the British Isles. This was an enormous decision. But though the world looked with horror and indignation at the sinking of merchant ships without a thought for the safety of passengers and crews, the British Admiralty felt no serious alarm. We knew that the Germans had only some twenty-five U-boats, and not more than one-third of them could be on the prowl at once. On hundreds of ships proceeding weekly in and out of scores of harbours, this handful of marauders could make no serious impression. It was like hundreds of rabbits running across a ride, with only two or three one-eyed poachers to shoot them. Nearly all the rabbits got across every time, and the poachers themselves were harassed by the gamekeepers. We actually announced in 1915 that we would publish all the sailings and sinkings every week, and Admiralty confidence was swiftly justified by events. No substantial or even noticeable injury was wrought upon British commerce by the first German submarine campaign. Upon the other hand, grave difficulties loomed up for the German Government. The torpedoes that sank neutral ships destroyed the goodwill of the neutral world. Finally, the sinking of the *Lusitania* roused a storm of wrath, and a Note from America which brought the campaign in British waters to a close.

The first U-boat attack ceased in June, 1915, and thereafter for more than a year—nearly two years in all from the declaration of war—the British command of the seas was absolute and unchallenged. Outside the land-locked waters of the Baltic and the Black Sea, not a single hostile vessel cleft salt water. Had the War ended in 1915 or 1916, history would have recorded—in spite of the broken-off encounter of the fleets at Jutland—that the domination of the British Navy had been undisturbed. Within this halycon period there was one, and only one, great naval opportunity of ending the War both by land and sea. That opportunity was lost for ever in April, 1915, when the Navy desisted finally from all attempts to force the passage of the Dardanelles. But even after all the misfortunes of the Allied armies in 1915, the naval calm continued, and a decisive victory of the British, French, and Russian armies in 1916 would have brought peace, with British naval power unquestioned and seemingly unquestionable.

All this time the Germans were building U-boats, and the German Admiralty staff clamoured unceasingly to be allowed to use them. The conflict between the Civil Power, terrified of bringing the United States and other neutrals into the War against them, and the German Admirals, sure that they had it in their power to free the Fatherland and its dependents from the stranglehold of the British blockade, is a long, cold, intense drama. Desperation alone turned the scale. In 1916 the miscarriage at Verdun, the strain of the Somme, the surprise of Brusilov's offensive, and finally the hostile entry of Roumania, constituted for Germany the second climacteric of the War. The men of dire decision were summoned to supreme control. Hindenburg and Ludendorff were given the helm. They threw their whole weight upon the side of the Admirals. The Chancellor and the Foreign Secretary were borne down by a new strong heave of the wheel. Their warnings that the United States would surely be drawn into the hostile ranks fell upon unheeding ears of ruthless, violent men fighting for national survival.

From October, 1916, onwards German submarine activities had been increasing, and sinkings had begun to rise sharply. On January 9, 1917, in conference with the Kaiser at Pless, the civilians abandoned their opposition to the extremist measures. A hundred submarines lay ready to proceed on fateful missions. The Admirals marshalled facts and figures to prove that unrestricted U-boat warfare would certainly yield a sinkage of 600,000 tons a month, and that five months of this would bring Great Britain, the Arch-enemy and soul of the hostile co-operation, to her knees. The Kaiser ratified the decision of his servants. The orders were issued; the declarations were made; unrestricted warfare began on February 1, and the United States became a mortal enemy. These prodigious stakes would never have been played if any of those who gathered at Pless had known that a few months later Russia would collapse, and that a new prospect of victory on land would open. It was their destiny to take the plunge just before they would have learnt that far less grievous hazards offered safety.

The first phase of the naval war was the tacit submission of the German sea-going fleets to the superior strength of Britain. There supervened upon this from October, 1916, with ever-growing intensity, the second phase, namely the life-and-death struggle of the Royal Navy with the German U-boats. It was a warfare hitherto undreamed-of among men, a warfare at once more merciless and complicated than had ever been conceived. All the known sciences, every adaptation of mechanics, optics, and acoustics that could play a part, were pressed into its service. It was a war of charts and calculations, of dials and switches, of experts who were also heroes, of tense, patient thought interrupted by explosions and death; of crews hunted and choked in the depths of the waters, and great ships foundering far from port without aid or mercy. And upon the workings of this grisly process turned the history of the world.

. . . .

November and December, 1916, had seen a tentative revival of the sinkings, but the public, and even the Government, had grown so confident of the security of our commerce that it was some time before they began to feel serious anxiety. This new attack would no doubt be speedily dealt with. To those concerned in the rising art of propaganda it was even pleasing, because of the effect on neutral and United States opinion. But the attack went on. The sinkings mounted month by month. On February 3, 1917, following the German declaration of unrestricted warfare, the American

Ambassador left Berlin. But it was not until April 6 that the United States entered the war. So enormous an accession of strength seemed to make victory certain. How could the Teutonic Empires, already hard-pressed, withstand this new surge of 120 millions against them? But suppose the American armies could not get across the Atlantic; nay, supposing the seas were barred to war materials, oil, and even food, what would happen to an island—the mainspring of the war— with 40 million mouths to feed, and often scarcely three weeks' supply in hand?

Hitherto British sea-power had been so unchallenged that its existence had been as unnoticed as the air we breathe. Then suddenly the air began to get horribly rarefied. The cannonade thundered on in Flanders, but in all the wide circles of the British Government a new preoccupation possessed men's minds. The sinkings of British, Allied and Neutral merchant shipping by submarines alone had crept up in October and November, 1916, to nearly 300,000 tons a month. In January this total was still 284,000 tons. With the opening of unrestricted warfare in February the dial mounted sharply to nearly 470,000 tons. The German Naval Staff had calculated that England, after providing for her own and allied military needs, had about $10\frac{1}{2}$ million tons of shipping for her supplies. She could not manage with less than $7\frac{1}{2}$ million tons. If the promised 600,000 tons could be sunk monthly, the fatal $7\frac{1}{2}$ million tons limit would be reached in five months, and by the plain logic of figures Germany's most formidable opponent must give in. The danger was mortal and near. No talk now of decisive battles at sea, or of the Dardanelles, or landings in the Baltic, or attacks on Heligoland. A blow was being aimed at the heart and a stranglehold was tightening round the throat. Would it succeed, or would it fail? This was the question that stood staring Whitehall in the face. April saw another tremendous rise, and the fateful finger moving remorselessly up. It was pointing to 837,000 tons of British, Allied, and Neutral sinkings, of which 516,000 tons were of British sinkings. It was, in fact, had we known it, only one-fifth short of the promised German Naval Staff figure! Every other aspect of the War declined and grew thin and pale before the U-boat menace.

This last volume of the Naval History describes its impact on the War Cabinet, the Admiralty and the Navy, and the measures taken to cope with the danger. The methods of defence fell into three categories. The first was mechanical. The preparations and counter-measures set on foot by the Board of Admiralty during the first abortive submarine attack in 1915 had not been neglected by their successors.

A great volume of small craft was built or building. The dodges and devices of 1915 had been elaborated and multiplied. Depth-charges to explode at set depths, hydrophones to detect the slightest sound of submarine engines; flotilla-hunting manœuvres, explosives, paravanes for towing under water; nets with tell-tale buoys, decoy ships, zig-zagging—all these were in full activity. The second category comprised the reorganization of the Naval Staff and the creation of an anti-submarine department. But it was the adoption of a third expedient, the tactics of convoy, that alone decided the fate of nations.

No story of the Great War is more remarkable or more full of guidance for the future than this. It was a long, intense, violent struggle between the amateur politicians, thrown by democratic Parliamentary institutions to the head of affairs, on the one hand, and the competent, trained, experienced experts of the Admiralty and their great sea officers on the other. The astonishing fact is that the politicians were right, and that the Admiralty authorities were wrong. The politicians were right upon a technical, professional question ostensibly quite outside their sphere, and the Admiralty authorities were wrong upon what was, after all, the heart and centre of their own peculiar job.

A second fact is not less noteworthy. The politicians, representing Civil Power at bay and fighting for the life of the State, overcame and pierced the mountains of prejudice and false argument which the Admiralty raised and backed with the highest naval authority. In no other country could such a thing have happened. In Germany, for instance, the Kaiser and his Ministers had to accept the facts, figures, and opinions of the naval experts as final. When Admiral Holtzendorff declared that unrestricted warfare would sink 600,000 tons of British shipping a month, and that five months would ruin England's war-making power; when he put that forward on his honour and conscience as the head of the German Naval Staff, there was no means of gainsaying him. Hindenburg and Ludendorff endorsed in professional loyalty the opinions of their naval colleagues, and the Civil Power, dumb before mysterious assertion, saw itself, if it did not adopt the technical advice, accused of timidity or weakness which might deprive Germany of victory and even life. Naturally they yielded, and all went forward to disaster.

But the British politicians—we apologize for their existence —were powerful people, feeling they owed their positions to no man's favour. They asked all kinds of questions. They did not always take 'No' for an answer. They did not accept the facts and figures put before them by their experts as necessarily unshakable. They were not under moral awe of professional authority, if it did not seem reasonable to the lay mind. They were not above obtaining secretly the opinions of the junior naval officers concerned with the problem, and of using these views to cross-examine and confute the naval chiefs. The sleuth-hound of the politicians was Sir Maurice Hankey, Secretary of the Committee of Imperial Defence and Secretary to the War Cabinet. He had a lawful foot in every camp—naval, military, professional, political—and while observing every form of official correctitude he sought ruthlessly 'the way out.' Above him stood Mr. Lloyd George, with Mr. Bonar Law at his side. Both these men had keen, searching minds for facts and figures. Neither of them was a stickler for professional etiquette. Neither was unduly impressed by gold-laced personages. Mr. Lloyd George in particular had grasped power by a strange combination of force and intrigue. He was sure he would be hanged if we did not win the War, and he was quite ready to accept the responsibility on such terms.

Both these Ministers, as early as November, 1916, when the sinkings began to rise, had suggested that the Admiralty should use convoys for merchant ships. There was nothing novel about the proposal. Convoy had been a usual method in former wars. It had been used at the beginning of the Great War to protect troopships against German cruisers, and had been completely successful. Not a single vessel had been sunk. The Grand Fleet or detached squadrons of battleships were invariably convoyed and protected against U-boats by escorts of destroyers.

Now let us see the mountain of objections which the Board of Admiralty and the heads of its expert departments built up against this proposal. The Admiralty argued that convoy would be no protection against submarine attack. First of all, it was not physically practicable. Merchant ships could not keep their stations in a convoy. They would certainly not be able to zig-zag in company. Their different speeds would make their pace that of the slowest. Time would be lost, danger increased, and tonnage capacity wasted. They would be readily thrown into confusion on a sudden attack. A submarine in the midst of a convoy might make tremendous havoc. We should be putting too many eggs in one basket. No fewer than 2,500 merchant ships, said the Admiralty, entered or left British ports every week. No convoy would be safe if it contained more than three or four merchantmen to every escorting warship. Where were the destroyers and small craft for this prodigious task? We had not got them. After the safety of the fighting fleets and the patrols of the Dover Straits and narrow seas had been provided, the destroyers left over would be hopelessly inadequate.

Such, in outline, was the monumental case which the Admiralty raised against the adoption of a convoy system against unrestricted U-boat attacks. It must be admitted that few stronger arguments were ever set forth on paper. And when the reasoning was backed by the sincere deep-rooted

convictions of able and experienced sailors who had spent
their lives upon the sea, and understood all the difficulties
and mysteries of which landsmen are necessarily ignorant,
it is amazing that any force should have been found within
the organism of the British State capable of overriding it
by command and overturning it by experiment. Yet that is
what happened; and unless it had happened America would
would have been cut off from Europe, England would have
been starved into submission, and Germany would have won
the War.

.   .   .   .

No part of the Official History is written with more
circumspection than the account of the conflict between
the War Cabinet and the Admiralty upon the adoption of
the convoy system. A layman might read these pages atten-
tively and remain quite unconscious of its intensity, or
indeed of what actually happened. All the main essential
facts are stated, but they are stated with such a studied
absence of emphasis, and often in so inverted a sequence, that
the conclusion to which they remorselessly point is hidden.
It is only when we decipher the cryptogram by the key of
chronology that the truth—to many the unwelcome truth—
emerges.

At the discussions on November 2, 1916, in the War Cabinet (Mr. Asquith being still Prime Minister) Mr. Lloyd George
had asked the Commander-in-Chief, Sir John Jellicoe, whether he had any plan against German submarines working
upon our trade routes. The Commander-in-Chief admitted
that he had not. Mr. Bonar Law then asked why they could
not use the system of convoy. He was answered by the Chief
of the Naval Staff that it did not do to send more than one
ship at a time under escort. The First Sea Lord, Sir Henry
Jackson, for his part added that merchant ships would never
be able to keep sufficiently together to enable a few destroyers
to screen them. The weight of adverse authority was for the
time being decisive. As the losses from sinkings grew con-

tinually, anxiety deepened, but the increasing apprehension in no way altered the Admiralty view. The arrival of Sir John Jellicoe as First Sea Lord confirmed it. The Admiralty Staff massed all their opinions and authority in a memorandum in January which condemned the convoy system with elaborately-marshalled reasons. There is no doubt, we are told, that this memorandum recorded the collective opinion of the Admiralty,

'for the minutes of those high officials who were more particularly concerned with the defence of trade are all expressive of the same, or nearly the same, view.'

On February 1, 1917, the unrestricted U-boat campaign began, and immediately the sinkings rose to an alarming pitch. It was at this point that Sir Maurice Hankey wrote his celebrated memorandum challenging all the main objections to the convoy system, and armed with this Mr. Lloyd George (now Prime Minister), on February 13, reopened the whole question with the Admiralty authorities. This masterly paper, and the pointed manner in which it was pressed upon the Admiralty by the new head of the Government, left the dominant and senior naval opinion unchanged. There can, of course, be no doubt that many of the facts and arguments upon which it had been built were those of the junior members of the Admiralty Staff departments dealing with the U-boat problem. In the Naval Service the discipline of opinion was so severe that had not the channel, or safety-valve, of the Committee of Imperial Defence been in existence, these opinions might never have borne fruit or even come to light. The firmly-inculcated doctrine that an admiral's opinion was more likely to be right than a captain's, and a captain's than a commander's, did not hold good when questions entirely novel in character, requiring keen and bold minds unhampered by long routine, were under debate.

Argument, however, was reinforced by practical experience. Ships engaged in the coal trade with France had suffered heavy losses in the closing months of 1916. The French immediately suggested convoy, and on February 7 the Admiralty deferred to their wishes. The colliers were dispatched in company and under escort. The new system was immediately effective. Out of 1,200 colliers convoyed to and fro in March, only three were lost. Still the Admiralty staff continued obdurate. But one cannot wonder at their tenacity, considering the data upon which their reasoning was based.

In the early part of the War, when we were publishing our losses from U-boats compared to our incoming and outgoing traffic, the number of ships arriving at or leaving British ports within a week had been magniloquently stated to amount to 2,500. How was it physically possible for the sixty or seventy destroyers which were at most available, supplemented by armed trawlers and other small craft, to deal with this vast inflow and outflow of thousands of ships? However, this damning figure of 2,500 was now itself attacked. A junior officer, Commander R. G. Henderson, working in the anti-submarine department and in close contact with the Ministry of Shipping, broke up this monstrous and long tamely-accepted obstacle. It was shown that the 2,500 voyages included all the repeated calls of coasters and short-sea traders of 300 tons and upwards. But these were not the ships upon which our life depended. It was the ocean-going traffic to and from all parts of the world that alone was vital. In the early days of April it was proved by Commander Henderson that the minimum arrivals and departures of ocean-going ships of 1,600 tons and upwards upon which everything hung did not exceed between 120 and 140 a week. The whole edifice of logical argument collapsed when the utterly unsound foundation of 2,500 was shorn away.

April saw a terrible intensity of the submarine war, and in every direction the secret graphs of the Cabinet showed the time-limits which were closing in upon the food supplies of the central island and the war supplies of its armies and of the Allied armies in the various theatres. Still the Admiralty in the ruins of their previous arguments resisted convoy. It may be that a dread of becoming responsible not only for the warships of the Navy, but for the safety of every merchant ship that sailed, lay heavy upon their minds. Whatever the root reason, they remained inflexible. On April 10, 1917, the United States having entered the War, Admiral Sims conferred with the First Sea Lord. The grim facts of the submarine campaign were put before the American sailor, and he was urged to procure all possible assistance in small craft. At the same time, he was induced to accept the Admiralty view that convoy was impossible. He conveyed this opinion to his own Government as the most authoritative expression of British naval science. To the cumulative pressure of events and reasons there were now added the conclusions of a committee of Officers from the Grand Fleet, who had sat for some weeks at Longhope in the Orkneys, on the question of the sinkings on the Scandinavian trade route. They unanimously recommended convoy. Nevertheless, the First Sea Lord, while agreeing to an experiment on this particular route, would only report to the War Cabinet that the question of its general use was still 'under consideration'.

Awful months had thus passed without relief. But now matters had reached a climax. On April 23 the War Cabinet debated the whole issue with their naval advisers. The results of the discussion were wholly unsatisfactory. On the 25th, therefore, the War Cabinet, sitting alone, resolved upon decisive action. It was agreed that the Prime Minister should personally visit the Admiralty 'to investigate all the means at present used in anti-submarine warfare, on the ground that recent inquiries had made it clear that there was not sufficient coordination in the present efforts to deal with the campaign.' The menace implied in this procedure was unmistakable. No greater shock could be administered to a responsible department or military profession. The naval authorities realized that it was a case of 'act or go.'

On the 26th the head of the anti-submarine department minuted to Admiral Jellicoe: 'It seems to me evident that the time has arrived when we must be ready to introduce a comprehensive scheme of convoy at any moment.' On the 27th Admiral Jellicoe approved the policy. When Mr. Lloyd George visited the Admiralty on April 30 in accordance with the Cabinet's decision, he was presented with a full acceptance of the demand of the Civil Power. He was able to report to his colleagues:

'As the views of the Admiralty are now in complete accord with the views of the War Cabinet on this question, and as convoys have just come into operation on some routes and are being organized on others, further comment is unnecessary . . .'

. . . .

Of course, as everyone knows, the adoption of the convoy system at sea defeated the German U-boat attack. By July, 1917, it was in working order. Five months of unrestricted submarine warfare had passed, and Great Britain had not been brought to her knees. In September the clouds began to break. Monthly sinkings had fallen from 800,000 to 300,000 tons. In February, 1918, the curve of building output crossed the sinkage curve. By October, 1918, 1,782 great ships had been convoyed across the seas with a loss of only 167. The war effort of the Allies had never slackened. The American armies had been carried safely across the seas, and the doom of Germany had for some months been only a matter of time.

This remarkable story had two suggestive sequels. When the Admiralty took their famous decision to adopt the convoy system, the First Sea Lord demanded in return from the War Cabinet that the naval task should be lightened by the abandonment of the Salonica operation and the withdrawal of the Allied armies from the Balkan theatre. He proved conclusively that 400,000 tons of shipping would be saved by this curtailment. Salonica and the Balkan campaign were Mr. Lloyd George's pet scheme. So relieved was he to obtain the Admiralty's consent to the adoption of convoy that he agreed on April 30, 1917, to sacrifice it. The French were also compelled to agree. However, a subordinate Minister, Sir Leo

Chiozza Money, working in the Foreign Trade Department, produced a paper, endorsed by the Ministry of Shipping, showing that this 400,000 tons saving could be effected by drawing the whole of the Allied supplies from the American Continent instead of from all parts of the world; and that the supplies would be forthcoming. The scheme was adopted, and the Salonican armies were therefore permitted to continue their campaign. As we all know now, it was the surrender of Bulgaria in October, 1918, which produced the final collapse of the Teutonic Empires. But for this, the German armies would have effected their retreat to the Meuse or the Rhine, and another bloody year might have dawned upon the world involving the killing and wounding of another two or three millions of men and the consumption of ten or twelve thousand more millions of our dwindling wealth.

The second incident is much smaller. Early in May, 1917, the Admiralty, having accepted the War Cabinet's decision in favour of convoy, asked the Navy Department at Washington to adopt it also. But the American naval authorities knew from Admiral Sims's reports that the convoy system had been forced upon the British sailors against their better judgment by political interference. They therefore refused to risk their ships upon what they knew was inexpert and unprofessional advice. It was some months before the vast and patent triumph of convoy removed their deep misgivings.

The reluctance of all the naval chiefs in every Allied country to adopt convoy finds its counterpart only in the reluctance of the military chiefs of all the armies, Allied and enemy, to comprehend the significance of the tank. In both cases these means of salvation were forced upon them from outside and from below.

THE DOVER BARRAGE

A SUBMARINE going round by the Orkneys took nearly a week to reach its hunting-grounds in the Channel or its approaches. If it ran the gauntlet of the Dover Straits, it took only a single day. It thus saved seven days of the fortnight that it could stay out. If the smaller U-boats could pass safely through the Dover Straits, the number which Germany possessed was for practical purpose almost doubled. The closure of the Straits and of the Belgian ports abutting on the Straits was therefore cardinal. The need to close the Straits against all enemy vessels had from the beginning of the War made Dover an important command. Admiral Bacon had come there in 1915, and in 1916 had laid a net barrage right across the Straits from the Goodwins to the Belgian sands.

Great results were expected from this barrage, and its reputation was established by a curious coincidence. On the very day that it was laid, April 24, 1916, Admiral Scheer, the German Commander-in-Chief, had been ordered to restrict submarine warfare. The German Government had decided that merchantmen were to be boarded before being sunk. In protest Scheer had called off his U-boats. None, therefore, passed the Straits for some months, and the cessation of their attempts gave rise at Dover to the idea that they had been stopped by the new net barrage.

A false confidence in this device was established in many able minds upon strong foundations. Admiral Bacon was the victim of the illusion that his net barrage could stop the U-boats. He was an able officer with a chequered history. The bent of his mind was technical. He was a brilliant formulator and exponent of complicated designs. His bombardments of

101

the Belgian coast were embodiments of higher mathematics. He had made a 15-in. howitzer in an incredibly short time at the beginning of the War. In everything that concerned machinery, invention, organization, precision, he had few professional superiors. He was a fine instrumentalist.

In the autumn of 1917 the newly-formed Plans Division of the Admiralty War Staff were quite sure that U-boats were habitually passing through the Dover barrage, and that it was neither an obstacle nor a deterrent. Rear-Admiral Keyes, in charge of this Division, began to press upon his superiors at the Admiralty first the reality of the evil, and secondly a number of remedial measures. The defence had originally consisted of a line of nets buoyed upon the surface, occasionally patrolled, and supported by elaborate minefields. Critics of our pre-war naval arrangements have justly censured the Admiralty mine. Lord Fisher, in his earlier peace-time administration, had been hostile to mines. The sub-department concerned had dwelt in a highly secret and secluded nook, defended on every side by abstruse technicalities. There is no doubt that it had produced at the beginning of the War a mine which would rarely keep its depth and very often not explode on being bumped. Even these defective instruments were not very numerous. The main strategy of the Admiralty had not contemplated elaborate minings and counter-minings. But now the War had gone on for nearly three years, and in the absence of any coherent scheme of a naval offensive, the mines played an ever-increasing part. By the middle of 1917 new and thoroughly-effective mines were flowing out from the factories, and in November fresh deep minefields were laid in the Dover Straits.

. . . .

A keen dispute arose in the winter of 1917 between the Plans Division of the Admiralty and the Dover Command. Admiral Keyes asserted that Admiral Bacon's existing arrangements were not stopping U-boat penetration. He declared that the minefields must be not only watched by trawlers and drifters with all available small craft patrolling above the mines, but that they must be brightly illuminated and actively defended. The movement of a U-boat, groping its way forward on the surface, ready to dive at any moment, would thus be detected. An alarm would be given, a hurroosh would be raised, cannon would fire, the submarine would dive and make its exit from the world by bumping into one of our good live mines. Admiral Bacon, on the other hand, contended that the lights would warn the submarines and teach them to avoid the minefields, and that if destroyers continually patrolled the Dover Straits it was only a question of time before the Germans sent out a strong force to devour the patrols. He argued, besides, that it was not true that submarines were passing the Dover Straits.

Anyone will see that the controversy thus outlined was well posed. Strong evidence was furnished by the Naval Intelligence that the Plans Division were right. A U-boat (U.C. 44) sunk in shoal water had been fished up, and her captain's log revealed the exact dates on which each of a continuous stream of U-boats had passed the Straits, and, indeed, their whole time-table and fortunes. In fact, the U-boat commanders were told in their instructions that they could dive under or go over the Dover barrage at will. It was possible, however, to be sceptical of the German figures, and though the Plans Division were convinced of their accuracy, the Dover Command continued obdurate and complacent.

When in the late autumn of 1917 the Plans Division began to criticize the efficacy of the Dover barrage, and alleged that German submarines were passing freely through Admiral Bacon's command, the Admiral was neither pleased nor polite. Many coldly-stated differences passed to and fro in official papers. The climax was reached upon the blunt issue of whether the minefields should be illuminated or not. The brightly-lighted picture of these large areas, picketed by almost defenceless trawlers manned by fishermen, seemed a most unwarlike proposition. One might almost have said that common sense repelled such a remedy. But on this point the

Admiralty Staff were right, and the Admiral on the spot was wrong. The simple truth emerged that the barrage and mine-fields were no use unless they were vigorously defended from above water.

Admiral Jellicoe (now First Sea Lord) had sided at the out-set with Admiral Bacon. But at length he was convinced by the Plans Division. On December 18, 1917, with the cordial approval of the First Lord, Sir Eric Geddes, he ordered Bacon to institute the 'Plans' Patrol system. By good luck it drew blood the very first night it was tried. On December 19 a German U-boat was destroyed. Admiral Jellicoe, who was greatly exhausted by the strain of his prolonged and valiant exertions in charge of the Fleet and later of the Admiralty, was relieved of his post. Admiral Wemyss, his deputy, an officer not greatly known, but of robust temper, and reputed to be willing to make full use of a Staff, was appointed in his stead. Admiral Bacon was dismissed from the Dover Command, and Keyes, the head of the Plans Division, hitherto the chief critic, was sent to see if he could do the job himself.

Here again the results of the change, even though perhaps favoured by fortune, were amazing. In the next six months eleven identified submarines perished in the Dover minefields or their approaches. The sinkings in the Channel, influenced also by convoy, rapidly declined. The German voyage through the Dover Straits became one of intolerable peril. In 1918 a Zeebrugge submarine could count on not more than six voyages before she met her inevitable doom. By the summer all attempts of U-boats to pass the Dover barrage had ceased.

The Official History is delicately careful not to emphasize the facts. But nevertheless all the salients are there. We see another clash between the new and somewhat irreverent junior brains of the Navy and august, old, honourable authority. Such cases reproduce themselves in civil life and in political affairs. We see them in the management of great businesses and in the structure and fortunes of Governments. But certainly the story of the Dover barrage forms a corroborating sequel to the story of the convoy system. It was the Prime

Minister, the War Cabinet and the First Lord who asserted the freedom of the new professional thought over embattled seniority. In both cases the Civil Power leaned, pressed, and finally thrust in the right direction.

There was, however, a bad moment for the new command at Dover. The patrolling of the illuminated minefields offered an obvious target to German attacks. The fishing craft on duty were vulnerable in the last degree. About a hundred little vessels of no military quality—trawlers burning flares, drifters, motor-launches, paddle mine-sweepers, old coal-burning destroyers, P-boats, with a monitor in their midst—all lay in the glare of the searchlights. The area was as bright as Piccadilly in peace time; and its occupants scarcely better armed. Some miles to the eastward five patrolling divisions of destroyers offered their only possible protection. But if these were evaded by a raiding enemy, a massacre seemed inevitable. The acceptance of this hideous liability was the essence of Keyes's conception. All the chances being balanced, this was the least bad to risk. But it was very bad.

On February 14, 1918, the Germans brought their best flotilla commander from the Heligoland Bight with their four latest and largest destroyers, and fell upon the trawlers of the Dover barrage with cruel execution. By a muddle in the darkness of mistaken signals, and what not, the six British destroyers on patrol inexcusably mistook them for friends and they escaped in triumph to the north. The fishermen were deeply angered. They thought the Royal Navy had failed to give them the protection which it had guaranteed, and which they deserved. They saw themselves exposed on any night to merciless attacks. For a while they lost confidence in the new Dover Command, and, indeed, in the Royal Navy.

Admiral Bacon, who had predicted this very event, saw his arguments justified. He felt himself entitled to say, 'I told you so.' Keyes's reputation hung on a thread. Luckily, resolute new-minded men more or less banded together upon a common scheme of thought had now got a grip of the Admiralty machine. Keyes survived the disaster, and the immortal epic of

Zeebrugge on St. George's Day restored alike the confidence of the Admiralty in their officer and the faith of the fishermen in their chief.

It also gained the plaudits of the public and very favourable references in the newspapers, neither of which, even in their excess, will be disputed by history.

LUDENDORFF'S 'ALL—OR NOTHING'

ONCE the War had begun, the only chance Germany had of making peace was during the winter of 1917. It was a good chance. Russia had fallen, the Treaty of Brest-Litovsk had been signed. The mighty 'steam-roller' lay a mass of scrap-iron in the ditch. For the first time the Central Empires had no fears about their Eastern front. Ludendorff could bring a million men and several thousand cannon across to the West. For the first time since the battles of 1914 Germany would outnumber the British and French.

The United States had entered the War. A new and almost unlimited source of man-power had been opened to the Allies. But the American armies were far away organizing, training, trickling only a few thousands at a time across the Atlantic Ocean. Many months must pass before the gigantic new combatant could appear in the arena. There must be a lengthy, deadly interval between the collapse of the Russia effort and the first effective manifestations of American power. It is in this interval that the crisis lies.

The mutinies in the French army which followed upon General Nivelle's disastrous offensive in April, 1917, had reduced France to the strictest form of defensive during the rest of the year. The British armies had had to shoulder the main responsibility. The fixed idea of the British High Command, spurred by French appeals and the danger of impending French collapse, spurred also by a phase of black pessimism at the Admiralty, had evoked a virtually continuous succession of desperate British attacks upon the German fortified lines.

The British Headquarters erroneously believed that they could break the German front, and they found in the temporary weakening of France a wealth of reasons to reinforce their convictions. 'We are sure we can break through; but even if we can't, we are bound to go on attacking to take the weight off the French in their present condition.' The result had been a series of well-planned, resolute, obstinate offensives at Arras in April, Messines in June, and Passchendaele in the autumn. These were pursued regardless of loss of life until at length in the winter battles of Passchendaele the spirit of the British army in France was nearly quenched under the mud of Flanders and the fire of the German machine-guns. 'Rain,' says the German official account, 'was Germany's ally all through.' When the last forlorn assault had been made across the indescribable crater-fields and bog-labyrinths of Passchendaele, the British army had been 'bled white'. Nearly 300,000 men had been killed or wounded. The Menin Memorial Arch records the names of scores of thousands whose bodies have never been recovered from the vast shell-churned morass in which the struggle had raged.

Thus the year closed. The French not yet revived; the British water-logged, the Americans remote. Meanwhile the fall of Russia, while it offered for the German High Command a gigantic reinforcement for the western front, presented to the German Government immense facilities for negotiation. All European Russia was within German power or reach. The Bolsheviks had ruptured all bonds with the Allies; they had repudiated all obligations, including the sacred obligations till then due from the Allies to their country. Who cared for Russia now? The Czar was in the hands of his murderers; the faithful officers and troops had been dispersed or destroyed; the liberal and intellectual elements which had, however ineffectually, tried to do their duty were massacred or in flight. Every tie between Russia and the Western Allies was severed. The German armies had saved their country in the field; now was the time for German statecraft to extricate the Empire from the hideous catastrophe into which it had blundered.

As the cannonades of Passchendaele died away and the British effort froze into a wintry stillness, every Government on both sides had time to count its own pulse. Even in resolute

England there was an intermittence in the beat. The very cessation of the fighting gave the peoples time to feel their wounds —grave and ghastly wounds indeed! Even as late as January or February, 1918, if Germany had offered the full restoration of Belgium, and a settlement with France about Alsace-Lorraine coupled with a scheme of German gains from Russia, a basis for negotiation might well have been established.

But First Quartermaster-General Ludendorff, mounted on the German General Staff, dominated not only the military but the political scene, and Ludendorff had other ideas. The realities of war had reduced the Emperor to a mere function of the war-time situation. The political system of Germany was not such as to throw up from the Parliamentary machine the audacious or rugged figures that had seized the helm of state in England or in France. Everything in Germany had been sacrificed to the military view. On every occasion the General Staff had had their way, and now this intense and mighty organism, at once the strength and ruin of the German Empire, focused itself in what for the actual guidance of events was virtually a Ludendorff Dictatorship.

And here we come to an essential characteristic of this extraordinary man. He loved his country, but he loved his task more. His task was to procure victory at all costs; to make sure that if defeat was certain, no resource should be left unconsumed, no chance untried, no boats unburned behind him. And what a chance yet remained!

. . . .

A million extra men, three thousand extra guns flung into the Western scale; the vast battering train of artillery which he and Hindenburg had been forging during the whole of 1917; the novel plan of attack by shock-troops and infiltration which had been conceived. Were these not to have their opportunity? Was it to be recorded that Germany gave up the game without playing the last card, and that perhaps the best card? No, the responsibilities of the General Staff ended only when they had reported to the Civil Government that every chance had been exhausted, and every vestige of strength consumed. Well has it been said, 'Thought which cools the minds of other peoples inflames the German.' The great design, a Kaiserschlacht—an attack in scale and intensity never before conceived, by methods and arts never before employed —might well snatch victory out of the slowly-closing jaws of disaster. And were not the Design in itself, and the Event to which it would give rise, mental propositions of rare quality? To make such plans, to set in motion such forces and trains of consequence, to play for such stakes—were not these good in themselves?

Accordingly, on November 11—fateful day, exactly one year before the end—Ludendorff held a conference at Mons— fateful place, where the first shots and the last were fired by the British Army in the Great War! This was a conclave of the real operators. The Kaiser, the kings and princes, the commanders of armies and groups of armies, the Chancellor of the Empire, the Foreign Minister, the leading figures of the Reichstag—all are banished.

Here we are dealing with business—precise, cold, grim, and titanic. Only the high confederacy of the General Staff; only men who know what they are talking about; only men who talk the same technical language; only men who are thinking of war propositions in war terms to the exclusion of all other considerations! Quite a small gathering, a rigidly limited few, competent experts in blinkers, their eyes riveted on the job, their own job, with supreme knowledge in their sphere and little inkling that other or larger spheres existed.

Kuhl, chief of the staff of Rupprecht's group of armies; Schulenberg, the Crown Prince's man and manager of his army group; Wetzell, Ludendorff's high plan-maker; and Ludendorff himself. The general premise: 'We are at last again strong enough in guns, munitions, and men to resume an offensive in the west. We can shake the life out of the French and British armies before the Americans can come. We have a clear run for six months.'

Resultant question: How are we to do it? Ludendorff declares: 'The British must be beaten' (*wir müssen die Engländer schlagen*).

Query: Shall they be attacked in Flanders towards Haze-brouck or southward near St. Quentin? There is much to be said for the northern attack. But one thing can be said against it which is decisive.

It cannot begin so early as March, the weather would be too bad, the ground would be too wet. We cannot afford to wait for April or May, for we are up against time. The Americans are coming, and we have taught the Allies how to make mustard gas. So we must attack the British as early as possible and as far south in their front as may be necessary to catch the weather. Ludendorff therefore proposed that the line of the Somme should be gained and held, and that then the main attack should turn north-westward so as to roll up the British front, and 'throw them into the sea.'

Kuhl advocated the Flanders attack, and was willing to wait a month longer if necessary for the sake of it. Wetzell was for resuming the attack on Verdun. During the six weeks' discussion which followed from the November 11 meeting he argued that the Verdun attack offered the best results, as it settled with the French who were 'strategically free'. The Flanders attack, according to him, had good prospects both tactical and strategic, but he regarded it as only suitable in the last phase of a great combined offensive. If the British were attacked in Flanders in March, the French could make a relieving offensive in the south; whereas if Verdun were attacked the state of the ground in March would prevent the British from bringing assistance. He strongly criticized the St. Quentin attack. Surprise would be difficult, as it was 'a quiet front and preparations would be noted.' The British and French could both bring help to the scene. The German advance would cross the devastated area of the Somme battlefields and run into a number of old defended lines, both German and Ally. Deferring no doubt to the view of his chief and ignoring the arguments he had himself advanced, Wetzell, by a strange inconsistency, finally proposed the double offensive against the British, first the St. Quentin attack in the third week in March (known in the secret patter of the confraternity as 'Michael and Mars'), and the second, a fortnight later, towards Hazebrouck (its token 'St. George').

Ludendorff, who had meanwhile visited the whole front with the two chiefs of staff, and had discussed the offensive with the five army commanders likely to be involved, decided definitely on January 21 against the attack on Verdun, and the attack on Hazebrouck, and chose the St. Quentin sector in spite of all that might be said against it. The choice was his, and his alone.

. . . .

The following was the artillery appointed to torture the British: 375 field, 297 heavy and 28 super-heavy batteries; or expressed in numbers of guns, Eighteenth Army 2,500 guns, Second Army, 1,800 guns, Seventeenth Army 1,900 guns; total, 6,200 guns.

And this was the method of the torture:

Beginning at 4.40 a.m.—Two hours: 50 minutes of gas against our batteries, trench mortars, headquarters, telephone exchanges, and dumps; then 10 minutes' surprise fire against the infantry position. These 50 and 10 minutes' fire were then to be repeated.

Three periods of 10 minutes' fire to verify ranges.

70 minutes' shooting for effect against the infantry position.

75 minutes' more, but with special sub-periods of 15 and 10 minutes of intense fire.

Finally, five minutes to prepare for the infantry assault.

Covered by this monstrous battery, 66 German divisions were to be launched in the dawn of March 21 against a front held by 19 British divisions.

. . . .

The reader will observe how low the art of war had sunk. In its supreme expression at this melancholy and degraded

112

epoch it represents little but the massing of gigantic agencies for the slaughter of men by machinery. It is reduced to a business like the stockyards of Chicago. On the whole this attack —a super-attack of the Haig-Passchendaele type, but far larger—represents the most terrific and most unhuman (in the sense of being wholly impersonal) of all the battles in the annals of war. But the scale and mechanism of the enterprise were the very features which captivated Ludendorff. These were the calculations on which he had spent his life. This was the quintessence of all he had learnt and wrought. Here were intense, precise, tangible propositions. The larger arguments about making peace with the Allies while time remained, and of compromising on both sides in the West at the expense of caitiff Russia, seemed quite unimportant. The practical warnings addressed to him in the winter by the ablest German industrialists upon the danger of continuing the war were brushed aside. All this was to him merely a vague, pale, tenuous mist, in the centre of which lay his own gigantic red-hot cannon-ball. To fire that shot, to pull that spring, and press that button, to let loose those mighty pent-up energies, must have seemed an end in itself.

Now this mood was very becoming in a military man. It is right in professional circles to isolate the subject, and you cannot blame a general for thinking as a general ought to think about his own job. This was the Ludendorff problem. It was certainly not the German problem. Germany, who from the very declaration of war had been horrified to find how many enemies she had, who had been continuously astounded by their unquenchable pugnacity, their will-power, the awe-inspiring crescendo of their wrath, all combined with a shortage of cereals, meat, and groceries, had been longing to find a way out; and there *was* a way out.

. . . . . .

The moment winter silenced the cannonade at Passchendaele all sorts of shrill, plaintive, bargaining voices became audible in the Allied countries. Was there no hope here? The

113

German house is on fire, thought the German people. The whole mighty mansion is aflame; the firemen are fighting the flames with dauntless vigour and the very best fire-engines; but the fire is gaining; there seems to be no end to the fire. At any moment the building may collapse and all in it perish with all their belongings. Now here suddenly above the eastern doorway are written quite clearly and illuminated the words 'Emergency Exit'. But they were not to be allowed to use it.

It was the fatal weakness of the German Empire that its military leaders, who knew every detail of their profession and nothing outside it, considered themselves, and became, arbiters of the whole policy of the State. In France throughout the War, even in its darkest and most convulsive hours, the civil government, quivering to its foundations, was nevertheless supreme. The President, the Premier, the Minister of War, the Chamber, and that amazing composite entity called 'Paris', had the power to break any military man and set him on one side. In England Parliament was largely in abeyance. The Press exalted the generals, or 'the soldiers' as they called themselves. But there existed a strong political caste and hierarchy which, if it chose to risk its official existence, could grapple with the 'brass hats'. In the United States the civil element was so overwhelmingly strong that its main need was to nurture and magnify the unfledged military-champions. In Germany there was no one to stand against the General Staff and to bring their will-power and special point of view into harmony with the general salvation of the State.

We may imagine a great ship of war steaming forward into battle. On the bridge there are only lay figures in splendid uniforms making gestures by clockwork and uttering gramophone speeches. The Engineer has taken charge of the vessel and, through the vessel, of the Fleet. He does not see a tithe of what is going on. How can he, locked in his engine-room far beneath the water-line and the armoured deck? He has stoked up all his boilers, he has screwed down all the safety-valves; he has jammed the rudder amidships. He utters nothing but the wild command, 'Full speed ahead'.

Alexander, Hannibal, Cæsar, Marlborough, Frederick the Great, Napoleon, all understood the whole story. But Ludendorff had only learnt one chapter, and he had it at his fingers' ends. One must not disparage the dire noble quality of risking all for the sake of victory. But other qualities besides this were required to carry nations through Armageddon. These other qualities were either non-existent or rigorously repressed in the German nation.

. . . .

This is not the time for an account of the stupendous battle of March 21. Everyone knows how the line of the British Fifth Army was bent backwards with a loss of 150,000 men and 1,000 guns, and how the Germans pressed into the ever-distending bulge in their march upon Amiens; how General Pétain resolved to break contact with the British Army and reserve the whole French forces for the defence of Paris; how, nevertheless, the thin line was never broken; how the British right-hand and the French left, joined as they had been during four shattering years, were destined not to be unclasped till victory was won. It is rather with the wider reactions that I am here concerned.

. . . .

The crisis and peril opened by Ludendorff's offensive galvanized the Allies and the United States into a superb activity. The long period of heart-breaking attacks upon the German fortified lines was over. In its place had come a stern fight for life. Ever since the Marne, the Allies had taken their victory for granted. It might be long delayed, it might be horribly costly, but that it was certain and would be complete they did not doubt. The slaughter of vain offensives, not for the purpose of winning the War (for that seemed won already), but for the purpose of imposing the most rigorous terms upon an enemy who was anxious for peace, offered a broadening field for differences of opinion even among those who had entered resolutely into the struggle. In the autumn of 1917 we had had

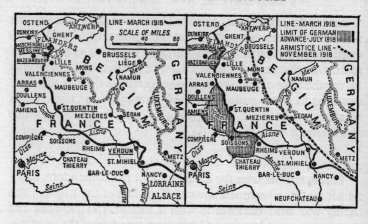

Lord Lansdowne's letter in the *Daily Telegraph*, we had had the Stockholm Conference of the Socialists. There had been the negotiations of Prince Sixte de Bourbon and the conversations between General Smuts and Count Mensdorff in Switzerland.

Now all doubts were cast away. No longer was it a question of fighting to impose hard terms upon the enemy. Actual defeat seemed to stare the Allies in the face; and defeat before the weight of the United States could be brought to bear. The disaster, heavy though it was, revived the morale and reinvigorated the military strength of Britain and France. It evoked from the United States the most strenuous efforts. No one thought of peace or peace negotiations. Never was the war resolve of the mighty confederacy against Germany more fierce and strong. A desperate 'comb-out' of munition factories, mines, and workshops throughout England, the raising of the age of compulsion to 55, the sending forward of the boys of 19, enabled nearly a quarter of a million men to be rapidly ferried across the Channel. The thousand guns were replaced within a month, and the British Army continued to sustain assault after assault from the German masses. After the fury of 'Mars and Michael' was spent, 'St. George' descended upon us before Hazebrouck. Nevertheless, the defence did not fail.

Up till the 21st March the United States was preparing its armies in an elaborate, methodical, and necessarily lengthy manner. Although the great Republic had been in the War for more than a year, only six American divisions were in France and only two in the line. The very natural object of the American Command was to place their forces in the field, if possible, by corps and armies, at least by divisions, and ultimately to gather all the American units into one great United States army. Training and preparation were ceaselessly proceeding on both sides of the Atlantic, but meanwhile the Allies were in grievous danger of collapsing under the German flail. The most vehement appeals were made by Lloyd George and Clemenceau for the acceleration of the movement of American troops to Europe, and that the infantry masses should be sent in advance, without waiting to be formed in divisions, and be incorporated in the line with British and French brigades, and even battalions.

On the morrow of the defeat General Pershing, with his military and civil colleagues, informed the French Government that the American troops in France would enter the fighting line, trained or half-trained, wherever they could render service. President Wilson, receiving the British demand for the dispatch of hundreds of thousands of American infantry, and the immense shipment of American divisions still only partially trained, across the Atlantic, replied to Lord Reading, in words which the British nation will always link with his memory: 'Ambassador, I'll do my damnedest!'

How this was made good can be seen from the recorded movements of United States divisions across the Atlantic. During February, March and April only four divisions had arrived. But from May onwards the President's resolve, supported as it was by the whole nation, began to take effect. Eight divisions, each of nearly 30,000 men, crossed in May, eight in June, four in July, six in August, and five in September. In all nearly a million men sailed, shielded by the British Navy from the submarines, during these four months from the New World to the aid of the Old. Although only a few American railway engineers had fought on the British front, and only four American divisions entered the line before Ludendorff's offensive against the British was decisively broken, nevertheless the constant landing in Europe of these enormous forces of vigorous manhood gave assurance to the Allies in their struggles that final victory was sure.

.   .   .   .

But the climax and turning-point of the Anglo-French recovery was reached at Doullens on March 26. Clemenceau, Poincaré, Foch, and Pétain for France, met Milner, Haig, and Wilson for England. Stark was the mood and bleak the air. These men, soldiers or statesmen, already marked and hardened by the War, were in the presence of the gravest realities. The French brooded with sombre eyes upon the immense defeat their Ally had sustained, upon soil of France so newly repurchased at prodigal sacrifices, once again fallen into the invaders' grip. Their military men judged severely the apparent failure of their Ally. Utterly exhausted, sleepless, haggard, the troops of the Fifth Army, recoiling before the overwhelming German tide, may well have seemed to be of little military value. Clemenceau told me one day, what he has since recorded in his Memoirs, that a French General of the highest rank said to him—indicating Haig—'There stands a commander who within a fortnight will be forced to capitulate or see his army broken up in the open field.' I wonder who that General was!

The British for their part remembered the exertions and slaughters of their unaided offensives of 1917; how their riddled and crippled divisions had been forced by French pressure to extend their line across this very disaster-front; how tardy and stinted had been the help which Pétain had sent to their aid. They were aghast at his cold resolve, announced two days before, to break contact and leave them, if need be, to be 'thrown into the sea'.

It was no time for reproaches. There were long silences between the few words that were spoken. Haig was ready to

acrifice the independent command he had held so long if by
o doing he could procure a greater effort from the French.
Clemenceau was determined that no effort should be wanting.
It is not a question,' he said, 'of what divisions can be spared
from the French front, but of how soon they can reach the
present battlefield.' Pétain, the cool, calm, perfectly-trained
commander, had already readjusted his ideas under the eye
of the 'Tiger'. Amiens, he now declared, must be defended to
he utmost. But it was Foch whose inexhaustible fighting
pirit met the need of the hour. Resolves were taken to hold
ogether at all hazards and to establish unity of command
upon the whole of the front in France and Flanders.

In the crisis of this stricken battle, whose advancing cannonade rumbled and thudded ceaselessly in all ears, Foch
received the august mission which he was to relinquish only
when it had been gloriously fulfilled.

A DAY WITH CLEMENCEAU

I N the days after the Germans broke our front on March 21, 1918, I used to sleep in my office at the Ministry of munitions, so that work could go forward at all times when I was awake. Early on the morning of the 28th the Prime Minister sent for me to Downing Street. I found him in bed, a grey figure amid a litter of reports and telegrams. He had been ploughing through them since daylight, scoring and scratching with a red pencil the points which struck him, and striving to reach a clear view from the mass of conflicting information which reached him upon high authority from all parts of the world. Only the best information came into his lap—the most vital matters collected and sifted through innumerable channels, each great sphere of action reducing its account to the smallest compass, the dominant facts, the most secret intelligence, the controlling opinions. Yet, however pruned and concentrated, the volume which reached the summit remained so considerable that two or three hours of rapid reading by an eye that had learnt to know what to look for were required merely to cover the daily budget.

Mr. Lloyd George said, 'Can you get away for a few days to France?'

I replied that measures had been taken to replace the munitions we had lost, and that while these were being carried out there was a certain lull so far as I was concerned.

'All right,' he said. 'I can't make out what the French are doing. Are they going to make a great effort to stop the German inrush? Unless they do, the Germans will break through between us to the sea. Our Headquarters don't seem to know what they are going to do. The reports show a few French divisions arriving here and a few there, but what is going on behind? Are armies moving? Are hundreds of thousands of men coming up? Where are they coming from, and when will they come up? That is what I want to know. Can't you go over and find out? Go and see everybody. Use my authority. See Foch. See Clemenceau. Find out for yourself whether they are making a really big move or not.'

I started about eleven o'clock with the Duke of Westminster as my sole companion. We crossed the Channel in a destroyer and stopped at the British General Headquarters at Montreuil on our motor journey to Paris. The rain streamed down in torrents in the silent, empty streets of this peaceful little old-world town. From this point sixty British divisions —more than half in bloody action—were being directed. From La Bassée southward the battle was at its intensest pitch. The remains of the Fifth Army were streaming back across the old crater-fields of the Somme towards Amiens. Byng with the Third Army was in full grapple. From every part of the British front, from every depôt and school in the rear, every division which could be spared, every reserve that could be discovered, every man who could shoulder a rifle, was being scraped together and rushed forward by rail and motor to stop the terrible tide of German advance. All this I knew. Yet how oddly the calm, almost somnolence, of this supreme nerve-centre of the Army contrasted with the gigantic struggle shattering and thundering on a fifty-thousand-yard front fifty or sixty miles away. The ordinary routine of the bureaus was proceeding. There was an utter absence of excitement or bustle. The Commander-in-Chief was taking his afternoon ride. No one not acquainted with the conditions of the Great War would have believed it possible that one of the largest and most bloody and critical battles in the history of the world was in fact being skilfully and effectively conducted from this spot.

I saw the Chief of the Staff in his office in the Military School. All his information had already been transmitted to London. The movement of a few divisions, clawed here and there from the disengaged sectors of the front, was dealt with by him on the telephone at interruptions in our conversation.

One felt in the presence of a man who knew he was in the hands of Fate. The battle was devouring his reserves; the enemy were still pouring through the gap; their front advanced continuously; every division taken from the quieter sectors invited a new blow in the weakened areas. Heavy evidences had come in of large accumulations of German divisions and artillery in the northern part of the British line. At any moment another formidable offensive might explode there. Already we had lost totally more than a hundred thousand men killed or captured, and more than a thousand guns, while scores of thousands of wounded were streaming through the hospitals to England, straining even that gigantic organization to its utmost capacity.

What were the French going to do? Were they going to react in decisive strength? Would they make a great punch up from the south into the southern flanks of the ever-extending German bulge? If not, the British and French armies would be forced apart. The Chief of the Staff showed me on the map the few French divisions which had actually come into action. But what their main intention was, or what their power to execute it was, he did not profess to know. At that moment a telegram came in stating that the Germans had occupied Montdidier. 'No doubt they are doing their best,' was all he could say.

Meanwhile outside, the rain streamed continuously down. We resumed our journey to Paris. Amiens was under bombardment, but we saw none of it in passing through; nor were any shells falling along the Amiens-Beauvais road. The mist and rain blanketed the flashes of the guns, and the throbbing of the motor drowned the distant cannonade. The streets of Beauvais were full of French troops; the hotel crowded with officers. The headquarters of an Army Corp had just arrived. Troop trains were disgorging continuously at the railway station. We reached Paris at midnight, and slept in the luxuries of an almost empty Ritz.

Early the next morning I requested General Sackville-West, the head of our military mission, to visit Monsieur Clemen

122

ceau and explain to him the object and character of my visit. At noon he returned. The 'Tiger's' answer was as follows:

'Not only shall Mr. Winston Churchill see everything, but I will myself take him to-morrow to the battle and we will visit all the Commanders of Corps and Armies engaged.'

I had Munitions work to do all the afternoon in connection with our Paris establishments, which at this time were on a very large scale. The German long-range gun flung its shells into the city at half-hourly intervals, and in the evening we were diverted by a vivid, noisy and comparatively harmless air-raid. At eight o'clock the next morning we were to start for the front from the Ministry of War.

On this morning, March 30, five military motor-cars, all decorated with the small satin tricolours of the highest authority, filled the courtyard of the rue St. Dominique. Monsieur Clemenceau, punctual to the second, descended the broad staircase of the Ministry, accompanied by his personal General and two or three other superior officers. He greeted me most cordially in his fluent English.

'I am delighted, my dear Mr. Wilson (sic) Churchill, that you have come. We shall show you everything. We shall go together everywhere and see everything for ourselves. We shall see Foch. We shall see Debeney. We shall see the Corps Commanders, and we will also go and see the illustrious Haig, and Rawlinson as well. Whatever is known, whatever I learn, you shall know.'

He got into the car accompanied by his General, and whirled off. Monsieur Loucheur, the Minister of Armaments and my opposite number in the Allied hierarchy, invited me to come with him in the second car. The staff officers filled the others. As soon as we had cleared the barriers of Paris we proceeded at a rate of about seventy kilometres an hour or over. The cars leapt and bounded on the muddy roads. The country, scarred by successive lines of entrenchments, flashed past as we racketed northward. While we sped along, Paris and its deep anxieties faded from the mind as from the eye. Loucheur and I had much to discuss. All our munitions business was interwoven in a hundred intricate ways. The German advance, if it arrived within regular bombarding distance of Paris, would confront us both with the most tremendous problems. All our great establishments, including some of the most important aeroplane factories, would have to move in good time, perhaps a hundred miles to the south. But the labour to prepare these new workshops could not be withdrawn from its present occupation without injuring our output; and the Paris factories had to function to the last minute, unless the aeroplane and other programmes on which the Armies were depending were to be seriously deranged. The hostile front was coming now so near to the capital that all these complications stared us in the face. Absorbed in these and other discussions we shook off the sense of disaster which in these days weighed heavily on the mind.

In rather less than two hours the spires of Beauvais Cathedral hove in sight, and we presently pulled up at the Town Hall. Clemenceau got out. We all got out. We marched quickly up the steps of a stone staircase to a big room on the first floor. The double doors were opened, and before us was Foch, newly created Generalissimo of all the Allied Armies on the western front. After brief greetings we entered the room. With Foch was Weygand, together with two or three other officers. Our party numbered about a dozen. The doors were shut. On the wall was a map about two yards square. It comprised only that portion of the front affected directly or indirectly by the German break-through, i.e. from the north of Arras to the approaches of Rheims. General Foch seized a large pencil as if it were a weapon, and without the slightest preliminary advanced upon the map and proceeded to describe the situation. I had heard of his extraordinary methods of exposition: his animation, his gestures, his habit of using his whole body to emphasize and illustrate as far as possible the action which he was describing or the argument which he was evolving; his vivid descriptiveness, his violence and vehemence of utterance. For this style he had been long wondered at, laughed at, and admired in all the schools of war at which he had been

124

Professor or Chief. He spoke so quickly and jumped from point to point by such large and irregular leaps that I could not make any exact translation of his words. But the whole impression was conveyed to the mind with perfect clearness by his unceasing pantomime and by his key phrases. I cannot attempt to reproduce his harangue, but this was his theme: 'Following the fighting of the 21st, the Germans broke through on the 22nd. See where they went. First stage of the invasion. Oh! oh! oh! How big!' He pointed to a line on the map.

'On the 23rd they advanced again. *Deuxième journée d'invasion. Ah! Ah!* Another enormous stride. On the 24th. *Troisième journée. Aïe! Aïe!*'

But the fourth day there was apparently a change. The lines on the map showed that the amount of territory gained by the enemy on the fourth day was less than that which they had gained on the third day. The Commander-in-Chief turned towards us and swayed from side to side, using his hands as if they were the scales of a balance.

'*Oho!*' he said. '*Quatrième journée. Oho! Oho!*'

We all knew that something had happened to the advancing flood. When he came to the fifth day, the zone was distinctly smaller. The sixth and the seventh zones were progressively smaller still. Foch's voice had dropped almost to a whisper. It was sufficient for him to point to the diminishing zones and with a wave of the hand or a shrug of the shoulder to convey the moral and meaning which he intended.

Until finally, '*Hier, dernière journée d'invasion,*' and his whole attitude and manner flowed out in pity for this poor, weak, miserable little zone of invasion which was all that had been achieved by the enemy on the last day. One felt what a wretched, petty compass it was compared to the mighty strides of the opening days. The hostile effort was exhausted. The mighty onset was coming to a standstill. The impulse which had sustained it was dying away. The worst was over. Such was the irresistible impression made upon every mind by his astonishing demonstration, during which every muscle and fibre of the General's being had seemed to vibrate with the excitement and passion of a great actor on the stage.

And then suddenly in a loud voice, 'Stabilization! Sure, certain, soon. And afterwards. Ah, afterwards. That is my affair.'

He stopped. Everyone was silent.

Then Clemenceau, advancing, '*Alors, Général, il faut que je vous embrasse.*'

They both clasped each other tightly without even their English companions being conscious of anything in the slightest degree incongruous or inappropriate. These two men had had fierce passages in the weeks immediately preceding these events. They had quarrelled before; they were destined to quarrel again. But, thank God, at that moment the two greatest Frenchmen of this awful age were supreme—and were friends. No more was said. We all trooped down the stairs, bundled into our cars, and roared and rattled off again to the north.

This time it was to Rawlinson's Headquarters that we proceeded. The Commander of the British Fourth Army, by whom the débris of our Fifth Army was being reorganized and the quivering, melting line as far as possible being maintained, was established in a small house on the Amiens-Beauvais road about twelve miles south of Amiens. Large new shell-holes in the surrounding fields showed how near the enemy had got to the Army Headquarters. The characteristic of Rawlinson as a Commander was that nothing ever changed his manner. Whatever the crisis, however great the success, however serious the catastrophe, he was always exactly the same man: good-humoured, jocular, cool, unpretentious: a typical English country gentleman and sportsman, but armed with a hard technical equipment in military affairs. It chanced during the War that I saw him at some of his worst moments of misfortune and in his hour of greatest triumph. I can testify that whether his front was crumbling away or in the moment of a dazzling victory, he was always exactly the same.

This day was one of his worst. He received Clemenceau

with the sincere respect and evident affection which the personality of the 'Tiger', above all his fellow-countrymen, always extorted from the leading soldiers of the British Army. An improvised but substantial collation (meat, bread, pickles, whisky and soda) was set out on the table. But Clemenceau would not have this until his contribution of chicken and sandwiches of the most superior type had been produced from the last of his cars.

'Haig will be here in a few minutes,' said Rawlinson as we ate our luncheon.

Almost immediately the long grey car of the British Commander-in-Chief pulled up at the door. Clemenceau and Haig went off together into the adjoining room, and Loucheur and I remained with Rawlinson.

'What is happening?' I asked.

'We have had a success,' Rawlinson replied. 'We have taken a wood. Jack Seely, with the Canadian Cavalry Brigade, has just stormed the Bois de Moreuil.'

'Will you be able to make a front?'

'No one can tell. We have hardly anything between us and the enemy except utterly exhausted, disorganized troops. There is a chap called Carey with a few thousand officers and men raked up anyhow from schools and depôts, who is holding about six miles of front here,' pointing to the map. 'The cavalry are doing their best to keep a line. We have a few batteries scattered about. All the Fifth Army infantry are dead to the world from want of sleep and rest. Nearly all the formations are mixed or dissolved. The men are just crawling slowly backwards; they are completely worn out. D. H.' (Sir Douglas Haig) 'is trying to get some reinforcements out of Clemenceau. Quite a lot of French troops are detraining to our right and rear. If these can come forward without delay in advance of their time-table, we may hold on till our own reserves come up. There are not many of them.'

I am giving of course only the gist of the conversation.

'Do you think you will be here to-morrow night?' I asked, wishing to take a sounding.

He made a grimace, the dominant effect of which was not encouraging to my mind.

Very soon Clemenceau returned with Sir Douglas Haig. Evidently all had gone well. The Tiger was in the greatest good humour. Sir Douglas, with all his reserve, seemed contented. The staff telephones were working vigorously in an adjoining room.

'Very well,' said Clemenceau in English to the company, 'then it is all right. I have done what you wish. Never mind what has been arranged before. If your men are tired and we have fresh men near at hand, our men shall come at once and help you. And now,' he said, 'I claim my reward.'

'What is that, sir?' asked Rawlinson.

'I wish to pass the river and see the battle.'

The Army Commander shook his head.

'It would not be right for you to go across the river,' he said.

'Why not?'

'Well, we are not at all sure of the situation beyond the river. It is extremely uncertain.'

'Good,' cried Clemenceau. 'We will re-establish it. After coming all this way and sending you two divisions, I shall not go back without crossing the river. You come with me, Mr. Winston Churchill (this time he got it right); and you, Loucheur. A few shells will do the General good,' pointing gaily to his military Chef de Cabinet.

So we all got into our cars again and set off towards the river and the cannonade. We soon began to pass long trickles and streams of British infantry in the last stages of fatigue; officers and men sometimes in formation but more often mingled. Many of these walked as if they were in a dream, and took no notice of our file of brightly-flagged cars. Others again, recognizing me, gave me a wave or a grin, even sometimes a fitful cheer, as they would no doubt have done to George Robey or Harry Lauder, or any other well-known figure which carried their minds back to vanished England and the dear days of peace and party politics.

At length we reached the river. The artillery fire was now fairly close. Near the bridge was a large inn. A French brigadier, pushing on in front of his troops, had already established himself in some of its rooms. The rest of the place was filled with British officers from twenty different units, for the most part prostrate with exhaustion and stunned with sleep. A Provost Marshal, I think, was serving out whisky to enable them to get up and crawl onwards as soon as possible. Clemenceau had a few minutes' talk with the French brigadier. As we got back into the motors he called to me, and I came to the side of his car.

'Now,' he said, 'Mr. Winston Churchill, we are in the British lines. Will you take charge of us? We will do what you say.'

I said, 'How far do you want to go?'

He replied, 'As far as possible. But you shall judge.'

So I made my car, which was now third in the procession, come up to the front, and seating myself next to the driver, map in hand, pushed on across the bridge. The straggling houses on the other side soon gave way to open country. At the first cross-roads I turned to the right, i.e. to the south, and followed an avenued road which ran roughly parallel to the river Luce, on the enemy's side of which we now were. This road led to the Bois de Moreuil, and I thought we might possibly get in touch with some of Seely's Canadians. The guns were firing now from every quarter. The flashes of the British and French batteries concealed in wooded heights behind the river were every moment more numerous. The projectiles whined to and fro overhead. On our left towards the enemy was a low ridge crowned with trees about three hundred yards away. Among these trees a few dark figures moved about. The study I had made of the map before leaving Rawlinson's Headquarters led to the presumption that these were the mixed forces scraped from the schools which Colonel Carey commanded. If so, it was at once our front line and our last line. What lay beyond that, I could not tell. Rifle fire was now audible in the woods, and shells began to burst in front of us

129

on the road and in the sopping meadows on either side. The rain continued, as always, to pour down, and the mists of evening began to gather.

I thought on the whole that we had gone quite far enough. If anything happened to this thin line on the top of the hill—and we had no means of knowing how near the enemy was to it or what would happen—it might be quite impossible to go back by the road, parallel with the front, by which we had come. It would be very awkward if a sudden retirement of the line made it necessary for the Prime Minister of France to retreat directly across the fields and ford the river (if indeed it was fordable—about which I knew nothing). And so I stopped the procession of cars and suggested to Monsieur Clemenceau that we could get as good a view of what was going on from the side of the road as from anywhere else. The Bois de Moreuil or its neighbouring woodlands lay before us at no great distance. The intervening ground was dotted with stragglers, and here and there groups of led horses—presumably of Seely's brigade—were standing motionless. Shrapnel continued to burst over the plain by twos and threes, and high explosive made black bulges here and there. The Tiger descended from his automobile and climbed a small eminence by the roadside. From here we could see as much as you can ever see of a modern engagement without being actually in the firing-line, that is to say, very little indeed.

We remained for about a quarter of an hour questioning the stragglers and admiring the scene. No shell burst nearer to us than a hundred yards. Loucheur and Clemenceau were in the highest spirits and as irresponsible as schoolboys on a holiday. But the French staff officers were increasingly concerned for the safety of their Prime Minister. They urged me to persuade him to withdraw. There was nothing more to see, and we had far to go before our tour of inspection was finished. The old Tiger was at that moment shaking hands with some weary British officers who had recognized and saluted him. We gave these officers the contents of our cigar-cases. I then said that I thought we ought to be off. He consented with

130

much good humour. As we reached the road a shell burst among a group of led horses at no great distance. The group was scattered. A wounded and riderless horse came in a staggering trot along the road towards us. The poor animal was streaming with blood. The Tiger, aged seventy-four, advanced towards it and with great quickness seized its bridle, bringing it to a standstill. The blood accumulated in a pool upon the road. The French General expostulated with him, and he turned reluctantly towards his car. As he did so, he gave me a sidelong glance and observed in an undertone, '*Quel moment délicieux!*'

We then returned without misadventure to the cross-roads. Here we found a staff officer in a car from Rawlinson's Headquarters with the news that they had now arranged for Monsieur Clemenceau to cross the river and go home by the quarter of Amiens which the German artillery had been demolishing. They evidently had wished him to turn northwards rather than southwards, if he was bent on crossing the bridge. Now he was going to have both treats! He beamed with pleasure but, as it turned out, there were no more shells that day.

It was dark when we were clear of Amiens on the road to General Debeney's headquarters. This General commanded the French Army, building up the front on the right of Rawlinson's slender line. A long animated discussion took place between the Commander and the two French Ministers. The General explained the situation with all the lucidity for which the French are distinguished. Like Rawlinson, he had hardly any troops between him and the advancing Germans. His leading formations were very heavily engaged, but he thought they could hold on till the next day when they would be reinforced.

From this point we set off again to General Pétain in the French Headquarters train in the siding of Beauvais railway station. Here all was calm and orderly. Pétain and his staff received the Prime Minister with the utmost ceremony. We were conducted into the sumptuous saloons of this travelling military palace, and a simple but excellent dinner was served

131

in faultless style. We had already been exactly twelve hours either touring along the roads at frantic speed or in constant exciting conversation with persons of high consequence. Personally I was quite tired. But the iron frame of the Tiger appeared immune from fatigue of any kind or in any form. He chaffed Loucheur and the Generals with the utmost vivacity, breaking at a bound from jokes and sallies into the gravest topics without an instant's interval, and always seeking the realities amid the cool sparkling ripple of his conversation.

When I had a chance I said to him apart: 'This sort of excursion is all right for a single day: but you ought not to go under fire too often.' He replied—and I record it—'*Cest mon grand plaisir.*'

Said Pétain at one moment, 'A battle like this runs through regular phases. The first phase, in which we now are, is forming a front of any kind. It is the phase of Men. The second phase is that of Guns. We are entering upon that. In forty-eight hours we shall have strong artillery organizations. The next is Ammunition-supplies. That will be fully provided in four days. The next phase is Roads. All the roads will be breaking up under the traffic in a week's time. But we are opening our quarries this evening. We ought just to be in time with the roads, if the front holds where it is. If it recedes, we shall have to begin over again.'

We reached Paris at one the next morning, having been seventeen hours in ceaseless activity and stress. Clemenceau, alert and fresh as when we started, dismissed me with a friendly gesture.

'To-morrow I must work. But Pétain has arranged for you to be received wherever you wish to go. There will always be dinner for you in his train.'

IN THE AIR

EXCEPT for the year 1916, I was continually in control of one or the other branch of the Air Service during the first eleven years of its existence. From 1911 to 1915 I was responsible at the Admiralty for the creation and development of the Royal Naval Air Service; from July, 1917, to the end of the War I was in charge of the design, manufacture and supply of all kinds of aircraft and air material needed for the War; and from 1919 to 1921 I was Air Minister as well as Secretary of State for War. Thus it happens to have fallen to my lot to have witnessed, and to some extent shaped in its initial phases, the whole of this tremendous new arm, undoubtedly destined to revolutionize war by land and sea, and possibly in the end to dominate or supersede armies and navies as we have known them.

At the very beginning in 1911 the Royal Navy possessed half a dozen aeroplanes and perhaps as many pilots. The art of flying was in its childhood, and flying for war purposes was a sphere about which only the vaguest ideas existed. The skill of the pilots, the quality of engines and machines, were alike rudimentary. Even the nomenclature had to be invented, and I may claim myself to have added the words 'seaplane' and 'flight' (of aeroplanes) to the dictionary.

From the outset I was deeply interested in the air and vividly conscious of the changes which it must bring to every form of war. On first going to the Admiralty I resolved to develop and extend the naval air service by every means in my power. I thus came into contact with a little band of adventurous young men who, under the leadership of Commander Samson, were the pioneers of naval flying. I was fascinated by the idea of flying, and yet side by side with desire

133

was also a dread of going into the air for the first time. Indeed it must have been three or four months before I made my first flight. We had already had several accidents, and I felt a very keen sympathy with these young officers who were risking their lives in time of peace. I thought it would be a stimulus to progress generally if I, as First Lord, participated to some extent. Other ministers in charge of the Air Service have usually taken the same view.

Accordingly early in 1912 I took my seat in a seaplane piloted by Commander Spenser Grey, and resigned myself to what was in those days at once a novel and a thrilling experience. I was astonished to find, after with some difficulty we had got off the water and had surged into the air, that looking down from seven or eight hundred feet did not make me dizzy. Still I am bound to confess that my imagination supplied me at every moment with the most realistic anticipations of a crash, and I remember in my ignorance that I hoped it would take place while we were flying over soft water instead of hard ground. However, we descended in due course with perfect safety. I have no compunction in relating the apprehensions which surrounded my first taste of the glorious sensations of flying. I am sure that when the secrets of all hearts are revealed, they will be found to have been shared by a good many others. I remember indeed a few weeks later going for a flight in a three-seater machine and asking a young officer if he would like to be my fellow-passenger. He accepted the invitation laconically, and after the flight was over told me he had spent the morning making his will! This officer subsequently gained the Victoria Cross in circumstances of extraordinary bravery. So I think my trepidations are at any rate countersigned by respectable authority.

The air is an extremely dangerous, jealous and exacting mistress. Once under the spell most lovers are faithful to the end, which is not always old age. Even those masters and princes of aerial fighting, the survivors of fifty mortal duels in the high air who have come scatheless through the War and all its perils, have returned again and again to their love and perished too often in some ordinary commonplace flight undertaken for pure amusement. Well do I remember presiding at the banquet given to the two British airmen who actually flew the broad Atlantic in their little machine and landed safely in Ireland in 1919, and saying to the pilot, then knighted as Sir John Allcock, 'You ought to stop now and leave off a winner; you must have used up all your luck.' In a few months this warning proved to be only too well founded.

Once I had started flying from motives in which a sense of duty, as well as excitement and curiosity, played its part, I continued for sheer joy and pleasure. I went up in every kind of machine and at every air station under the Admiralty. The '*vol plané*' or descending glide with the engine off was in those days a comparative novelty, and I must say its silent downward rush through the soft air, amid the glories of the sunset and with the earth as a map spread beneath, was a delightful experience when first enjoyed. I soon became ambitious to handle these machines myself, and took many lessons both at the Naval and Military Schools. Dual-control machines were developing fast in 1912, and I had one made where pilot and passenger could sit side by side and take control alternately. In this machine, the type of which was particularly useful for instructional purposes, I made many delightful flights, and it was ultimately the means of revealing in an exceedingly unpleasant manner the dangers of a particular form of rudder and spin which we thereafter avoided.

Curiously enough my apprehensions about going into the air were apparently confirmed by a long series of dangerous or fatal accidents in which I narrowly missed being involved. The young Pilot Instructor who gave me my first lesson at Eastchurch was killed the day after we had been flying together. I was sitting in the Treasury Board Room discussing the details of the Naval Estimates of 1912 with the Chancellor of the Exchequer, when a slip of paper was put before me acquainting me with the fact that my companion of yesterday had perished in the same machine in which we had been practising for two or three hours. A few weeks later a seaplane of a new and experimental type was produced in Southampton Water, and I made a prolonged flight in it while it was being tested. It manœuvred perfectly under every condition, and I sailed away in the Admiralty yacht *Enchantress* to Sheerness. I had no sooner arrived than I learnt that the machine had nose-dived into the sea with three officers, all of whom were killed. I was going out to fly, as I frequently did, in the sociable dual-control machine which I have mentioned, and was prevented by press of public business. The machine having flown perfectly all the morning suddenly took it into its head to plunge into a spin of a kind then quite unknown, and smashed itself to pieces on the ground, thereby gravely injuring the two officers, both personal friends of mine, who were flying it.

As I began to know more about flying, I began to understand the enormous number of hazards which beset every moment of the airman's flight—(I suppose it is all different now)—and I noticed on several occasions defects in the machine in which we had been flying—a broken wire, a singed wing, a cracked strut—which were the subject of mutual congratulation between my pilot and myself once we had returned safely to *terra firma*. However, having been thoroughly bitten, I continued to fly on every possible occasion when my other duties permitted.

Then came the episode of Gustave Hamel in the spring of 1914. If ever there was a man born to fly, three parts a bird and the rest genius, it was Hamel. He belonged to the air rather than to the earth, and handled the primitive machines of those days in what was then an unknown element, with a natural gift and confidence quite indescribable. Hamel was a civilian, but far ahead in the art of flying of any of our naval fliers. He it was who, when the dangerous spins first began to kill our pilots, went up 10,000 feet, put his machine deliberately into what had hitherto been considered a fatal movement, and was whirled round and round at 100 miles an hour towards the ground until at last he found the way of breaking the frightful rotation and sailing out of it into a smooth *vol plané*. These discoveries once made were immediately imparted as common property to airmen, and the fatal and uncontrollable spin of 1912 became a usual manœuvre in the air fighting of the War when the aviator wished to lose two or three thousand feet with the utmost rapidity, or to baffle the aim of a pursuing machine-gun by gyrations which human eye could never calculate.

I brought Hamel down to Sheerness, as I wanted him to show the naval fliers his wonderful command of a machine in the air. He came as my guest on the *Enchantress*, arriving in a hurricane through which few in those days would have dared to fly. And that afternoon and the next morning he gave us exhibitions in the art of flying never previously seen in England. He would throw himself into the then awful 'side-slip out of control' and fall like a stone in a nose-dive for a thousand feet while the air sang with a loud shriek through his wires, and then come out of this fearful descent terribly close to the ground or to the sea and emerge frolicking and serene in graceful pirouettes. We were exploring an unknown world then, and the value of these demonstrations was inestimable. Looping the loop had just been discovered by Pégoud, and Hamel performed this feat for us again and again, and performed it, I am sorry to say, far too low down, 'so that everybody could see how it was done.'

I spent a delightful day flying with him. Morning, afternoon and evening we sailed about in his little 'Voisin' monoplane. Although I have flown hundreds of times, probably with a hundred pilots, I have never experienced that sense of the poetry of motion which Hamel imparted to those who were privileged to fly with him. It was like the most perfect skater on the rink, but the skating was through three dimensions, and all the curves and changes were faultless, and faultless not by rote and rule but by native instinct. He would bank his machine so steeply that there was nothing between us and the world far below, and would continue circling downwards so gently, so quietly, so smoothly, in such true harmony with the element in which he moved, that one would have believed that one wing-tip was fastened to a pivot. As for the grim force of gravity—it was his slave. In all his flying there was no sense of struggle with difficulties, or effort at a complicated feat; everything happened as if it could never have happened in any other way. It seemed as easy as pouring water out of a jug.

But our acquaintance had a tragic conclusion. I wanted him to repeat to the Calshot (Portsmouth) Air Station the kind of demonstration he had given with so much advantage at Sheerness, and with a select body of our pioneer pilots I awaited him in the *Enchantress* in Southampton Water. He would fly from Paris, he said, and be with us at sundown. In those days a cross-Channel journey was in itself quite an adventure. Darkness fell before he arrived. After a long wait we went in to dinner without him. We went to bed thinking he must have had a forced landing. Morning brought no telegram. By midday we began to get anxious. In the afternoon we learned that he had started across the Channel in mist and storm and had not returned to the French coast. In the evening he was reported missing. By the next day it seemed certain that he was missing for ever. And so indeed it proved. He had flown off in the fading light, into the squalls and mists of the Channel, confident that there was no difficulty and no danger he could not surmount, and from that moment he vanished for ever from human ken.

. . . .

Then came the War, and entirely different standards of the value of human life ruled in the world. Death became a commonplace, and everybody acted and lived, week in week out, on the basis that they might be killed. In all the history of the world, in the dim carnage and confusions of the Stone Age, in the intense struggles which proceed among the animalculæ in a single drop of water, risks have never been run more recklessly by living beings than were challenged day after day, month after month, by the air fighters. I had no time to fly while I was First Lord during the War, but as Minister of Munitions in 1917-18 I had to be alternately on each side of the Channel and I usually travelled by air, landing at the exact

138

point on the front where I had to see people or where I wished to witness particular operations. My pilot in these days was a young officer who had been so shattered by wounds at Gallipoli and on the Somme that he could not endure explosions. He was insensible to any other form of danger, and as a flying officer he was as fine and skilful a pilot as one could ever wish to fly with. In this period all the best machines were of course needed for the Front, and one could not make appreciable claims upon our supply of mechanics. I remember returning from General Headquarters one afternoon to London, when we broke down twice in very awkward conditions. The first time was over the Channel. There was a sharp crack, or rather intense click, followed by a splutter from the engine. A valve had burst. We began to descend. The smooth grey Channel lay beneath us. We were five miles out from the French shore. It was a dull afternoon, and we were flying only at about 2,000 feet. If the engine did not pick up again, we must reach the sea on a slant of under two miles. Usually when you look at the Channel it is crowded with traffic, but as always happens at a crucial moment, not a steamer, not a trawler, not a 'fishing-smack could be seen except paddling along on dim horizons. We had no means of flotation, no 'bathing suits' as the inflatable air-jackets were called. My pilot made a gesture with his hand indicating that he could do nothing, and I wondered how long I could keep myself afloat in my thick clothes and heavy boots or whether it would be worth while to try to take them off. Certainly for half a minute, or it may have been a minute—it seemed quite a long time—I thought extinction certain and near. And then the old engine began to cough and splutter again with many misfires and jerks. The pilot swung the aeroplane back towards the coast of France, and after ten anxious minutes we passed over the headland of Gris Nez. We just managed to make the aerodrome of Marquise with about a hundred feet to spare, and landed safely in that gigantic war-time receiving-station for British and American outward-bound machines.

The larger resources of the Marquise aerodrome soon provided us with another indifferent aeroplane, and then we started off for the second time, with about an hour of daylight across the Channel. The wind was against us and the engine pulling poorly, and we were nearly forty minutes before we reached the British shore. About a quarter of an hour later another snap in the engine led to a repetition on the part of my pilot of those gestures which indicated that we had no choice but to descend. He side-slipped artistically between two tall elms, just avoiding the branches on either side, and made a beautiful landing in a small field. I missed my London engagement.

.   .   .   .

Flying on the fighting line had an interest all its own. Apart from the ordinary risks of aviation, every cloud had to be scrutinized with the possibility that a Fokker would suddenly swoop from it. And here and there the 'Archie' shells with their white puffs indicated other dangers from which it would be well to turn aside. The only time I witnessed these conditions was during the progress of a general battle, in August or September 1918. I was most anxious to gain an impression of the movements of our advancing troops; but at 7,000 feet nothing but the fat bulges of big shells bursting far below and the barrages of shrapnel indicated anything unusual in the landscape. And as we were moving ourselves at eighty miles an hour, one could not trace any alteration in the positions of these sufficient to enable the progress of the action to be followed. My pilot, a Squadron Leader, suggested by signs a closer examination, but I thought on the whole I would rest content with the general view, and after forty or fifty minutes we returned to our aerodrome near Arras.

I must record an incident which revealed to me that after noon the severity of the life which flying officers lived in the War. We had just returned from our flight on the line when a wounded machine struggled down into the aerodrome. It was riddled with bullets. I counted myself over thirty holes in the fuselage and wings. But the engine was still intact, and none of the vital wires was severed. The observer was wounded in the leg, and sopping with blood. I was an auditor of the following dialogue:

Squadron Leader: 'Well, what do you come down here for?'

Pilot: 'I lost an observer last week through hæmorrhage, and I thought I had better get first aid as soon as possible for him.'

Squadron Leader: 'Where is your own aerodrome?' A name was mentioned. 'Well, that's only a quarter of an hour on.'

Pilot: 'I thought you could give me transport on and we would come over for the machine in the morning.'

Squadron Leader: 'Well, all right, but it's very inconvenient. Do try to get home another time.'

While they were lifting the wounded officer out of his seat, I tried to speak a few words expressive of sympathy and admiration to the pilot who had emerged a few minutes before from a frightful ordeal. I clasped his hand and said, 'You have been splendid,' or words to that effect. But he did not seem in the least surprised by his chilly reception; he took it as a matter of course. 'It upsets their arrangements if all the casualties come down here,' he said.

Never has the human race displayed the fortitude which was the ordinary habit of the men in the Great War.

．　．　．　．　．　．　．　．

After the War, when I was Air Minister, I flew for a time more frequently than ever before. And now my pilot was the heroic Jack Scott who at the age of thirty-eight, though shattered at the outset of the War by a fearful aeroplane accident, won for himself by his skill and prowess a reputation in the very first rank of our military airmen. We used to fly everywhere on business, and often on pleasure, in a dual-control machine, and I had become capable, with supervision, of flying under ordinary conditions and performing the usual vertical turns.

I had to travel frequently from London to Paris during the

Peace Conference, and I almost invariably went by air. Very lovely it was on a bright clear day to flash across, at twelve or fourteen thousand feet, the sixty-mile stretch of sea from Dungeness to Etaples, and to sail down in long spirals in the evening light to the Paris Aerodromes at Buc or Le Bourget. No tedious railway journey, no delays of transhipment, no apprehensions of seasickness! In these very fast war machines one travelled as on a magic carpet.

But some of our journeys were less smooth and easy. I remember one morning starting to fly back from the Buc Aerodrome to London with low, thick clouds and gathering mist on all sides. Scott suggested through the speaking apparatus that we should get above the clouds and fly by the compass in the clear sunlight. Accordingly I climbed, and soon entered a bank of blank grey vapour which closed us in on every side and made it very difficult to keep the machine level. Higher and higher we went, and the dial marked successively ten, twelve and fourteen thousand feet. Still there was nothing but mist wrapping us in thick impenetrable clouds. At last at 15,000 feet it began to be so cold that we thought we had better come down. And now we were confronted with one of those dangers of flying which it will be most difficult, if not impossible, to eliminate. Where were we? We must have flown nearly an hour, frequently losing direction in the fog. In what part of the country should we descend, and how near to the ground would the mist lie? These uncertainties impressed themselves sternly upon the mind as we glided silently, swiftly and blindly downwards.

We had originally entered the clouds at about 2,000 feet, but descending we could see nothing of the earth at 800. I handed the machine over to my pilot, and we descended as gradually as possible to 300 feet. Here we plunged through driving rain-storms, and still there was no sign of the ground. We knew that between Paris and Amiens there were many eminences with trees on them which were certainly higher than that, and at any moment we might crash at seventy miles an hour into a forest or on to the face of a hill with disastrous consequences. Yet, on the other hand, there was no use flying around in the fog for hours and hours until the petrol was exhausted.

At last at about 150 feet the earth appeared. We were in a narrow valley with wooded hills on each side, with houses here and there and a factory chimney towering up almost, it looked, at our height, a hundred yards away. Ahead the mist and raging squalls seemed to lie on the ground. Such a situation, reached so soon after a casual, cheerful start, is the inevitable experience from time to time of everyone who flies much. Quoth Scott through the microphone, 'We'll claw our way through all right.' Our dials registered less than a hundred feet, and the ground was spinning away at seventy or eighty miles an hour. We followed the valley. And as the mist drove us nearer and nearer to earth, we finally were scarcely 50 feet above it. Suddenly Scott said, 'Hurrah, the railway line!' The machine dived violently to the left, avoiding a mist-swathed bank of fir trees which rose like a wall before us, and I saw beneath me the track of a railway. This at any rate we could follow, quite low down, with the certainty, bar tunnels, of not running into hills. Accordingly for nearly half an hour we followed the windings of this railway—which was not the main line—through the misty valleys. Presently to my great delight I discerned a luminous patch high up in the vapour ahead of us. We immediately began to fly towards it, losing our railway line and rising fast. It brightened rapidly, and all of a sudden there appeared before us a little bright gleaming cloud silhouetted on a delicious scrap of blue. In less than a minute we slid out of the cloud bank into clear air. Behind us lay mountains of storm-laden vapour. Above the sun shone brightly through rain-cleaned air. Large black and white islands of cloud, the rearguard of the storm, presented themselves before us, through which and around which we easily flew, rising gradually to three or four thousand feet. Then we picked up Beauvais Cathedral, and presently the silver ribbon of the Somme shone beneath us near Pecquigny. A few minutes more and the sea at Abbeville came in sight. We had been more than two hours and a half covering a distance often accomplished in fifty minutes.

But now new cloud armies began to concentrate and consolidate themselves before us, and soon the whole situation was changed again to our disadvantage. Again we had to crawl down to 100 feet. But this time we flew over the sea, keeping the line of the surf on our right hand, and so groped a way along the coast in the new storm until we reached Boulogne. Here once more we emerged into sunlight, and turning out across the Channel, reached the Lympne Aerodrome without mishap. We had now been four hours in flight, and decided to land for lunch and petrol. Lympne Aerodrome, though shorn of its enormous war-time throng of planes ferrying across to the front, was still in the spring of 1919 a busy air station, and we soon found all we needed for man and machine.

At about three o'clock we started on again for London. We rose rapidly to about 1,500 feet. Then I noticed that the machine, instead of heading inland, was making a wide sweep seawards, and the next moment we side-slipped, as it seemed to me, out of control. 'What's the matter?' I asked through the microphone. No answer. The machine, now evidently unguided, was falling rapidly towards the ground and seemed about to go into a nose dive. The pace increased to 120 miles an hour, and the smooth expanse of the aerodrome which we had so lately quitted rushed up towards us full of menace. At the same time I saw a long wisp of smoke curling from the left-hand side of the fuselage by the pilot's seat. Almost simultaneously with this dread discovery the aeroplane came again into control and swung out of her nose dive 200 feet from the ground. I heard my companion's voice, 'We have been on fire. I've put it out. I'm going to land.' This then was the explanation of our erratic fall of a thousand feet, during which Scott, leaving the machine to take care of itself, had by pumping the liquid from the fire-extinguisher stopped the fatal flames from reaching the petrol tanks which they were already licking.

I was extremely glad to find myself once more on *terra*

irma. The cause of the fire was soon apparent. The exhaust pipe which discharges the flaming gases from the engine, instead of being turned away from the side of the fuselage, had through the snapping of a small steel pin swung round inboard and was actually darting its flames against the metal and canvas of our side. Only a few seconds more before discovery, and we should have burst into a sheet of flame. Only a few seconds more in extinguishing the fire, and we should not have pulled out of the nose dive before reaching the ground. As it was, no harm was done except for a black patch of charred canvas. The machine was intact, and after our exhaust pipe had been replaced and fastened in its proper position, we set off again for a third time on our journey to London. This time at least we had no adventures, but it was nearly five o'clock when we landed at Croydon, after a journey from Paris which had taken at least as long as the train and was undeniably diversified with many more uncertainties. As I quitted my seat and clambered down on to the aerodrome, I felt as if I had done a hard day's work.

.   .   .   .

I had only a few weeks to wait for another exciting experience. I was going for a practice flight from the Buc Aerodrome. My pilot (Colonel Scott was not with me on this occasion) sat in the leading seat of an Avro biplane with the dominating control, and I sat behind him. We started, and soon began to gain speed. The machine was slow in rising from the ground owing to the fact that the grass of the aerodrome was more than a foot high, and we developed a speed of over fifty miles an hour before lifting at all. Suddenly, just as I supposed we were about to quit the ground, there was a violent shock accompanied by the extraordinary sensation—it is necessary to use a contradiction in terms in order to describe it—of one's body being driven irresistibly forward by the momentum and at the same time being effectually held back by the belt. In ordinary experience there is nothing like this feeling of being in the grip of apparently uncontrollable forces. Simultaneously with this sensation the machine stood on its head and turned a complete somersault exactly like a rabbit shot in full career. In much less than a second I found myself hanging head downwards, still fastened to my seat by the belt, and looking back saw my pilot in a similar plight, our positions being exactly reversed. The aeroplane was smashed to pieces. Although I found myself afterwards cut and bruised, I experienced at the time no sense of injury, nor did I hear any noise of the crash. My pilot was equally fortunate. So ridiculous did our attitudes appear as we dangled motionless upside down from the fuselage that we burst out laughing.

We quickly unfastened our belts, and had extricated ourselves from the wreckage in time to arrest by reassuring gestures the throng of rescuers and stretcher-bearers who rushed to our assistance from the aerodrome shed. The cause of the accident was obvious. Concealed in the high grass lay a disused road sunken nearly two feet below the general level of the plain. We had not been warned of its existence, and on its further bank the strong wooden skid underneath Avro machines had struck with tremendous force, causing the aeroplane at this great speed to whirl completely over. In all the circumstances we were very lucky to escape serious injury, either from the shock or from an explosion of fire following upon it.

. . . .

It was not, and still is not, common for men over forty to become good and trustworthy pilots. Youth with its extraordinary quickness and aptitudes was almost always the first qualification for the attainment of 'Flying Sense.' I persevered, however, in my endeavours and continued, as I thought, to make steady progress. I was thus fated to have a much more melancholy adventure before I decided to relinquish, at any rate for the time being, the fascinating study of the art of flight. This event occurred in the summer of 1919. I had had a long day's work at the War Office, and motored down with Colonel Scott to the Croydon Aerodrome for an evening flight. I took the machine off the ground myself. The engine was pulling well, and we rose to 70 or 80 feet smoothly and swiftly. The Croydon Aerodrome was in those days bordered at several points by high elm trees, and it was necessary to make two half circles, first to the right and then to the left, in order to gain a safe height to pass over these.

The machine took its first turn perfectly, and the dial marked over sixty miles an hour, a thoroughly trustworthy flying speed. I now turned her to the left, as I had so often done before, and having put her on her bank, I began to centre the guiding-stick slowly and gently in order to resume an even keel. Anyone who has handled an aeroplane knows how delicate are its controls and how instantaneously it responds when all is well to the smallest movement. To my surprise the stick came home at least a foot without producing the slightest effect. The aeroplane remained inclined at about 45 degrees and began gradually to increase its list. 'She is out of control,' I said through the microphone to my pilot. Instantly I felt the override of his hand and feet on stick and rudders, as by a violent effort he sought to plunge the machine head-downwards in the hope of regaining our lost flying speed. But it was too late. We were scarcely 90 feet above the ground, just the normal height for the usual side-slip fatal accident, the commonest of all. The machine rushed earthwards helplessly. Above two hundred feet there would have been no danger; in fact at a thousand or fifteen hundred feet we had over and over again deliberately stalled the machine, made it fall out of control, waited till the side-slip turned (as all side-slips do) into the ultimate nose dive, and then as the speed increased to eighty or a hundred miles an hour and the controls began again to answer, had pulled her gently out into a normal flight.

But there was no time now. I saw the sunlit aerodrome close beneath me, and the impression flashed through my mind that it was bathed in a baleful yellowish glare. Then in another flash a definite thought formed in my brain, 'This is

147

very likely Death.' And swift upon that I felt again in imagination the exact sensations of my smash on the Buc Aerodrome a month before. Something like that was going to
happen NOW! I record these impressions exactly as they
occurred, and they probably occupied in reality about the
same time as they take to read. Apart from the sinister impression of a differently-lighted world, there was no time for
fear. Luckily we can only take in a certain amount at a time
whatever happens.

The aeroplane was just turning from its side-slip into the
nose dive when it struck the ground at perhaps fifty miles
an hour with terrific force. Its left wing crumpled, and its
propellor and nose plunged into the earth. Again I felt myself driven forward as if in some new dimension by a frightful
and overwhelming force, through a space I could not measure.
There was a sense of unendurable oppression across my
chest as the belt took the strain. Streams of petrol vapour
rushed past in the opposite direction. I felt, as a distinct phase,
the whole absorption of the shock. Suddenly the pressure
ceased, the belt parted, and I fell forward quite gently on to
the dial board in front of me. Safe! was the instantaneous
realization. I leapt out of the shattered fuselage and ran to
my companion. He was senseless and bleeding. I stood by
ready to try and pull him out should the machine catch fire.
Otherwise it was better to leave him till skilled help arrived.

No fire or explosion followed the crash. A year before
Lord Hugh Cecil, himself an aviator, speaking to me of Jack
Scott, had said, 'Anyone can fly an aeroplane when things
are going all right, but it is when things go wrong that the
great qualities of a man like Scott are decisive.' These words
had indeed come true. With unfailing presence of mind he
had switched off the electric current in the few seconds before
the machine struck the ground, and had thus prevented the
clouds of petrol vapour from exploding in flame. It was only
another example of those commanding gifts which, in spite
of the disabilities of his age and of the injuries he had sustained in his accident at the outset of the War, had won him

the widespread fame which he enjoyed throughout the Royal Air Force.

I had two hours later to preside and speak at a House of Commons dinner to General Pershing. I managed to do this; but next day I found myself black and blue all over. Colonel Scott recovered completely from his injuries, which were severe, and actually walked better after his second accident than before. But I reproached myself with having been the cause of his sufferings, and from that day to this I have rarely been in the air. Certainly I have not flown a dozen times. Yet they tell me it is quite safe now.

ELECTION MEMORIES

IF you wish to know about elections I am the person to tell you. I have actually fought more parliamentary elections than any living member of the House of Commons. I have fought fifteen. Think of that! Fifteen elections, each taking at least three weeks, with a week beforehand when you are sickening for it, and at least a week afterwards when you are convalescing and paying the bills. Since I came of age I have lived thirty-five years, and taking an election as dominating one month of your life, I have spent considerably more than a whole year of this short span under these arduous and worrying conditions. In fact I have devoted one day in thirty of my whole adult life to these strange experiences.

One has got by now pretty well to know the routine. First the negotiations and ceremonial with the local fathers and magnates, then the interviews with the Committee and the Council and the Executive: and finally confrontation with the full Association for the adoption meeting. Next the visits to the prominent people, the tour of the constituency, and study of its industries, interests, character and particular idiosyncrasies. Then decision as to the main line of the campaign. Writing the election address: alarums and excursions in the local Press! Opening of the contest! Nomination day! You walk with your principal friends to the Town Hall or other appointed place. Here you meet your opponent or opponents for the first time. Smiles of forced geniality are interchanged. 'Good morning, I am delighted to meet you. I hope we shall have a very pleasant contest.' 'The weather is rather cold (or hot) for this time of year, isn't it?' 'Mind you let me know if there is anything I can do for your convenience,' and so on. Then the fight in earnest. Every morning between nine and ten the Committee, i.e. the General Staff Meeting; all the heads of departments represented—posters, canvassers, the reports from the different committee-rooms, progress of the canvass, press-notices, advertisements, motor-cars, meetings, prevention of disorder (at your own meetings), cautioning everyone about the election laws, prominent persons who require to be attended to, and so on.

Then out and about around the constituency. When I first began, this had to be done in a two-horse landau, at about seven miles an hour. Nowadays in a whirling motor-car one sometimes goes a good deal faster. Both sides do more, so it makes no difference except that the candidates work harder. Meetings early in the mornings when the workmen have their lunch, meetings in their dinner-hour, meetings in the afternoon. Nowadays three meetings every evening, rushing from one to the other. You arrive on the platform, the other speakers sit down when the candidate is seen. (Loud cheers or boos!) Sometimes when there are only twenty or thirty extremely stolid-looking persons in a hall which will hold six or seven hundred, this is a trial to the speaker. But think of his poor friends, of his wife and daughter who follow him round from place to place and hear the same speech let off, with variations to suit the local circumstances, again and again. Well do I know the loyal laughter of the faithful chairman or vice-chairman of the Association as he hears the same old joke trotted out for the thirty-third time. My dear friend, I sympathize with you, my heart bleeds for you. Think of all the other meetings where I shall have to make this joke, and you will have to give your enthusiastic Ha! ha! ha! —Hear, hear—Bravo! Never mind. It cannot be helped. It is the way the Constitution works. We are all galley-slaves chained to our toil. We swing forward and back, and forward again. The overseer cracks his whip and the galley goes forward through waters increasingly sullen.

Of course there are the rowdy meetings. These are a great relief. You have not got to make the same old speech. Here you have excited crowds, Green-eyed opponents, their jaws twitching with fury shouting interruptions, holloing, bellowing insults of every kind, anything they can think of that will hurt your feelings, any charge that they can make against your consistency or public record, or sometimes, I am sorry to say, against your personal character; and loud jeers and scoffs arising now on all sides, and every kind of nasty question carefully thought out and sent up to the Chair by vehement-looking pasty youths or young short-haired women of bull-dog appearance. An ordeal? Certainly: but still these sort of meetings make themselves. You have not got to worry beforehand to prepare a speech. A few of the main slogans are quite enough to start with. The rest is—not silence. But how your supporters enjoy it! How much more effectually are they stimulated by the interruptions of their opponents, than convinced by the reasonings of their candidate! A long sagacious argument makes the audience yawn, a good retort at a turbulent meeting makes friends by the dozen, even sometimes of the enemy. My advice to candidates in rowdy meetings is this. First of all grin, or, as they say, 'smile.' There is nothing like it. Next be natural, and quite easy, as if you were talking to a single friend in some quiet place about something in which you were both much interested. Thirdly, cultivate a marked sense of detachment from the clatter and clamour proceeding around you. After all, nothing is so ludicrous as a large number of good people in a frantic state, so long as you are sure they are not going to hurt you. In Great Britain they very rarely try to hurt you. If they do, well then it becomes a simple proposition of self-defence. Harry Cust, at a meeting in his fight for South Lambeth, suddenly noticed an enormous man advancing on him in a pugilistic attitude. He took off his coat and squared up to him, whispering to his friends behind him, 'Hold me back! hold me back!' Above all, never lose your temper. The worse it goes, the more you must treat it as a puppet show. Cultivate the feeling of Mr. Punch's pheasant who, as he sailed on expanded wings from cover to cover, remarked to his friend, 'I wonder why that funny little man down there makes that sharp noise every time I fly over him.'

The late Duke of Devonshire, the famous Lord Hartington, talked to me about public meetings on several occasions. He was once accused of yawning in the middle of an important speech of his own in the House of Commons. When asked if this was true he replied: 'Did you hear the speech?' On another occasion he went still further: 'I dreamt,' he said, 'that I was making a speech in the House. I woke up, and by Jove I was!' In the great Free Trade split I had once to go into action with him at a very big meeting in Liverpool. He was to deliver the principal speech, and I was to move a vote of thanks in twelve minutes. We spent the previous night in Lord Derby's comfortable abode at Knowsley. We drove in to the meeting together. It was in 1904, and I think it must have been in a carriage-and-pair. 'Are you nervous?' he said. I admitted I was a bit worried. 'Well,' he said, 'I have always found it a good rule when you come before a very large audience to take a good look at them and say to yourself with conviction, "I have never seen such a lot of d——d fools in all my life." ' However, he made a massive speech to a magnificent audience, and whether he used this recipe or not I cannot tell. But I am digressing.

After ten days or it may be a fortnight of meetings of every kind, including sometimes even tramway-men at 1 a.m., we reach Polling Day. This is always passed entirely in a vehicle. From early morning till night we circulate and peregrinate among polling-booths and committee-rooms. A candidate is allowed to enter any polling-station, and this is the usual practice, though what good he can do I cannot tell. You watch the electors coming up, getting their ballot papers and going off into their little pen to put their fateful cross in the right (or wrong) place. You do not need to be a reader of thought or character to make a shrewd guess at how the bulk of them have voted. An averted look or a friendly wink will usually tell you all you need to know. As the day wears on, the voters become more numerous and the excitement rises. Large crowds of yelling children waving party colours salute or assail the candidates. By nine o'clock

153

at latest all is over. In the old days the count was nearly always taken in boroughs the same night. Now in many boroughs as well as counties the constituencies have become so vast and unmanageable that you have a night of exhaustion and suspense before the declaration. Once you have entered the counting-room, you must not leave again till all is over. It is therefore wise not to go too early, and to be well provided with refreshments when you do. Usually after two hours of counting a pretty good estimate can be formed. You see the votes neatly stacked in thousands on the returning officer's table, and looks corresponding to those piles may be read in the eyes of your friends or opponents. But sometimes when the result is very close the last few scraps of paper hold their secret till the end. What is it—victory or defeat? And a short speech for either event!

I have nearly always had agreeable relations with my opponents. I do not go so far as a candidate the other day in Islington who actually kissed the victorious lady; but I have almost always shaken hands. I have always tried to avoid mentioning their names or indeed noticing their existence during the contest. But after it is over, whatever has happened, one can afford to be good-tempered. If you win, you dwell upon the fair manner in which the contest has been conducted (never mind what you feel) and express your determination to be a father to the whole constituency without respect to party. If you have lost, you congratulate the victor and say what an ornament he will be to Parliament. I have seen men very broken and bitter in these circumstances, and some of the great men of the past—John Morley and Sir William Harcourt in particular—showed great emotion in defeat. But it does no good, it only pleases the other side. It is far better to pretend that the matter is of trifling consequence. Most painful is the grief of your supporters. This is sometimes poignant. Men and women who have given weeks of devoted and utterly disinterested labour, with tears streaming down their cheeks and looking as if the world had come to an end! This is the worst part of all. Still sometimes

—more often indeed—one wins. Out of my fifteen elections have lost five and won ten, and then what jubilation! What rousing cheers, pattings on the back and shaking of hands and throwing of caps into the air! As the reader may have gathered, I do not like elections, but it is in my many elections that I have learnt to know and honour the people of this island. They are good all through. Liberals, Tories, Radicals, Socialists, how much kindliness and good sportsmanship there is in all!

I have already described in my autobiography my two elections at Oldham. The first was a sharp rebuff, the second—after the South African campaign and the glamour then attached to those who had served in such easy wars—a decisive recovery. But by the time the Parliament was ended convulsion had occurred in British politics the consequences of which are with us to-day. Mr. Chamberlain's attack upon the Free Trade system had become not only the dominant feature in politics but the supreme test and focus by which everything else was judged. I was chosen candidate for the Liberal party in the central division of Manchester, the Exchange division, considered the Blue Ribbon of the city. My individual fight was part of a vehement national revolt against the Conservative Government. Nothing like it had been seen before in the memory of mortal man, and nothing like it was seen till 1931. Mr. Balfour had succeeded Lord Salisbury as Prime Minister at a time when the twenty years' reign of Conservatism was drawing to its inevitable close. The death of Lord Salisbury ended a definite and recognizable period in English history. Many mistakes were made by the Conservatives, and many violences done. But nothing done or undone could have saved them from grave defeat. Folly and pride converted this defeat into ruin. In those days elections took five or six weeks between the results of the earliest boroughs and of the later counties. Manchester polled on the first or second day. There were nine seats in the city and in the neighbouring borough of Salford. Mr. Balfour, the Prime Minister of a few weeks before, led the

Conservatives in the battle. I was certainly the most prominent figure on the Liberal side. The contest was strenuous,
but from the outset it was clear the popular favour lay with
us. No one however could possibly suppose that the final
result would be so sweeping. Even the most ardent Liberal
would never have believed it. When we rose up in the morning
all the nine seats were held by Conservatives. When we went
to bed that night all had been won by Liberals. I went back
to my hotel through streets which were one solid mass of
humanity. Arthur Balfour was down and out, and with him
all his friends. His sister, Miss Alice, was deeply distressed.
We had only communicated by none too cordial salutations.

Some of us belonging to the victorious party had a supper
at the Midland Hotel, then a brand-new mammoth up-to-
date erection, vaunting the wealth and power of the Lan-
cashire of those days. There was a gallant little man, a Mr
Charles Hands, on the staff of the *Daily Mail*, who had been
a correspondent in the South African War and whom I had
known there. He had been shot through the breast in the
Relief of Mafeking. He wrote extremely well, but of course
on the Conservative side. I invited him to supper. 'What do
you think of that?' 'It is,' he said, 'a grand slam in doubled
no trumps.' It certainly seemed very like it. And the next
day a whole tribe of lackey papers, fawning on success, declared that my victory had been a triumph of moral standards
over the vacillations and cynicism of Mr. Balfour. He had
been very wrong and had made great mistakes, but I was
wise enough even then not to be taken in by such talk.

Lord James of Hereford has described in his recent
memoirs the scene at Sandringham when these surprising
results flowed in to King Edward. To me he wrote: 'You
must have thought "*I walked on clouds, I stood on thrones.*"
The Manchester results were endorsed throughout the
island. The Conservative party which had ruled the nation
for so many years was shattered to pieces; barely a hundred
representatives came back to the chamber which they had left
nearly four hundred strong.

Seats wrested by a great wave of public opinion from the side to which they normally belong usually return to their old allegiance at the first opportunity. In the spring of 1908 I entered the Cabinet as President of the Board of Trade. In those days this entailed a by-election. The Liberal Government had been two years in office and as is usual with governments had disappointed its friends and aroused its enemies. The contest was unusually difficult, and all the forces hostile to the Government concentrated upon one of its most aggressive representatives. It was most memorable however as marking the beginning of the Votes for Women campaign in its violent form. Manchester was the home of the Pankhursts. The redoubtable Mrs. Pankhurst, aided by her daughters Christabel and Sylvia, determined upon violent courses. In those days it was a novelty for women to take a vigorous part in politics. The idea of throwing a woman out of a public meeting or laying rough hands upon her was rightly repulsive to all. Painful scenes were witnessed in the Free Trade Hall when Miss Christabel Pankhurst, tragical and dishevelled, was finally ejected after having thrown the meeting into pandemonium. This was the beginning of a systematic interruption of public speeches and the breaking up and throwing into confusion of all Liberal meetings. Indeed, it was most provoking to anyone who cared about the style and form of his speech to be assailed by the continued, calculated, shrill interruptions. Just as you were reaching the most moving part of your peroration or the most intricate point in your argument, when things were going well and the audience was gripped, a high-pitched voice would ring out, 'What about the women?' 'When are you going to give women the vote?' and so on. No sooner was one interrupter removed than another in a different part of the hall took up the task. It became extremely difficult to pursue connected arguments. All this developed during my second fight in North-West Manchester, in which I was eventually defeated by a few hundred votes by the same opponent, Mr. Joynson-Hicks, afterwards Lord Brentford, whom I had defeated two years before.

It took only five or six minutes to walk from the City Hall, where the poll was declared, to the Manchester Reform Club. I was accompanied there by tumultuous crowds. As I entered the club a telegram was handed to me. It was from Dundee, and conveyed the unanimous invitation of the Liberals of that city that I should become their candidate in succession to the sitting member, Mr. Edmund Robertson, who held a minor position in the Government, and was about to be promoted to the House of Lords. It is no exaggeration to say that only seven minutes at the outside passed between my defeat at Manchester and my invitation to Dundee. This was, of course, one of the strongest Liberal seats in the island. The Conservatives had never yet succeeded since the Reform Bill of 1832 in returning a member. The Labour movement was still in its adolescence. Here I found a resting place for fifteen years, being five times returned by large majorities during all the convulsions of peace and war which marked that terrible period. Nevertheless my first contest was by no means easy. The Conservative party in the city was full of combative spirit. At the other extreme of politics appeared a Labour candidate (an able representative of the Post Office Trade Union), and finally a quaint and then dim figure in the shape of Mr. Scrimgeour, the Prohibitionist, who pleaded for the kingdom of God upon earth with special reference to the evils of alcohol.

For the first week I fought the Conservatives and completely ignored the Labour attack. At the end of the first week, when the Liberals had been marshalled effectively against the Conservatives, it was time to turn upon the Socialists. Accordingly on the Monday preceding the poll I attacked Socialism in all its aspects. I think this was upon the whole the most successful election speech I have ever made. The entire audience, over 2,000 persons, escorted me cheering and singing, through the streets of Dundee to my hotel. Thereafter we never looked back, but strode on straight victory. There was indeed on polling day a wave of panic among friends and helpers from London, and the large staff of press correspondents who had followed the contest. It was said I was out again, and that this would be final. But the old Scotch Chairman of the Liberal Association, Sir George Ritchie, only smiled a wintry smile and observed, 'The majority will be about three thousand.' and so it was.

I had now been electioneering for nearly two months. Both contests had been most strenuous. The Suffragettes, as they were beginning to be called, had followed me from Manchester to Dundee, and a peculiarly virulent Scotch virago armed with a large dinner-bell interrupted every meeting to which she could obtain access. The strain and anxiety, so continued and so prolonged, had exhausted me. By-elections are always much harder than fights in a General Election. Both these by-elections following one upon the other without an interval had riveted the attention of the country. I had had to speak many times each day, and columns had appeared in all the newspapers. To produce a stream of new material and to keep up electioneering enthusiasm, while at the same time I was a member of a Cabinet, and head of an important department, had taxed me to the full. It was with the greatest relief that I returned to London, was introduced into the House of Commons by the Prime Minister, Mr. Asquith, took my seat as a member in the Cabinet, and settled down to enjoy the Board of Trade.

I should not forget to add that Mr. Scrimgeour, the Prohibitionist, scored three or four hundred votes only out of the thirty thousand that were cast. However, he persevered. He entered the lists in the two General Elections of 1910. He opposed me in the by-election of 1917, when I re-entered the Government as Minister of Munitions. He fought again in 1918 in the 'Victory' election. On every occasion he increased his poll, and at the fifth attempt his original three hundred had grown to four or five thousand. The great extensions of the franchise which were made during the War fundamentally altered the political character of Dundee.

These effects were veiled for the moment in 1918 by the jo
of victory and peace and by hatred for the Germans. But i
1922, when Mr. Lloyd George's Coalition Government wa
broken up, the whole strength of the new electorate becam
manifest. Three days before the contest opened I was struc
down by appendicitis. I had a very serious operation pe
formed only just in time, and an abdominal wound seve
inches long. My wife and a few friends had to keep the battl
going as well as they could.

The tide flowed fierce and strong against us. Meeting
were everywhere interrupted and disorderly, not through th
efforts of individuals, but—far worse—from general di
content and ill-will. It was not till two days before the po
that I was allowed to travel from London to the scene. O
the twenty-first day after my operation I addressed two grea
assemblies. The first, a ticket meeting, was orderly and I wa
able to deliver my whole argument. The evening meetin
in the Drill Hall was a seething mass of eight or nir
thousand people, among whom opponents greatly predom
inated. I was unable to stand and my wound was sti
open. I had to be carried in an invalid chair on to th
platform and from place to place. There is no doubt a majo
operation is a shock to the system. I felt desperately wea
and ill. As I was carried through the yelling crowd c
Socialists at the Drill Hall to the platform I was struck b
looks of passionate hatred on the faces of some of the younge
men and women. Indeed but for my helpless condition I ai
sure they would have attacked me. Although I had enjoye
for the previous eight years the whole-hearted support of th
Dundee Conservatives, both Conservatives and Libera
together were swept away before the onslaught of the ne
electorate. Enormous masses of people hitherto disfranchise
through not paying the rates, and great numbers of ver
poor women and mill-girls, streamed to the poll during th
last two hours of the voting, besieging the polling-station i
solid queues. My majority at the 'Victory' election of fiftee
thousand was swept away, and I was beaten by over te

160

thousand votes. And who was the victor? It was the same Mr. Scrimgeour who at the sixth time at last had increased his original poll of three hundred to a total of thirty-five thousand.

I felt no bitterness towards him. I knew that his movement represented after a fashion a strong current of moral and social revival. During the fifteen years of his efforts to gain the seat he had visited several times almost every household in the city. He was surrounded and supported by a devoted band of followers of the Christian Socialist type. He lived a life of extreme self-denial; he represented the poverty and misery of the poorer parts of the city and the strong movement towards prohibition of all sorts of alcoholic liquor. When it came to his duty to move the customary vote of thanks to the returning officer, Mr. Scrimgeour moved it instead to Almighty God. I was too ill to be present, and quitting Dundee for ever I was carried back to a long convalescence in London and the south of France.

Here is a good instance of the ups and downs of politics. I had been a prominent member of the Coalition Government to which both Liberals and Conservatives were giving allegiance. I had in two years successfully conducted the settlement of our affairs in Palestine and Irak, and had carried through the extremely delicate and hazardous arrangements necessitated by the Irish treaty. I think I may say that the session of 1922 was the most prosperous I have ever had as a minister in the House of Commons. Suddenly everything broke in pieces. I was hurried off in an ambulance to the hospital, and had hardly regained consciousness before I learnt that the Government was destroyed and that our Conservative friends and colleagues, with whom we had been working so loyally, had in a night turned from friends to foes. I was no longer a minister. And then a few weeks later the constituency which had sustained me so long repudiated and cast me out in the most decisive manner. And all this, mind you, at the close of a year when I had been by general consent more successful in Parliament and in administration than

161

at any other time in my life. In a twinkling of an eye I found myself without an office, without a seat, without a party, and without an appendix.

But incomparably the most exciting, stirring, sensational election I have ever fought was the Westminster election of 1924. The eighteen months that had passed since the breaking up of the Coalition had produced great and lamentable changes in the political situation. Mr. Bonar Law had died, his successor Mr. Baldwin had suddenly appealed to the country upon the protectionist issue. He had been decisively defeated, and to the deep alarm of the general public the Liberal Party decided to put the Socialists in power for the first time in our history. On a vacancy occurring in the Abbey division of Westminster I decided to stand as a Liberal who wished to join with Conservatives in arresting the march of Socialism. This seemed at first a very forlorn hope. I had no organization, and no idea how to form one. All the three great parties, Conservatives, Liberals and Labour, brought forward their official candidates and backed them with their whole resources. The polling day was fixed for the earliest possible date, and less than a fortnight was available for the fight. However, I immediately felt the exhilarating sensation of being supported by a real and spontaneous movement of public opinion. From all sides men of standing and importance came to join me. With scarcely a single exception the whole London Press gave its support. The Conservative Association, torn between conflicting views, split in twain. This fissure rapidly extended through the whole Conservative party. Everyone took sides, families were divided; nearly thirty Conservative members of Parliament appeared upon my platform and worked on the committees. Energetic friends laid hold of the organization. By the end of the first week Captain Guest, my chief lieutenant, a most experienced electioneer, was able to report to me that my candidature was seriously supported.

The constituency, which includes the Houses of Parliament, the seat of government, Buckingham Palace, the principal clubs and theatres, St. James's Street, the Strand, Soho, Pimlico and Covent Garden, is one of the strangest and most remarkable in the world. The poorest and the richest are gathered there, and every trade, profession and interest finds its representative and often its headquarters in this marvellous square mile. To and fro throughout its streets flow the tides of mighty London. As the campaign progressed I began to receive all kinds of support. Dukes, jockeys, prize-fighters, courtiers, actors and business men, all developed a keen partisanship. The chorus girls of Daly's Theatre sat up all night addressing the envelopes and dispatching the election address. It was most cheering and refreshing to see so many young and beautiful women of every rank in life ardently working in a purely disinterested cause not unconnected with myself. The leaders of the Conservative party were themselves divided. Mr. Baldwin supported the official candidate. Lord Balfour with his acquiescence wrote a letter in my support. The count at the finish was the most exciting I have ever seen. Up to the very end I was assured I had won. Someone said as the last packet was being carried up to the table: 'You're in by a hundred.' A loud cheer went up. The sound was caught by the crowds waiting outside and the news was telegraphed all over the world. A minute later the actual figures showed that I was beaten by forty votes out of nearly forty thousand polled. I must confess I thoroughly enjoyed the fight from start to finish.

I had now been defeated three times in succession— Dundee, West Leicester and Westminster—and it was a relief to be returned by a majority of ten thousand for West Essex at the end of the General Election of 1924. This made four elections in under two years! That is certainly enough to satisfy anyone, and makes me earnestly hope that I have now found a resting-place amid the glades of Epping which will last me as long as I am concerned with mundane affairs.

THE IRISH TREATY

No act of British State policy in which I have been concerned aroused more violently-conflicting emotions than the negotiations which led to the Irish settlement. For a system of human government so vast and so variously composed as the British Empire, a compact with open rebellion in the peculiar form in which it was developed in Ireland was an event which might well have shaken to its foundations that authority upon which the peace and order of hundreds of millions of people and of many races and communities were erected. Humble agents of the Crown in the faithful exercise of their duty had been and were being cruelly murdered as a feature in a deliberately-adopted method of warfare. Officers, soldiers, policemen, officials—often unarmed—were shot down at close quarters by persons who, though they considered themselves as belonging to a hostile army, bore no distinguishing mark and conformed in no respect to the long-established laws and customs of war. It was only possible to say of those responsible for these acts that they were not actuated by selfish or sordid motives, that they were ready to lay down their own lives, and that in the main they were supported by the sentiment of their fellow-countrymen. To receive the leaders of such men at the Council Board, to attempt to form through their agency the government of a civilized and worthy state, must be regarded as one of the most questionable and hazardous experiments upon which a great empire in the plenitude of its power and on the morrow of its greatest victory could ever have embarked.

On the other hand stood the history of Ireland, the unending quarrel and mutual injuries done each other by sister

164

countries and close neighbours generation after generation, and the earnest desire of every liberal heart in Britain to end this odious feud. During the nineteenth century both England and Ireland had restated their cases in forms far superior to those of the dark times of the past. England had lavished remedial measures and conciliatory procedure upon Ireland; Ireland in the main had rested herself upon constitutional and parliamentary action to support her claim. It would have been possible in 1886 to have reached a solution on a basis infinitely less perilous both to Ireland and Great Britain than that to which we were ultimately drawn. Said Mr. Gladstone in the House of Commons before the fateful division on the Home Rule Bill, 'Ireland stands at your bar, expectant, hopeful, almost suppliant. Her words are the words of truth and soberness. She asks a blessed oblivion of the past, and in that oblivion our interest is deeper than even hers. . . . Think, I beseech you—think well, think wisely, think not for a moment but for the years that are to come, before you reject this Bill.' In 1903 the Irish claim had been accorded by the vote of the House of Commons, and the measure embodying it had been destroyed only by the vote of the House of Lords. In 1914, when after four years of the fiercest Party strife a third Home Rule Bill seemed to be approaching a successful conclusion, doctrines of unconstitutional action had rightly or wrongly been proclaimed and preached by the great Conservative Party. Our country had been brought to the verge almost of civil war when this hateful issue was drowned in the cannonade of Armageddon. When at last the Home Rule Bill reached the Statute Book it was only under guarantee that it should not be brought into operation until the close of the War. And in 1920, in spite of unceasing effort, the problem was still unsolved and Ireland had become ungovernable except by processes of terror and violent subjugation deeply repugnant to British institutions and to British national character.

Both of these pictures must be gazed upon by those who attempt to form a true and fair judgment of the Irish Treaty

Settlement. Both are needed to explain the perplexities of the British Government and the causes which led them to grasp the larger hope.

. . . .

The actual event which led to negotiations was the opening of the Northern Parliament by the King in person. It would not have been right for Ministers to put in the mouth of the Sovereign words which could only apply to the people of Northern Ireland. It is well known that the King, acting in harmony not only with the letter but with the spirit of the Constitution, earnestly desired that language should be used which would appeal to the whole of his Irish subjects—South as well as North, Green as well as Orange. The outlook of the Sovereign, lifted high above the strife of Parties, the clash of races and religions and all sectional divergences of view, necessarily and naturally comprised the general interest of the Empire as a whole— and nothing narrower. Already the Prime Minister of Northern Ireland, Sir James Craig, alone and unarmed, had sought out Mr. De Valera in his hiding-places, and with equal statesmanship and courage had laboured in the cause of peace. The Government, therefore, took the responsibility which rested with them and with them alone of inserting in the Royal speech what was in effect a sincere appeal for a common effort to end the odious and disastrous conflict which was every day spreading more widely and bringing more discredit upon the name not only of Ireland but of the British Empire. The response in the opinion of both islands to that appeal was deep and widespread, and from that moment events moved forward in unbroken progression to the establishment of the Irish Free State.

. . . .

From the outset it became of the utmost importance to convince those who were now accepted as the Irish leaders of the sincerity and goodwill of the Imperial Government.

The issue was too grave for bargaining and haggling. We stated from the very beginning all that we were prepared to give, and that in no circumstances could we go any further. We also made it clear that if our offer were accepted, we would unhesitatingly carry it through without regard to any political misfortune which might in consequence fall upon the Government or upon its leading members. On this basis, therefore, and in this spirit the long and critical negotiations were conducted.

We found ourselves confronted in the early days not only with the unpractical and visionary fanaticism and romanticism of the extreme Irish secret societies, but also with those tides of distrust and hatred which had flowed between the two countries for so many centuries. An essential element in dynamite and every other high explosive is some intense acid. These terrible liquids slowly and elaborately prepared unite with perfectly innocent carbon compounds to give that pent-up, concentrated blasting power which shatters the structures and the lives of men. Hatred plays the same part in Government, as acids in chemistry. And here in Ireland were hatreds which in Mr. Kipling's phrase would 'eat the live steel from a rifle butt,' hatreds such as, thank God, in Great Britain had not existed for a hundred years. All this we had to overcome.

. . . .

The personal relationships which were established gradually between the British Ministers charged with the negotiations and the Irish representatives were of real importance in achieving the settlement. If I touch lightly upon a few incidents in these long parleys, it is only to illustrate how prejudice on both sides was largely disarmed, and how a mutual confidence and understanding grew up to bridge the abyss which had yawned between us.

Mr. Griffith was a writer who had studied deeply European history and the polity of States. He was a man of great firmness of character and of high integrity. He was that unusual figure—a silent Irishman; he hardly ever said a word. But no word that issued from his lips in my presence did he ever unsay. Mr. Lloyd George has described how in the supreme crisis of the negotiations, when rupture and resumption by both sides of whatever hostilities were possible to them seemed about to leap upon us, Mr. Griffith quietly declared that he for his part, whatever others might do, would accept the offer of the British Government and would return to Ireland to urge it upon the Irish people.

Michael Collins had not enjoyed the same advantages in education as his elder colleague. But he had elemental qualities and mother-wit which were in many ways remarkable. He stood far nearer to the terrible incidents of the conflict than his leader. His prestige and influence with the extreme parties in Ireland for that reason were far higher, his difficulties in his own heart and with his associates were far greater.

'I am sure,' I said during one of our meetings, 'you would much rather have fought properly in the field.'

His eye responded gratefully.

'I have written a paper,' he replied, 'on the limitation of our power to conform to the status of belligerents. We had not got even a county in which we could organize a uniformed force.'

And later: 'In the 1916 rebellion when you had millions of soldiers in arms our few hundreds in Dublin thought they were going to certain death. That was the nearest we could get to a military operation.'

'What will be the position,' I asked him, 'if after we have withdrawn all the police and most of the troops, the Treaty is broken and the Republic proclaimed?'

'Well,' he said, 'you will still have a great many troops in the most important places, and our country is accessible from every side. Personally I will do my best against such a breach. If it were only the wild men, we should be able to hold them in. But if the great majority of Ireland went to war with the British Empire, I could not fight against them. I would give up all authority and would fight as a private soldier on their side till I was killed, which would not be long. You would be entitled to do everything against us that may be done in war. And all the world would say we were in the wrong. And anyhow it will not happen. It will not be so bad as that.'

To Mr. Griffith I said one day:

'I would like us to have beaten you beyond all question, and then to have given you freely all that we are giving you now.'

'*I* understand that,' he answered, 'but would your countrymen?'

I wonder. It is extraordinary how rarely in history have victors been capable of turning in a flash to all those absolutely different processes of action, to that utterly different mood, which alone can secure them for ever by generosity what they have gained by force. In the hour of success, policy is blinded by the passion of the struggle. Yet the struggle with the enemy is over. There is only then the struggle with oneself. That is the hardest of all. So the world moves on only very slowly and fitfully with innumerable set-backs, and the superior solutions, when from time to time as the result of great exertions they are open, are nearly always squandered. Two opposite sides of human nature have to be simultaneously engaged. Those who can win the victory cannot make the peace; those who make the peace would never have won the victory. Have we not seen this on the most gigantic scale drawing out before our eyes in Europe? Still, after all, we have the gesture of Grant at Appomatox sending the sorely-needed rations of his own army apace into the starving Confederate camp and telling Lee to take his artillery horses home to plough the devastated Southern fields. We have the statecraft of Bismarck driving King, Cabinet, and Generals of Prussia into war with Austria in 1866, and then on the morrow of Sadowa, when Austria was at his mercy, slipping round in an hour and driving them all in the opposite direction. We have the great Castlereagh—so ignorantly traduced—after a generation of struggle with France, threatening in the day of triumph to go to war with his Prussian and Russian allies rather than have France dismembered or oppressed. And we have in our own time South Africa, where decisive victory in arms was swiftly followed by complete concession in policy, with results marvellous to this day.

Our settlement with the Boers, with my own vivid experiences in it, was my greatest source of comfort and inspiration in this Irish business. Indeed it was a help to all. I remember one night Mr. Griffith and Mr. Collins came to my house to meet the Prime Minister. It was at a crisis, and the negotiations seemed to hang only by a thread. Griffith went upstairs to parley with Mr. Lloyd George alone. Lord Birkenhead and I were left with Michael Collins meanwhile. He was in his most difficult mood, full of reproaches and defiances, and it was very easy for everyone to lose his temper.

'You hunted me night and day,' he exclaimed. 'You put a price on my head.'

'Wait a minute,' I said. 'You are not the only one.' And I took from my wall the framed copy of the reward offered for my recapture by the Boers. 'At any rate it was a good price— £5,000. Look at me—£25 dead or alive. How would you like that?'*

He read the paper, and as he took it in he broke into a hearty laugh. All his irritation vanished. We had a really serviceable conversation, and thereafter—though I must admit that deep in my heart there was a certain gulf between us— we never to the best of my belief lost the basis of a common understanding.

Michael Collins acted up to his word in his relations with the British Government. The strains and stresses upon him at times were unimaginable. Threatened always with death from those whose methods he knew only too well, reproached by darkly-sworn confederates with treason and perjury, the object of a dozen murder conspiracies, harassed to the depth of

* Actually no such reward had ever been offered by the British Government, but this I did not know at the time.

his nature by the poignant choices which thrust themselves upon him, swayed by his own impulsive temperament, nevertheless he held strictly to his engagements with the Ministers of a Government he had so long hated, but at last learned to trust. He was determined that the Irish name should not be dishonoured by the breach of the Treaty made in all good faith and goodwill.

'I expect,' he said to me towards the end, 'that I shall soon be killed. It will be a help. My death will do more to make peace than I could do by living.'

He was indeed soon to seal the Treaty of Reconciliation with his life's blood. 'Love of Ireland' are the words which Sir John Lavery has inscribed on his picture of the dead Irish leader. They are deserved, but with them there might at the end be written also, 'To England Honour and Goodwill.' A great Act of Faith had been performed on both sides of the Channel, and by that Act we dearly hoped that the curse of the centuries would at last be laid.

PARLIAMENTARY GOVERNMENT AND
THE ECONOMIC PROBLEM*

THE title of this lecture might suggest a connexion with contemporary party controversies. Dismiss any such apprehensions from your mind. Once I have assumed the academic panoply, I present myself before you as a Seeker after Truth; and if haply in my quest I should discern some glimpses of the more obvious forms of truth, the seeker will not hesitate to become the guide.

It has been accepted generally until quite recent times that the best way of governing states is by talking. An assemblage of persons who represent, or who claim to represent, the nation meet together face to face and argue out our affairs. The public at large having perforce chosen these persons from among those who were put before them submits itself in spite of some misgivings and repinings to their judgment. The public are accustomed to obey the decisions of Parliament, and the rulers who rest upon a parliamentary majority are not afraid to use compulsion upon recalcitrants. Of this method the English may not be the inventors; but they are undoubtedly the patentees. Here in this island have sprung and grown all those representative and parliamentary institutions which so many countries new and old alike have adopted and which still hold the field in the more powerful communities of the world.

However, we have seen that this system of government seems to lose much of its authority when based upon universal

* This paper was delivered as the Romanes Lecture in the Sheldonian Theatre at Oxford on June 19, 1930. It has already been published separately by the Clarendon Press, and is printed here by permission of the University of Oxford.

suffrage. So many various odd and unwritten processes are interposed between the elector and the assembly, and that assembly itself is subjected to so much extraneous pressure, that the famous phrase 'Government of the people by the people for the people' has in many states proved a mere illusion. Many of the parliaments so hopefully erected in Europe in the nineteenth century have already in the first quarter of the twentieth century been pulled down. Democracy has shown itself careless about those very institutions by which its own political status has been achieved. It seems ready to yield up the tangible rights hard won in rugged centuries to party organizations, to leagues and societies, to military chiefs or to dictatorships in various forms. Nevertheless, we may say that representative institutions still command a consensus of world opinion. In the United States representative institutions have expressed themselves almost entirely through the machinery of party; but here at home, although the party organization is necessary and powerful, the parliamentary conception is still dominant.

I see the Houses of Parliament—and particularly the House of Commons—alone among the senates and chambers of the world a living and ruling entity; the swift vehicle of public opinion; the arena—perhaps fortunately the padded arena— of the inevitable class and social conflict; the College from which the Ministers of State are chosen, and hitherto the solid and unfailing foundation of the executive power. I regard these parliamentary institutions as precious to us almost beyond compare. They seem to give by far the closest association yet achieved between the life of the people and the action of the State. They possess apparently an unlimited capacity of adaptiveness, and they stand an effective buffer against every form of revolutionary or reactionary violence. It should be the duty of faithful subjects to preserve these institutions in their healthy vigour, to guard them against the encroachment of external forces, and to revivify them from one generation to another from the springs of national talent, interest, and esteem.

We must, however, recognize in good time the great change which since the War has come over our public life in Great Britain. Before the War the issues fought out in Parliament were political and social. The parties fought one another heartily in a series of well-known stock and conventional quarrels, and the life of the nation proceeded underneath this agitated froth. Since the War, however, the issues are not political; they are economic. It is no longer a case of one party fighting another, nor of one set of politicians scoring off another set. It is the case of successive governments facing economic problems, and being judged by their success or failure in the duel. The nation is not interested in politics, it is interested in economics. It has in the main got the political system it wants; what it now asks for is more money, better times, regular employment, expanding comfort, and material prosperity. It feels that it is not having its share in the development of the modern world, and that it is losing its relative position. It feels that science and machinery ought to procure a much more rapid progress. It complains that the phenomena of production, consumption, and employment are at this time in our country exceptionally ill-related. It turns to Parliament asking for guidance, and Parliament, though voluble in so many matters, is on this one paramount topic dumb.

Never was a body more capable of dealing with political issues than the House of Commons. Its structure has stood the strain of the most violent contentions. Its long tradition, its collective personality, its flexible procedure, its social life, its unwritten inviolable conventions have made an organism more effective for the purpose of assimilation than any of which there is record. Every new extension of the franchise has altered the character, outlook, and worldly wealth of its members. The Whig and Tory squires of the eighteenth century and the gifted nominees or sprigs of the nobility have given place to the mercantile and middle classes, and these in turn receive into their midst hundreds of working men. Yet though the human element has undergone these substantial changes, the nature and spirit of the assembly is the same. We may be sure that Fox or Burke, that Disraeli or Gladstone, if they returned to-day, would in a few months feel quite at home and speedily reclaim their rightful place. Indeed, they might find it an all-too-easy conquest.

In the present period the House of Commons is engaged in digesting and assimilating a large new party founded, in theory at any rate, upon the basis of manual labour. It is a very heavy meal and the process of deglutition must take time. The constitutional boa-constrictor which has already devoured and absorbed the donkeys of so many generations only requires reasonable time to convert to its own nourishment and advantage almost any number of rabbits. And similarly the House of Commons tames, calms, instructs, reconciles, and rallies to the fundamental institutions of the State all sorts and conditions of men; and even women! But these latter dainty morsels are not always so tender as one would suppose. Taking a general view, we may say that in dealing with practical politics the House of Commons has no rival.

But it is otherwise when we come to economic problems. Members elected as the result of the antagonisms and partisanship of class and party may find in Parliament the means of adjusting their differences and providing a continual process by which the necessary changes in national life can be made. Political questions can be settled to a very large extent by counting noses, and by the recognized rough-and-tumble of electioneering. One feels grave doubt whether our economic problems will be solved by such methods. One may even be pardoned for doubting whether institutions based on adult suffrage could possibly arrive at the right decisions upon the intricate propositions of modern business and finance. Of course if the House of Commons shut itself up for three or four weeks to debate upon a long and profoundly-considered series of resolutions on the present new and serious economic position of this island, and of the Empire of which it is the heart, it might well be that when the doors were opened someone would emerge with a bold plan and a resolute majority. But the attempt to find the best way out of our economic difficulties by party politicians urgently looking for popular election cries, or the means to work up prejudice against those cries, is hardly likely to lead to a successful result. Yet we do most grievously need to find in a reasonably short time a national policy to reinvigorate our economic life and achieve a more rapid progress in the material well-being of the whole people. It might well be that the measures which in the course of several years would vastly improve our economic position actually and relatively, and open broadly to us the high roads of the future, would be extremely unpopular, and that no single party, even if they possessed the secret, would be able to carry their policy in the face of opposition by the others. In fact it would probably be safe to say that nothing that is popular and likely to gather a large number of votes will do what is wanted and win the prize which all desire.

Let us now look at some of the economic issues about which our partisans contend so loudly and about which great numbers of intelligent people are in honest doubt.

The classical doctrines of economics have for nearly a century found their citadels in the Treasury and the Bank of England. In their pristine vigour these doctrines comprise among others the following tenets: Free imports, irrespective of what other countries may do and heedless of the consequences to any particular native industry or interest. Ruthless direct taxation for the repayment of debt without regard to the effects of such taxation upon individuals or their enterprise or initiative. Rigorous economy in all forms of expenditure whether social or military. Stern assertion of the rights of the creditor, national or private, and full and effectual discharge of all liabilities. Profound distrust of State-stimulated industry in all its forms, or of State borrowing for the purpose of creating employment. Absolute reliance upon private enterprise, unfettered and unfavoured by the State. These principles, and others akin to them, are all part of one general economic conception, amplified and expounded in all the Victorian textbooks, and endorsed by most modern histories extant and current.

Whatever we may think about these doctrines—and I am not to-day pronouncing upon them—we can clearly see that they do not correspond to what is going on now. No doubt each political party picks out unconsciously from these tables of economic law the tenets which they think will be most agreeable to the crowd that votes for them, or which they hope will vote for them. They ignore or transgress the others. They then proceed to plume themselves upon their orthodoxy. But the growth of public opinion, and still more of voting opinion, violently and instinctively rejects many features in this massive creed. No one, for instance, will agree that wages should be settled only by the higgling of the market. No one would agree that modern world-dislocation of industry through new processes, or the development of new regions, or the improvement of international communications, or through gigantic speculations, should simply be met by preaching thrift and zeal to the displaced worker. Few would agree that private enterprise is the sole agency by which fruitful economic undertakings can be launched or conducted. An adverse conviction on all these points is general, and practice has long outstripped conviction. The climate of opinion in which we live to-day assigns the highest importance to minimum standards of life and labour. It is generally conceded that the humble local toiler must be protected or insured against exceptional external disturbance. It is admitted increasingly every day that the State should interfere in industry—some say by tariffs, some by credits, some say by direct control, and all by workshop regulations; and far-reaching structures of law are already in existence under several of these heads. Enormous expenditures have grown up for social and compassionate purposes. Direct taxation has risen to heights never dreamed of by the old economists and statesmen, and at these heights has set up many far-reaching reactions of an infrugal and even vicious character. We are in presence of new forces not existing when the text-books were written. There are the violent changes in world prices and in the localities where the leadership of particular industries is situated, all unmitigated by any steady up-

177

tide of British population and consuming power. There is the power of vast accumulations of capital to foresee and to fore-stall beneficial expenditure in new regions or upon new pro-cesses. There are the remarkable economies with their conse-quent competitive dominance which flow from scientific mass production. There is the vast network of cartels and trading agreements which has grown up irrespective of frontiers, na-tional sentiments, and fiscal laws. All these are new factors. These examples could be multiplied, but enough will suffice. It is certain that the economic problem with which we are now confronted is not adequately solved, indeed is not solved at all, by the teachings of the text-books, however grand may be their logic, however illustrious may be their authors.

But a harder task lies before us than the mere breaking up of old-established conclusions. It may well be indeed that these conclusions are sound, that they are the true foundations of the palace in which we seek some day to dwell. Our task is not to break up these foundations and use the fragments as missiles in party warfare. Our task is to build another storey upon them equally well-proportioned, symmetrical and uni-fied. This, then, and nothing else is the dangerous puzzle with which you now confront your ancient and admirable Parlia-mentary institutions and the harassed managers or leaders of your political parties. If the doctrines of the old economists no longer serve for the purposes of our society, they must be replaced by a new body of doctrine equally well-related in it-self, and equally well-fitting into a general theme. There is no reason that the new system should be at variance with the old. There are many reasons why it should be a consistent, but a more complex, secondary application.

I will take a sharp illustration. On the one hand we are told that imports injure our prosperity, and that we should insu-late ourselves against them and substantially abate their vol-ume. Something like this, you will remember, was done for us in the War by the German submarines. On the other hand there is the view that it is what comes into the island, rather than what goes out of it, that we enjoy: and that to refuse imports is to refuse the payment for your exports and consequently to impede your exports, or else it is to refuse to receive the interest upon your immense foreign investments. Therefore, it is argued, the more imports the merrier. But why should we accept this bleak dichotomy? Could we not by a selective process so handle the matter that while the volume of imports actually increased or remained constant, its character would be changed, and the commodities which compose it and the sources from which they come would be quite differently proportioned? What is required is not a simple Aye or No, but a discriminating process based upon systematized principles. These principles, no doubt, exist; but they are hardly likely to be discovered for regulating either imports or exports, by candidates for Parliament promising to protect their local industries; or by any favours which Ministers may bestow upon the mining constituencies whose support they enjoy.

It is evidently a matter requiring high, cold, technical, and dispassionate or disinterested decision. It is a matter requiring stiff rules to which local and individual interests can be made to conform.

I cannot believe that the true principles will be discovered by our excellent Parliamentary and electoral institutions—not even if they are guided by our faithful and energetic Press. We might have a General Election in which eight million voters were taught to sing in chorus, 'Make the foreigner pay,' and eight million more to chant in unison, 'Give the rich man's money to the poor, and so increase the consuming power'; and five other millions to intone, 'Your food will cost you more.' We might have all this; we probably shall! But even so we may be none the wiser or the better off.

Beyond our immediate difficulty lies the root problem of modern world economics; namely, the strange discordance between the consuming and producing power. Is it not astonishing that with all our knowledge and science, with the swift and easy means of communication and correspondence which exist all over the world, the most powerful and highly organized communities should remain the sport and prey of these perverse tides and currents? Who could have thought that it would be easier to produce by toil and skill all the most necessary or desirable commodities than it is to find consumers for them? Who could have thought that cheap and abundant supplies of all the basic commodities would find the science and civilization of the world unable to utilize them? Have all our triumphs of research and organization bequeathed us only a new punishment—the Curse of Plenty? Are we really to believe that no better adjustment can be made between supply and demand? Yet the fact remains that every attempt has so far failed. Many various attempts have been made, from the extremes of Communism in Russia to the extremes of Capitalism in the United States. They include every form of fiscal policy and currency policy. But all have failed, and we have advanced little further in this quest than in barbaric times. Surely it is this mysterious crack and fissure at the basis of all our arrangements and apparatus upon which the keenest minds throughout the world should be concentrated. Lasting fame and great advantage would attend the nation which first secured the prize. But here again it is doubtful whether Democracy or Parliamentary government, or even a General Election, will make a decisively helpful contribution.

Are we not capable of a higher and more complex economic, fiscal, and financial policy? Are we not capable of evolving a united body of doctrine adapted to our actual conditions and requirements? Could not such a system of policy be presented and accepted upon a national and not a party basis? Could it not when devised be taken out of the political brawling and given a fair trial by overwhelming national consent? Here then is the crux for Parliament. Many dangers threaten representative institutions once they have confided themselves to adult suffrage. There are dangers from the right and dangers from the left. We see examples of both in Europe to-day. But the British Parliamentary system will not be overthrown by political agitation: for that is what it specially comprehends. It will pass only when it has shown itself incapable of dealing with some fundamental and imperative economic need; and such a challenge is now open.

It must be observed that economic problems, unlike political issues, cannot be solved by any expression, however vehement, of the national will, but only by taking the right action. You cannot cure cancer by a majority. What is wanted is a remedy. Everyone knows what the people wish. They wish for more prosperity. How to get it? That is the grim question, and neither the electors nor their representatives are competent to answer it. Governments and the various parties moving in the political sphere are not free to proclaim the proper remedies in their completeness, even if they knew them. All kinds of popular cries can be presented for an election, and each may contain some measure of the truth. None in itself will provide us with the key. For this reason opinion has been turning towards the treatment of the subject on national and non-party lines. The leaders of parties, we are told, should meet together and arrive at a common policy. But these leaders, having their being in the political sphere, would not be able at such a conference to do much more than to restate in civil terms the well-known differences and antagonisms which they represent.

It would seem, therefore, that if new light is to be thrown upon this grave and clamant problem, it must in the first instance receive examination from a non-political body, free altogether from party exigencies, and composed of persons possessing special qualifications in economic matters. Parliament would, therefore, be well advised to create such a body subordinate to itself, and assist its deliberations to the utmost. The spectacle of an Economic sub-Parliament debating day after day with fearless detachment from public opinion all the most disputed questions of Finance and Trade, and reaching conclusions by voting, would be an innovation, but an innovation easily to be embraced by our flexible constitutional system. I see no reason why the political Parliament should not choose in proportion to its party groupings a subordinate Economic Parliament of say one-fifth of its numbers, and composed of persons of high technical and business qualifications. This idea has received much countenance in Germany. I see no reason why such an assembly should not debate in the open light of day and without caring a halfpenny who won the General Election, or who had the best slogan for curing Unemployment, all the grave economic issues by which we are now confronted and afflicted. I see no reason why the Economic Parliament should not for the time being command a greater interest than the political Parliament; nor why the political Parliament should not assist it with its training and experience in methods of debate and procedure. What is required is a new *personnel* adapted to the task which has to be done, and pursuing that task day after day without the distractions of other affairs and without fear, favour, or affection. The conclusions of such a body, although themselves devoid of legal force, might well, if they commanded a consensus of opinion, supply us with a comprehensive and unified view of high expert authority, which could then be remitted in its integrity to the political sphere.

Let me recapitulate the argument I have submitted to you upon this aspect of political science. The economic problem for Great Britain and her Empire is urgent, vital, and dominant. There exists at the present time no constitutional machinery for dealing with it on its merits, with competent examination and without political bias and antagonisms. The House of Commons, to which the anxious nation looks to provide a solution, is unsuited both by its character and the conditions which govern its life to fulfil such a task. Nevertheless, the task has to be done. Britain is unconquerable, and will not fail to find a way through her difficulties. Parliament is therefore upon its trial, and if it continues to show itself incapable of offering sincere and effective guidance at this juncture, our Parliamentary institutions, so admirable in the political sphere, may well fall under a far-reaching condemnation. If Parliament, and the Ministries dependent upon Parliament, cannot proclaim a new policy, the question arises whether they should not, while time remains, create a new instrument specially adapted for the purpose, and delegate to that instrument all the necessary powers and facilities.

I hope you will feel I have been justified in troubling you to-day with these anxious matters. These eventful years through which we are passing are not less serious for us than the years of the Great War. They belong to the same period. The grand and victorious summits which the British Empire won in that war are being lost, have indeed largely been lost in the years which followed the peace. We see our race doubtful of its mission and no longer confident about its principles, infirm of purpose, drifting to and fro with the tides and currents of a deeply-disturbed ocean. The compass has been damaged. The charts are out of date. The crew have to take it in turns to be Captain; and every captain before every movement of the helm has to take a ballot not only of the crew but of an ever-increasing number of passengers. Yet within this vessel there abide all the might and fame of the British race and all the treasures of all the peoples in one-fifth of the habitable globe. Let this University bear her part in raising our economic thought to the height of the situation with which we are confronted, and thereafter in enforcing action, without which such thought is vain.

SHALL WE ALL COMMIT SUICIDE?*

THE story of the human race is War. Except for brief and precarious interludes, there has never been peace in the world; and before history began, murderous strife was universal and unending. But up to the present time the means of destruction at the disposal of man have not kept pace with his ferocity. Reciprocal extermination was impossible in the Stone Age. One cannot do much with a clumsy club. Besides, men were so scarce and hid so well that they were hard to find. They fled so fast that they were hard to catch. Human legs could only cover a certain distance each day. With the best will in the world to destroy his species, each man was restricted to a very limited area of activity. It was impossible to make any effective progress on these lines. Meanwhile one had to live and hunt and sleep. So on the balance the life-forces kept a steady lead over the forces of death, and gradually tribes, villages, and governments were evolved.

The effort at destruction then entered upon a new phase. War became a collective enterprise. Roads were made which facilitated the movement of large numbers of men. Armies were organized. Many improvements in the apparatus of slaughter were devised. In particular the use of metal, and above all steel, for piercing and cutting human flesh, opened out a promising field. Bows and arrows, slings, chariots, horses, and elephants lent valuable assistance. But here again another set of checks began to operate. The governments were not sufficiently secure. The armies were liable to violent internal disagreements. It was extremely difficult to feed large numbers of men once they were concentrated, and consequently the efficiency of the efforts at destruction became fit

* Published in 1925.

184

ful and was tremendously hampered by defective organization. Thus again there was a balance on the credit side of life. The world rolled forward, and human society entered upon a vaster and more complex age.

It was not until the dawn of the twentieth century of the Christian era that War really began to enter into its kingdom as the potential destroyer of the human race. The organization of mankind into great States and Empires and the rise of nations to full collective consciousness enabled enterprises of slaughter to be planned and executed upon a scale and with a perseverance never before imagined. All the noblest virtues of individuals were gathered together to strengthen the destructive capacity of the mass. Good finances, the resources of world-wide credit and trade, the accumulation of large capital reserves, made it possible to divert for considerable periods the energies of whole peoples to the task of Devastation. Democratic institutions gave expression to the will-power of millions. Education not only brought the course of the conflict within the comprehension of everyone, but rendered each person serviceable in a high degree for the purpose in hand. The Press afforded a means of unification and of mutual encouragement; Religion, having discreetly avoided conflict on the fundamental issues, offered its encouragements and consolations, through all its forms, impartially to all the combatants. Lastly, Science unfolded her treasures and her secrets to the desperate demands of men, and placed in their hands agencies and apparatus almost decisive in their character.

In consequence many novel features presented themselves. Instead of merely starving fortified towns, whole nations were methodically subjected to the process of reduction by famine. The entire population in one capacity or another took part in the War; all were equally the object of attack. The Air opened paths along which death and terror could be carried far behind the lines of the actual armies, to women, children, the aged, the sick, who in earlier struggles would perforce have been left untouched. Marvellous organizations of railroads, steamships, and motor vehicles placed and maintained tens of millions of men continuously in action. Healing and surgery in their exquisite developments returned them again and again to the shambles. Nothing was wasted that could contribute to the process of waste. The last dying kick was brought into military utility.

But all that happened in the four years of the Great War was only a prelude to what was preparing for the fifth year. The campaign of the year 1919 would have witnessed an immense accession to the power of destruction. Had the Germans retained the morale to make good their retreat to the Rhine, they would have been assaulted in the summer of 1919 with forces and by methods incomparably more prodigious than any yet employed. Thousands of aeroplanes would have shattered their cities. Scores of thousands of cannon would have blasted their front. Arrangements were being made to carry simultaneously a quarter of a million men, together with all their requirements, continuously forward across country in mechanical vehicles moving ten or fifteen miles each day. Poison gases of incredible malignity, against which only a secret mask (which the Germans could not obtain in time) was proof, would have stifled all resistance and paralysed all life on the hostile front subjected to attack. No doubt the Germans too had their plans. But the hour of wrath had passed. The signal of relief was given, and the horrors of 1919 remain buried in the archives of the great antagonists.

The War stopped as suddenly and as universally as it had begun. The world lifted its head, surveyed the scene of ruin, and victors and vanquished alike drew breath. In a hundred laboratories, in a thousand arsenals, factories, and bureaus, men pulled themselves up with a jerk, turned from the task in which they had been absorbed. Their projects were put aside unfinished, unexecuted; but their knowledge was preserved; their data, calculations, and discoveries were hastily bundled together and docketed 'for future reference' by the War Offices in every country. The campaign of 1919 was never fought; but its ideas go marching along. In every Army they are being explored, elaborated, refined under the surface of peace, and

186

should war come again to the world it is not with the weapons and agencies prepared for 1919 that it will be fought, but with developments and extensions of these which will be incomparably more formidable and fatal.

It is in these circumstances that we have entered upon that period of Exhaustion which has been described as Peace. It gives us at any rate an opportunity to consider the general situation. Certain sombre facts emerge solid, inexorable, like the shapes of mountains from drifting mist. It is established that henceforward whole populations will take part in war, all doing their utmost, all subjected to the fury of the enemy. It is established that nations who believe their life is at stake will not be restrained from using any means to secure their existence. It is probable—nay, certain—that among the means which will next time be at their disposal will be agencies and processes of destruction wholesale, unlimited, and perhaps, once launched, uncontrollable.

Mankind has never been in this position before. Without having improved appreciably in virtue or enjoying wiser guidance, it has got into its hands for the first time the tools by which it can unfailingly accomplish its own extermination. That is the point in human destinies to which all the glories and toils of men have at last led them. They would do well to pause and ponder upon their new responsibilities. Death stands at attention, obedient, expectant, ready to serve, ready to shear away the peoples *en masse*; ready, if called on, to pulverize, without hope of repair, what is left of civilization. He awaits only the word of command, He awaits it from a frail, bewildered being, long his victim, now—for one occasion only—his Master.

Let it not be thought for a moment that the danger of another explosion in Europe is passed. For the time being the stupor and the collapse which followed the World War ensure a sullen passivity, and the horror of war, its carnage and its tyrannies, has sunk into the soul, has dominated the mind, of every class in every race. But the causes of war have been in no way removed; indeed they are in some respects aggravated

187

by the so-called Peace Treaties and the reactions following thereupon. Two mighty branches of the European family will never rest content with their existing situation. Russia, stripped of her Baltic Provinces, will, as the years pass by, brood incessantly upon the wars of Peter the Great. From one end of Germany to the other an intense hatred of France unites the whole population. The enormous contingents of German youth growing to military manhood year by year are inspired by the fiercest sentiments, and the soul of Germany smoulders with dreams of a War of Liberation or Revenge. These ideas are restrained at the present moment only by physical impotence. France is armed to the teeth. Germany has been to a great extent disarmed and her military system broken up. The French hope to preserve this situation by their technical military apparatus, by their shield of fortresses, by their black troops, and by a system of alliances with the smaller States of Europe; and for the present at any rate overwhelming force is on their side. But physical force alone, unsustained by world opinion, affords no durable foundation for security. Germany is a far stronger entity than France, and cannot be kept in permanent subjugation.

'Wars,' said a distinguished American to me some years ago, 'are fought with Steel: weapons may change, but Steel remains the core of all modern warfare. France has got the Steel of Europe, and Germany has lost it. Here, at any rate, is an element of permanency.' 'Are you sure,' I asked, 'that the wars of the future will be fought with Steel?' A few weeks later I talked with a German. 'What about Aluminium?' he replied. 'Some think,' he said, 'that the next war will be fought with Electricity.' And on this a vista opens out of electrical rays which could paralyse the engines of a motor-car, could claw down aeroplanes from the sky, and conceivably be made destructive of human life or human vision. Then there are Explosives. Have we reached the end? Has Science turned its last page on them? May there not be methods of using explosive energy incomparably more intense than anything heretofore discovered? Might not a bomb no bigger than an orange be found to possess a secret power to destroy a whole block of buildings—nay, to concentrate the force of a thousand tons of cordite and blast a township at a stroke? Could not explosives even of the existing type be guided automatically in flying machines by wireless or other rays, without a human pilot, in ceaseless procession upon a hostile city, arsenal, camp, or dockyard?

As for Poison Gas and Chemical Warfare in all its forms, only the first chapter has been written of a terrible book. Certainly every one of these new avenues to destruction is being studied on both sides of the Rhine, with all the science and patience of which man is capable. And why should it be supposed that these resources will be limited to Inorganic Chemistry? A study of Disease—of Pestilences methodically prepared and deliberately launched upon man and beast—is certainly being pursued in the laboratories of more than one great country. Blight to destroy crops, Anthrax to slay horses and cattle, Plague to poison not armies only but whole districts—such are the lines along which military science is remorselessly advancing.

It is evident that whereas an equally-contested war under such conditions might work the ruin of the world and cause an immeasurable diminution of the human race, the possession by one side of some overwhelming scientific advantage would lead to the complete enslavement of the unwary party. Not only are the powers now in the hands of man capable of destroying the life of nations, but for the first time they afford to one group of civilized men the opportunity of reducing their opponents to absolute helplessness.

In barbarous times superior martial virtues—physical strength, courage, skill, discipline—were required to secure such a supremacy; and in the hard evolution of mankind the best and fittest stocks came to the fore. But no such saving guarantee exists to-day. There is no reason why a base, degenerate, immoral race should not make an enemy far above them in quality, the prostrate subject of their caprice or tyranny, simply because they happened to be possessed at a given

189

moment of some new death-dealing or terror-working process and were ruthless in its employment. The liberties of men are no longer to be guarded by their natural qualities, but by their dodges; and superior virtue and valour may fall an easy prey to the latest diabolical trick.

In the sombre paths of destructive science there was one new turning-point which seemed to promise a corrective to these mortal tendencies. It might have been hoped that the electro-magnetic waves would in certain scales be found capable of detonating explosives of all kinds from a great distance. Were such a process discovered in time to become common property, War would in important respects return again to the crude but healthy limits of the barbarous ages. The sword, the spear, the bludgeon, and above all *the fighting man*, would regain at a bound their old sovereignty. But it is depressing to learn that the categories into which these rays are divided are now so fully explored that there is not much expectation of this. All the hideousness of the Explosive era will continue; and to it will surely be added the gruesome complications of Poison and of Pestilence scientifically applied.

Such, then, is the peril with which mankind menaces itself. Means of destruction incalculable in their effects, wholesale and frightful in their character, and unrelated to any form of human merit: the march of Science unfolding ever more appalling possibilities; and the fires of hatred burning deep in the hearts of some of the greatest peoples of the world, fanned by continual provocation and unceasing fear, and fed by the deepest sense of national wrong or national danger! On the other hand, there is the blessed respite of Exhaustion, offering to the nations a final chance to control their destinies and avert what may well be a general doom. Surely if a sense of self-preservation still exists among men, if the will to live resides not merely in individuals or nations but in humanity as a whole, the prevention of the supreme catastrophe ought to be the paramount object of all endeavour.

Against the gathering but still distant tempest the League of Nations, deserted by the United States, scorned by Soviet

Russia, flouted by Italy, distrusted equally by France and Germany, raises feebly but faithfully its standards of sanity and hope. Its structure, airy and unsubstantial, framed of shining but too often visionary idealism, is in its present form incapable of guarding the world from its dangers and of protecting mankind from itself. Yet it is through the League of Nations alone that the path to safety and salvation can be found. To sustain and aid the League of Nations is the duty of all. To reinforce it and bring it into vital and practical relation with actual world-politics by sincere agreements and understanding between the great Powers, between the leading races, should be the first aim of all who wish to spare their children torments and disasters compared with which those we have suffered will be but a pale preliminary.

MASS EFFECTS IN MODERN LIFE

Is the march of events ordered and guided by eminent men;
or do our leaders merely fall into their places at the heads
of the moving columns? Is human progress the result of
the resolves and deeds of individuals, or are these resolves and
deeds only the outcome of time and circumstance? Is history
the chronicle of famous men and women, or only of their res-
ponses to the tides, tendencies and opportunities of their age?
Do we owe the ideals and wisdom that make our world to the
glorious few, or to the patient anonymous innumerable many?
The question has only to be posed to be answered. We have
but to let the mind's eye skim back over the story of nations,
indeed to review the experience of our own small lives, to observe the decisive part which accident and chance play at every
moment. If this or that had been otherwise, if this instruction
had not been given, if that blow had not been struck, if that
horse had not stumbled, if we had not met that woman, or
missed or caught that train, the whole course of our lives
would have been changed; and with our lives the lives of
others, until gradually, in ever-widening circles, the movement of the world itself would have been affected. And if this
be true of the daily experience of ordinary average people,
how much more potent must be the deflection which the
Master Teachers—Thinkers, Discoverers, Commanders—
have imparted at every stage. True, they required their background, their atmosphere, their opportunity; but these were
also the leverages which magnified their power. I have no
hesitation in ranging myself with those who view the past
history of the world mainly as the tale of exceptional human
beings, whose thoughts, actions, qualities, virtues, triumphs,
weaknesses and crimes have dominated the fortunes of the
race. But we may now ask ourselves whether powerful changes

are not coming to pass, are not already in progress or indeed far advanced. Is not mankind already escaping from the control of individuals? Are not our affairs increasingly being settled by mass processes? Are not modern conditions—at any rate throughout the English-speaking communities—hostile to the development of outstanding personalities, and to their influence upon events: and lastly if this be true, will it be for our greater good and glory? These questions merit some examination from thoughtful people.

Certainly we see around us to-day a marked lack of individual leadership. The late Mr. John Morley, statesman and philanthropist, man of letters and man of affairs, some years ago towards the close of his life delivered an oration in which he drew attention to the decline in the personal eminence of the leaders in almost all the important spheres of thought and art. He contrasted the heads of the great professions in the early twentieth century with those who had shone in the mid-Victorian era. He spoke of 'the vacant Thrones' in Philosophy, History, Economics, Oratory, Statecraft, Poetry, Literature, Painting, Sculpture, and Music, which stood on every side. He pointed—as far as possible without offence—to the array of blameless mediocrities, who strutted conscientiously around the seats of the mighty decked in their discarded mantles and insignia. The pith and justice of these reflections were unwelcome, but not to be denied. They are no less applicable to the United States. With every natural wish to be complimentary to our own age and generation, with every warning against 'singing the praises of former times', it is difficult to marshal to-day in any part of the English-speaking world an assembly of notables, who either in distinction or achievement can compare with those to whom our grandfathers so gladly paid attention and tribute.

It must be admitted that in one great sphere the thrones are neither vacant nor occupied by pygmies. Science in all its forms surpasses itself every year. The body of knowledge ever accumulating is immediately interchanged and the quality and fidelity of the research never flags. But here again the mass effect largely suppresses the individual achievement. The throne is occupied; but by a throng.

In part we are conscious of the enormous processes of collectivization which are at work among us. We have long seen the old family business, where the master was in direct personal touch with his workmen, swept out of existence or absorbed by powerful companies, which in their turn are swallowed by mammoth trusts. We have found in these processes, whatever hardships they may have caused to individuals, immense economic and social advantages. The magic of mass production has carried all before it. The public have a cheaper and even better article or a superior service, the workmen have better wages and greater security.

The results upon national character and psychology are more questionable. We are witnessing a great diminution in the number of independent people who had some standing of their own, albeit a small one, and who if they conducted their affairs with reasonable prudence could 'live by no man's leave underneath the law.' They may be better off as the salaried officials of great corporations; but they have lost in forethought, in initiative, in contrivance, in freedom and in effective civic status.

These instances are but typical of what is taking place in almost every sphere of modern industrial life, and of what must take place with remorseless persistency, if we are to enjoy the material blessings which scientific and organized civilization is ready to bestow in measureless abundance.

In part again these changes are unconscious. Public opinion is formed and expressed by machinery. The newspapers do an immense amount of thinking for the average man and woman. In fact they supply them with such a continuous stream of standardized opinion, borne along upon an equally inexhaustible flood of news and sensation, collected from every part of the world every hour of the day, that there is neither the need nor the leisure for personal reflection. All this is but a part of a tremendous educating process. But it is an education which passes in at one ear and out at the other. It is an education at once universal and superficial. It produces enormous numbers of standardized citizens, all equipped with regulation opinions, prejudices and sentiments, according to their class or party. It may eventually lead to a reasonable, urbane and highly-serviceable society. It may draw in its wake a mass culture enjoyed by countless millions, to whom such pleasures were formerly unknown. We must not forget the enormous circulations at cheap prices of the greatest books of the world, which is a feature of modern life in civilized countries, and nowhere more than in the United States. But this great diffusion of knowledge, information and light reading of all kinds may, while it opens new pleasures to humanity and appreciably raises the general level of intelligence, be destructive of those conditions of personal stress and mental effort to which the masterpieces of the human mind are due.

It is a curious fact that the Russian Bolsheviks in carrying by compulsion mass conceptions to their utmost extreme seem to have lost not only the guidance of great personalities, but even the economic fertility of the process itself. The Communist theme aims at universal standardization. The individual becomes a function: the community is alone of interest: mass thoughts dictated and propagated by the rulers are the only thoughts deemed respectable. No one is to think of himself as an immortal spirit, clothed in the flesh, but sovereign, unique, indestructible. No one is to think of himself even as that harmonious integrity of mind, soul and body, which, take it as you will, may claim to be 'the Lord of Creation.' Sub-human goals and ideals are set before these Asiatic millions. The Beehive? No, for there must be no queen and no honey, or at least no honey for others. In Soviet Russia we have a society which seeks to model itself upon the Ant. There is not one single social or economic principle or concept in the philosophy of the Russian Bolshevik which has not been realized, carried into action, and enshrined in immutable laws a million years ago by the White Ant.

But human nature is more intractable than ant-nature.

195

The explosive variations of its phenomena disturb the smooth working out of the laws and forces which have subjugated the White Ant. It is at once the safeguard and the glory of mankind that they are easy to lead and hard to drive. So the Bolsheviks, having attempted by tyranny and by terror to establish the most complete form of mass life and collectivism of which history bears record, have not only lost the distinction of individuals, but have not even made the nationalization of life and industry pay. We have not much to learn from them, except what to avoid.

Mass effects and their reactions are of course more pronounced in the leading nations than in more backward and primitive communities. In Great Britain, the United States, Germany, and France, the decline in personal pre-eminence is much more plainly visible than in societies which have less wealth, less power, less freedom. The great emancipated nations seem to have become largely independent of famous guides and guardians. They no longer rely upon the Hero, the Commander, or the Teacher as they did in bygone rugged ages, or as the less advanced peoples do to-day. They wend their way ponderously, unthinkingly, blindly, but nevertheless surely and irresistibly towards goals which are ill-defined and yet magnetic. Is it then true that civilization and democracy, when sufficiently developed, will increasingly dispense with personal direction: that they mean to find their own way for themselves; and that they are capable of finding the right way? Or are they already going wrong? Are they off the track? Have they quitted the stern, narrow high-roads which alone lead to glorious destinies and survival? Is what we now see in the leading democracies merely a diffusion and squandering of the accumulated wisdom and treasure of the past? Are we blundering on together in myriad companies, like innumerable swarms of locusts, chirping and devouring towards the salt sea, or towards some vast incinerator of shams and fallacies? Or have we for the first time reached those uplands whence all of us, even the humblest and silliest equally with the best, can discern for ourselves the

196

beacon lights? Surely such an enquiry deserves an idle hour.

In no field of man's activities is the tendency to mass effects and the suppression of the individual more evident than in modern war. The Armageddon through which we have recently passed displays the almost complete elimination of personal guidance. It was the largest and the latest of all wars. It was also the worst, the most destructive, and in many ways the most ruthless. Now that it is over we look back, and with minute and searching care seek to find its criminals and its heroes. Where are they? Where are the villains who made the War? Where are the deliverers who ended it? Facts without number, growing libraries, clouds of contemporary witnesses, methods of assembling and analysing evidence never before possessed or used among men are at our disposal. The quest is keen. We ought to know; we mean to know. Smarting under our wounds, enraged by our injuries, amazed by our wonderful exertions and achievements, conscious of our authority, we demand to know the truth, and to fix the responsibilities. Our halters and our laurels are ready and abundant.

But what is the answer? There is no answer. On the one hand, the accusations eagerly pressed now against this man or Government or nation, now against that, seem to dissipate themselves as the indictment proceeds. On the other, as the eager claimants for the honour of being the man, the Government, the nation THAT ACTUALLY WON THE WAR multiply and as their self-advocacy becomes more voluble, more strident, we feel less and less convinced. The Muse of History to whom we all so confidently appeal has become a Sphinx. A sad, half-mocking smile flickers on her stone war-scarred lineaments. While we gaze, we feel that the day will never come when we shall learn the answer for which we have clamoured. Meanwhile the halters rot and the laurels fade. Both the making and the winning of the most terrible and the most recent of earthly struggles seems to have been a co-operative affair!

Modern conditions do not lend themselves to the production of the heroic or super-dominant type. On the whole they are fatal to pose. The robes, the wigs, the ceremonies, the grades that fortified the public men and ruling functionaries of former centuries have fallen into disuse in every country. Even 'the Divinity that doth hedge a King' is considered out of place except on purely official occasions. Sovereigns are admired for their free and easy manners, their readiness to mingle with all classes, their matter-of-fact work-a-day air, their dislike of pomp and ritual. The Minister or President at the head of some immense sphere of business, whose practical decisions from hour to hour settle so many important things, is no longer a figure of mystery and awe. On the contrary he is looked upon, and what is more important for our present purpose, looks upon himself, as quite an ordinary fellow, who happens to be charged for the time being with a peculiar kind of large-scale work. He hustles along with the crowd in the public conveyances, or attired in 'plus fours' waits his turn upon the links. All this is very jolly, and a refreshing contrast to the ridiculous airs and graces of the periwigged potentates of other generations. The question is whether the sense of leadership, and the commanding attitude towards men and affairs, are likely to arise from such simple and unpretentious customs and habits of mind: and further whether our public affairs will now for the future run on quite happily without leaders who by their training and situation, no less than by their abilities, feel themselves to be uplifted above the general mass.

The intense light of war illuminates as usual this topic more clearly than the comfortable humdrum glow of peace. We see the modern commander entirely divorced from the heroic aspect by the physical conditions which have overwhelmed his art. No longer will Hannibal and Cæsar, Turenne and Marlborough, Frederick and Napoleon, sit their horses on the battlefield and by their words and gestures direct and dominate between dawn and dusk the course of a supreme event. No longer will their fame and presence cheer their struggling soldiers. No longer will they share their perils, rekindle their spirits and restore the day. They will not be there. They have been banished from the fighting scene, together with their plumes, standards and breast-plates. The lion-hearted warrior, whose keen eye detected the weakness in the foeman's line, whose resolve outlasted all the strains of battle, whose mere arrival at some critical point turned the tide of conflict, has disappeared. Instead our Generals are to be found on the day of the battle at their desks in their offices fifty or sixty miles from the front, anxiously listening to the trickle of the telephone for all the world as if they were speculators with large holdings when the market is disturbed.

All very right and worthy. They are at their posts. Where else indeed should they be? The tape-machine ticks are recording in blood-red ink that railways are down or utilities up, that a bank has broken here, and a great fortune has been captured there. Calm sits the General—he is a high-souled speculator. He is experienced in finance. He has survived many market crashes. His reserves are ample and mobile. He watches for the proper moment, or proper day—for battles now last for months—and then launches them to the attack. He is a fine tactician, and knows the wiles of bull and bear, of attack and defence to a nicety. His commands are uttered with decision. Sell fifty thousand of this. Buy at the market a hundred thousand of that. Ah! No, we are on the wrong track. It is not shares he is dealing in. It is the lives of scores of thousands of men. To look at him at work in his office you would never have believed that he was fighting a battle in command of armies ten times as large and a hundred times as powerful as any that Napoleon led. We must praise him if he does his work well, if he sends the right messages, and spends the right troops, and buys the best positions. But it is hard to feel that he is the hero. No; he is not the hero. He is the manager of a stock-market, or a stock-yard.

The obliteration of the personal factor in war, the stripping from high commanders of all the drama of the battlefield, the reducing of their highest function to pure office work, will have profound effects upon sentiment and opinion.

Hitherto the great captain has been rightly revered as the genius who by the firmness of his character, and by the mysterious harmonies and inspirations of his nature, could rule the storm. He did it himself: and no one else could do it so well. He conquered there and then. Often he fell beneath the bolts and the balls, saviour of his native land. Now, however illogical it may seem and even unjust, his glamour and honours will not readily descend upon our calculating friend at the telephone. This worthy must assuredly be rewarded as a useful citizen, and a faithful perspicacious public servant; but not as a hero. The heroes of modern war lie out in the cratered fields, mangled, stifled, scarred; and there are too many of them for exceptional honours. It is mass suffering, mass sacrifice, mass victory. The glory which plays upon the immense scenes of carnage is diffused. No more the blaze of triumph irradiates the helmets of the chiefs. There is only the pale light of a rainy dawn by which forty miles of batteries recommence their fire, and another score of divisions flounder to their death in mud and poison gas.

That was the last war. The wars of the future will be even less romantic and picturesque. They will apparently be the wars not of armies but of whole populations. Men, women and children, old and feeble, soldiers and civilians, sick and wounded—all will be exposed—so we are told—to aerial bombardment, that is to say to mass destruction by lethal vapour. There will not be much glory for the general in this process. My gardener last spring exterminated seven wasp's nests. He did his work most efficiently. He chose the right poison. He measured the exact amount. He put it stealthily in the right place, at the right time. The entire communities were destroyed. Not even one wasp got near enough to sting him. It was his duty and he performed it well. But I am not going to regard him as a hero.

So when some spectacled 'brass hat' of a future world-agony has extinguished some London or Paris, some Tokio or San Francisco, by pressing a button, or putting his initials neatly at the bottom of a piece of foolscap, he will have to wait a long time for fame and glory. Even the flashlights of the photographers in the national Ministry of Propaganda will be only a partial compensation. Still our Commander-in-Chief may be a man of exemplary character, most painstaking and thorough in his profession. He may only be doing what in all the circumstances some one or other would have to do. It seems rather hard that he should receive none of the glory which in former ages would have been the attribute of his office and the consequence of his success. But this is one of the mass effects of modern life and science. He will have to put up with it.

From this will follow blessed reactions. The idea of war will become loathsome to humanity. The military leader will cease to be a figure of romance and fame. Youth will no longer be attracted to such careers. Poets will not sing nor sculptors chisel the deeds of conquerors. It may well be that the chemists will carry off what credit can be found. The budding Napoleons will go into business, and the civilization of the world will stand on a surer basis. We need not waste our tears on the mass effects in war. Let us return to those of peace.

Can modern communities do without great men? Can they dispense with hero-worship? Can they provide a larger wisdom, a nobler sentiment, a more vigorous action, by collective processes, than were ever got from the Titans? Can nations remain healthy, can all nations draw together, in a world whose brightest stars are film stars and whose gods are sitting in the gallery? Can the spirit of man emit the vital spark by machinery? Will the new problems of successive generations be solved successfully by 'the common sense of most'; by party caucuses; by Assemblies whose babble is no longer heeded? Or will there be some big hitch in the forward march of mankind, some intolerable block in the traffic, some vain wandering into the wilderness; and will not then the need for a personal chief become the mass desire?

We see a restlessness around us already. The cry of 'Measures, not Men' no longer commands universal sympathy. There is a sense of vacancy and of fatuity, of incompleteness.

We miss our giants. We are sorry that their age is past. The general levels of intelligence and of knowledge have risen. We are upon a high plateau. A peak of 10,000 feet above the old sea-level is scarcely noticeable. There are so many such eminences that we hardly bother about them. The region seems healthy; but the scenery is unimpressive. We mourn the towering grandeur which surrounded and cheered our long painful ascent. Ah! if we could only find some new enormous berg rising towards the heavens as high above our plateau as those old mountains down below rose above the plains and marshes! We want a monarch peak, with base enormous, whose summit is for ever hidden from our eyes by clouds, and down whose precipices cataracts of sparkling waters thunder. Unhappily the democratic plateau or platform does not keep that article in stock. Perhaps something like it might be worked up by playing spot-lights upon pillars of smoke or gas, and using the loud-speaker apparatus. But we soon see through these pretences.

No, we must take the loss with the gain. On the uplands there are no fine peaks. We must do without them while we stay there. Of course we could always if we wished go down again into the plains and valleys out of which we have climbed. We may even wander thither unwittingly. We may slide there. We may be pushed there. There are still many powerful nations dwelling at these lower levels—some contentedly—some even proudly. They often declare that life in the valleys is preferable. There is, they say, more variety, more beauty, more grace, more dignity—more true health and fertility than upon the arid highlands. They say this middle situation is better suited to human nature. The arts flourish there, and science need not be absent. Moreover it is pleasing to look back over the plains and morasses through which our path has lain in the past, and remember in tradition the great years of pilgrimage. Then they point to the frowning crag, their venerated 'El Capitan' or 'Il Duce,' casting its majestic shadow in the evening light; and ask whether we have anything like that up there. We certainly have not.

FIFTY YEARS HENCE

THE great mass of human beings, absorbed in the toils, cares and activities of life, are only dimly conscious of the pace at which mankind has begun to travel. We look back a hundred years, and see that great changes have taken place. We look back fifty years, and see that the speed is constantly quickening. This present century has witnessed an enormous revolution in material things, in scientific appliances, in political institutions, in manners and customs. The greatest change of all is the least perceptible by individuals; it is the far greater numbers which in every civilized country participate in the fuller life of man. 'In those days,' said Disraeli, writing at the beginning of the nineteenth century, 'England was for the few and for the very few.' 'The twice two thousand for whom,' wrote Byron, 'the world is made' have given place to many millions for whom existence has become larger, safer, more varied, more full of hope and choice. In the United States scores of millions have lifted themselves above primary necessities and comforts, and aspire to culture—at least for their children. Europe, though stunned and lacerated by Armageddon, presents a similar if less general advance. We all take the modern conveniences and facilities as they are offered to us without being grateful or consciously happier. But we simply could not live, if they were taken away. We assume that progress will be constant. 'This 'ere progress,' Mr. Wells makes one of his characters remark, 'keeps going on. It's wonderful 'ow it keeps going on.' It is also very fortunate, for if it stopped or were reversed, there would be the catastrophe of unimaginable horror. Mankind has gone too far to go back, and is moving too fast to stop. There are too many people maintained not merely in comfort but in existence by processes unknown a century ago, for us to afford even a temporary check, still less a general set-back, without experiencing calamity in its most frightful form.

When we look back beyond a hundred years over the long trails of history, we see immediately why the age we live in differs from all other ages in human annals. Mankind has sometimes travelled forwards and sometimes backwards, or has stood still even for hundreds of years. It remained stationary in India and in China for thousands of years. What is it that has produced this new prodigious speed of man? Science is the cause. Her once feeble vanguards, often trampled down, often perishing in isolation, have now become a vast organized united class-conscious army marching forward upon all the fronts towards objectives none may measure or define. It is a proud, ambitious army which cares nothing for all the laws that men have made; nothing for their most time-honoured customs, or most dearly-cherished beliefs, or deepest instincts. It is this power called Science which has laid hold of us, conscripted us into its regiments and batteries, set us to work upon its highways and in its arsenals; rewarded us for our services, healed us when we were wounded, trained us when we were young, pensioned us when we were worn out. None of the generations of men before the last two or three were ever gripped for good or ill and handled like this.

Man in the earliest stages lived alone and avoided his neighbours with as much anxiety and probably as much reason as he avoided the fierce flesh-eating beasts that shared his forests. With the introduction of domestic animals the advantages of co-operation and the division of labour became manifest. In the neolithic times when cereals were produced and agriculture developed, the bleak hungry period whilst the seeds were germinating beneath the soil involved some form of capitalism, and the recognition of those special rights of landed proprietors the traces of which are still visible in our legislation. Each stage involved new problems legal, sociological and moral. But progress only crawled, and often rested for a thousand years or so.

The two ribbon States in the valley of the Nile and the Euphrates produced civilizations as full of pomp and circumstance and more stable than any the world has ever known. Their autocracies and hierarchies were founded upon the control and distribution of water and corn. The rulers held the people in an efficiency of despotism never equalled till Soviet Russia was born. They had only to cut off or stint the water in the canals to starve or subjugate rebellious provinces. This, apart from their granaries, gave them powers at once as irresistible and as capable of intimate regulation as the control of all food supplies gives to the Bolshevik commissars. Safe from internal trouble, they were vulnerable only to external attack. But in these states man had not learnt to catalyse the forces of nature. The maximum power available was the sum of the muscular efforts of all the inhabitants. Later empires, scarcely less imposing but far less stable, rose and fell. In the methods of production and communication, in the modes of getting food and exchanging goods, there was less change between the time of Sargon and the time of Louis XIV than there has been between the accession of Queen Victoria and the present day. Darius could probably send a message from Susa to Sardis faster than Philip II could transmit an order from Madrid to Brussels. Sir Robert Peel, summoned in 1841 from Rome to form a government in London, took the same time as the Emperor Vespasian when he had to hasten to his province of Britain. The bathrooms of the palaces of Minos were superior to those of Versailles. A priest from Thebes would probably have felt more at home at the Council of Trent two thousand years after Thebes had vanished, than Sir Isaac Newton at a modern undergraduate physical society, or George Stephenson in the Institute of Electrical Engineers. The changes have been so sudden and so gigantic that no period in history can be compared with the last century. The past no longer enables us even dimly to measure the future.

* * * * * * *

The most wonderful of all modern prophecies is found in Tennyson's 'Locksley Hall':

'For I dipt into the future, far as human eye could see,
Saw the Vision of the world, and all the wonder that would be;

Saw the heavens fill with commerce, argosies of magic sails,
Pilots of the purple twilight, dropping down with costly bales;

Heard the heavens fill with shouting, and there rain'd a ghastly dew
From the nation's airy navies grappling in the central blue;

Far along the world-wide whisper of the south-wind rushing warm,
With the standards of the peoples plunging thro' the thunder-storm;

Till the war-drum throbb'd no longer, and the battle-flags were furl'd
In the Parliament of man, the Federation of the world.

. . . .

Slowly comes a hungry people, as a lion creeping nigher,
Glares at one that nods and winks behind a slowly-dying fire.'

These six couplets of prediction, written eighty years ago, have already been fulfilled. The conquest of the air for commerce and war, the League of Nations, the Communist movement—all divined in their true sequence by the great Victorian—all now already in the history-books and stirring the world around us to-day! We may search the Scriptures in vain for such precise and swiftly-vindicated forecasts of the future. Jeremiah and Isaiah dealt in dark and cryptic parables pointing to remote events and capable of many varied interpretations from time to time. A Judge, a Prophet, a Redeemer would arise to save his chosen People; and from age to age the Jews asked, disputing, 'Art thou he that should come or do we look for another?' But 'Locksley Hall' contains an exact foretelling of stupendous events, which many of those who

206

knew the writer lived to see and endure! The dawn of the Victorian era opened the new period of man; and the genius of the poet pierced the veil of the future.

·   ·   ·   ·   ·   ·   ·   ·

There are two processes which we adopt consciously or unconsciously when we try to prophesy. We can seek a period in the past whose conditions resemble as closely as possible those of our day, and presume that the sequel to that period will, save for some minor alterations, be repeated. Secondly, we can survey the general course of development in our immediate past, and endeavour to prolong it into the near future. The first is the method of the historian; the second that of the scientist. Only the second is open to us now, and this only in a partial sphere. By observing all that Science has achieved in modern times, and the knowledge and power now in her possession, we can predict with some assurance the inventions and discoveries which will govern our future. We can but guess, peering through a glass darkly, what reactions these discoveries and their applications will produce upon the habits, the outlook and the spirit of men.

Whereas formerly the utmost power that man could guide and control was a team of horses, or a galleyful of slaves; or possibly, if they could be sufficiently drilled and harnessed, a gang of labourers like the Israelites in Egypt: it is to-day already possible to control accurately from the bridge of a battle cruiser all the power of hundreds of thousands of men: or to set off with one finger a mine capable in an instant of destroying the work of thousands of man-years. These changes are due to the substitution of molecular energy for muscular energy, and its direction and control by an elaborate, beautifully-perfected apparatus. These immense new sources of power, and the fact that they can be wielded by a single individual, have made possible novel methods of mining and metallurgy, new modes of transport and undreamed-of machinery. These in their turn enable the molecular sources of power to be extended and used more efficiently. They facilitate also the improvement of ancient methods. They substitute the hundred-thousand-kilowatt turbo-generators at Niagara for the mill-wheel of our fore-fathers. Each invention acted and reacted on other inventions, and with ever-growing rapidity that vast structure of technical achievement was raised which separates the civilization of to-day from all that the past has known.

There is no doubt that this evolution will continue at an increasing rate. We know enough to be sure that the scientific achievements of the next fifty years will be far greater, more rapid and more surprising, than those we have already experienced. The slide-lathe enabled machines of precision to be made, and the power of steam rushed out upon the world. And through the steam-clouds flashed the dazzling lightning of electricity. But this is only a beginning. High authorities tell us that new sources of power, vastly more important than any we yet know, will surely be discovered. Nuclear energy is incomparably greater than the molecular energy which we use to-day. The coal a man can get in a day can easily do five hundred times as much work as the man himself. Nuclear energy is at least one million times more powerful still. If the hydrogen atoms in a pound of water could be prevailed upon to combine together and form helium, they would suffice to drive a thousand horse-power engine for a whole year. If the electrons—those tiny planets of the atomic systems—were induced to combine with the nuclei in the hydrogen the horse-power liberated would be 120 times greater still. There is no question among scientists that this gigantic source of energy exists. What is lacking is the match to set the bonfire alight, or it may be the detonator to cause the dynamite to explode. The Scientists are looking for this.

The discovery and control of such sources of power would cause changes in human affairs incomparably greater than those produced by the steam-engine four generations ago. Schemes of cosmic magnitude would become feasible. Geography and climate would obey our orders. Fifty thousand tons of water, the amount displaced by the *Berengaria*, would, if exploited as described, suffice to shift Ireland to the middle of the Atlantic. The amount of rain falling yearly upon the Epsom race-course would be enough to thaw all the ice at the Arctic and Antarctic poles. The changing of one element into another by means of temperatures and pressures would be far beyond our present reach, would transform beyond all description our standards of values. Materials thirty times stronger than the best steel would create engines fit to bridle the new forms of power. Communications and transport by land, water and air would take unimaginable forms, if, as is in principle possible, we could make an engine of 600 horsepower weighing 20 lb. and carrying fuel for a thousand hours in a tank the size of a fountain-pen. Wireless telephones and television, following naturally upon their present path of development, would enable their owner to connect up with any room similarly installed, and hear and take part in the conversation as well as if he put his head in through the window. The congregation of men in cities would become superfluous. It would rarely be necessary to call in person on any but the most intimate friends, but if so, excessively rapid means of communication would be at hand. There would be no more object in living in the same city with one's neighbour than there is to-day in living with him in the same house. The cities and the countryside would become indistinguishable. Every home would have its garden and its glade.

Up till recent times the production of food has been the prime struggle of man. That war is won. There is no doubt that the civilized races can produce or procure all the food they require. Indeed some of the problems which vex us today are due to the production of wheat by white men having exceeded their own needs, before yellow men, brown men and black men have learnt to demand and become able to purchase a diet superior to rice. But food is at present obtained almost entirely from the energy of the sunlight. The radiation from the sun produces from the carbonic acid in the air more or less complicated carbon compounds which give us our plants and vegetables. We use the latent chemical energy of these to keep our bodies warm, we convert it into muscular effort. We employ it in the complicated processes of digestion to repair and replace the wasted cells of our bodies. Many people of course prefer food in what the vegetarians call 'the second-hand form', i.e. after it has been digested and converted into meat for us by domestic animals kept for this purpose. In all these processes however ninety-nine parts of the solar energy are wasted for every part used.

Even without the new sources of power great improvements are probable here. Microbes which at present convert the nitrogen of the air into the proteins by which animals live, will be fostered and made to work under controlled conditions, just as yeast is now. New strains of microbes will be developed and made to do a great deal of our chemistry for us. With a greater knowledge of what are called hormones, i.e. the chemical messengers in our blood, it will be possible to control growth. We shall escape the absurdity of growing a whole chicken in order to eat the breast or wing, by growing these parts separately under a suitable medium. Synthetic food will, of course, also be used in the future. Nor need the pleasures of the table be banished. That gloomy Utopia of tabloid meals need never be invaded. The new foods will from the outset be practically indistinguishable from the natural products, and any changes will be so gradual as to escape observation.

If the gigantic new sources of power become available, food will be produced without recourse to sunlight. Vast cellars in which artificial radiation is generated may replace the cornfields or potato-patches of the world. Parks and gardens will cover our pastures and ploughed fields. When the time comes there will be plenty of room for the cities to spread themselves again.

. . . .

But equally startling developments lie already just beyond our finger-tips in the breeding of human beings, and the shaping of human nature. It used to be said, 'Though you have

aught the dog more tricks, you cannot alter the breed of the
dog.' But that is no longer true. A few years ago London was
surprised by a play called *Roosum's Universal Robots*. The
production of such beings may well be possible within fifty
years. They will not be made, but grown under glass. There
seems little doubt that it will be possible to carry out in artificial surroundings the entire cycle which now leads to the
birth of a child. Interference with the mental development of
such beings, expert suggestion and treatment in the earlier
years, would produce beings specialized to thought or toil.
The production of creatures, for instance, which have admirable physical development with their mental endowment
stunted in particular directions, is almost within the range of
human power. A being might be produced capable of tending a
machine but without other ambitions. Our minds recoil from
such fearful eventualities, and the laws of a Christian civilization will prevent them. But might not lop-sided creatures of
this type fit in well with the Communist doctrines of Russia?
Might not the Union of Soviet Republics armed with all the
power of science find it in harmony with all their aims to produce a race adapted to mechanical tasks and with no other
ideas but to obey the Communist State? The present nature
of man is tough and resilient. It casts up its sparks of genius
in the darkest and most unexpected places. But Robots could
be made to fit the grisly theories of Communism. There is
nothing in the philosophy of Communists to prevent their
creation.

I have touched upon this sphere only lightly, but with the
purpose of pointing out that in a future which our children
may live to see, powers will be in the hands of men altogether
different from any by which human nature has been moulded.
Explosive forces, energy, materials, machinery will be available upon a scale which can annihilate whole nations. Despot-
isms and tyrannies will be able to prescribe the lives and even
the wishes of their subjects in a manner never known since
time began. If to these tremendous and awful powers is added
the pitiless sub-human wickedness which we now see embodied

in one of the most powerful reigning governments, who shall say that the world itself will not be wrecked, or indeed that it ought not to be wrecked? There are nightmares of the future from which a fortunate collision with some wandering star, reducing the earth to incandescent gas, might be a merciful deliverance.

. . . .

It is indeed a descent almost to the ridiculous to contemplate the impact of the tremendous and terrifying discoveries which are approaching upon the structure of Parliamentary institutions. How can we imagine the whole mass of the people being capable of deciding by votes at elections upon the right course to adopt amid these cataclysmic changes? Even now the Parliaments of every country have shown themselves quite inadequate to deal with the economic problems which dominate the affairs of every nation and of the world. Before these problems the claptrap of the hustings and the stunts of the newspapers wither and vanish away. Democracy as a guide or motive to progress has long been known to be incompetent. None of the legislative assemblies of the great modern states represents in universal suffrage even a fraction of the strength or wisdom of the community. Great nations are no longer led by their ablest men, or by those who know most about their immediate affairs, or even by those who have a coherent doctrine. Democratic governments drift along the line of least resistance, taking short views, paying their way with sops and doles and smoothing their path with pleasant-sounding platitudes. Never was there less continuity or design in their affairs, and yet towards them are coming swiftly changes which will revolutionize for good or ill not only the whole economic structure of the world but the social habits and moral outlook of every family. Only the Communists have a plan and a gospel. It is a plan fatal to personal freedom and a gospel founded upon Hate.

. . . .

Certain it is that while men are gathering knowledge and power with ever-increasing and measureless speed, their virtues and their wisdom have not shown any notable improvement as the centuries have rolled. The brain of a modern man does nor differ in essentials from that of the human beings who fought and loved here millions of years ago. The nature of man has remained hitherto practically unchanged. Under sufficient stress,—starvation, terror, warlike passion, or even cold intellectual frenzy, the modern man we know so well will do the most terrible deeds, and his modern woman will back him up. At the present moment the civilizations of many different ages co-exist together in the world, and their representatives meet and converse. Englishmen, Frenchmen, or Americans with ideas abreast of the twentieth century do business with Indians or Chinese whose civilizations were crystallised several thousands of years ago. We have the spectacle of the powers and weapons of man far outstripping the march of his intelligence; we have the march of his intelligence proceeding far more rapidly than the development of his nobility. We may well find ourselves in the presence of 'the strength of civilization without its mercy.'

It is therefore above all things important that the moral philosophy and spiritual conceptions of men and nations should hold their own amid these formidable scientific evolutions. It would be much better to call a halt in material progress and discovery rather than to be mastered by our own apparatus and the forces which it directs. There are secrets too mysterious for man in his present state to know; secrets which once penetrated may be fatal to human happiness and glory. But the busy hands of the scientists are already fumbling with the keys of all the chambers hitherto forbidden to mankind. Without an equal growth of Mercy, Pity, Peace and Love, Science herself may destroy all that makes human life majestic and tolerable. There never was a time when the inherent virtue of human beings required more strong and confident expression in daily life; there never was a time when the hope of immortality and the disdain of earthly power and achievement were more necessary for the safety of the children of men.

After all, this material progress, in itself so splendid, does not meet any of the real needs of the human race. I read a book the other day which traced the history of mankind from the birth of the solar system to its extinction. There were fifteen or sixteen races of men which in succession rose and fell over periods measured by tens of millions of years. In the end a race of beings was evolved which had mastered nature. A state was created whose citizens lived as long as they chose, enjoyed pleasures and sympathies incomparably wider than our own, navigated the inter-planetary spaces, could recall the panorama of the past and foresee the future. But what was the good of all that to them? What did they know more than we know about the answers to the simple questions which man has asked since the earliest dawn of reason—'Why are we here? What is the purpose of life? Whither are we going?' No material progress, even though it takes shapes we cannot now conceive, or however it may expand the faculties of man, can bring comfort to his soul. It is this fact, more wonderful than any that Science can reveal, which gives the best hope that all will be well. Projects undreamed of by past generations will absorb our immediate descendants; forces terrific and devastating will be in their hands; comforts, activities, amenities, pleasures will crowd upon them, but their hearts will ache, their lives will be barren, if they have not a vision above material things. And with the hopes and powers will come dangers out of all proportion to the growth of man's intellect, to the strength of his character or to the efficacy of his institutions. Once more the choice is offered between Blessing and Cursing. Never was the answer that will be given harder to foretell.

MOSES

THE LEADER OF A PEOPLE

'And there arose not a prophet since in Israel like unto Moses, whom the Lord knew face to face, in all the signs and wonders which the Lord sent him to do in the land of Egypt to Pharaoh, and to all his servants, and to all his land, and in all that mighty hand, and in all the great terror which Moses shewed in the sight of all Israel.'

THESE closing words of the Book of Deuteronomy are an apt expression of the esteem in which the great leader and liberator of the Hebrew people was held by the generations that succeeded him. He was the greatest of the prophets, who spoke in person to the God of Israel; he was the national hero who led the Chosen People out of the land of bondage, through the perils of the wilderness, and brought them to the very threshold of the Promised Land; he was the supreme law-giver, who received from God that remarkable code upon which the religious, moral, and social life of the nation was so securely founded. Tradition lastly ascribed to him the authorship of the whole Pentateuch, and the mystery that surrounded his death added to his prestige.

Let us first retell the Bible story.

The days were gone when Joseph ruled in Egypt. A century had passed. A new Pharaoh had arisen who knew not Joseph. The nomadic tribe of Bedouins who, in the years of dearth preceding the Great Famine, had sought asylum by the ever-fertile banks of the Nile, had increased and multiplied. From being a band of strangers hospitably received into the wealth of a powerful kingdom, they had become a social, political, and industrial problem. There they were in the 'Land of Goshen,' waxing exceedingly, and stretching out every day long arms and competent fingers into the whole life of Egypt.

215

There must have arisen one of those movements with which the modern world is acquainted. A wave of anti-Semitism swept across the land. Gradually, year by year and inch by inch, the Children of Israel were reduced by the policy of the State and the prejudices of its citizens from guests to servants and from servants almost to slaves.

Building was the mania then, and here were strong, skilful, industrious builders. They were made to build. They built for Pharaoh by forced labour treasure cities or store cities, for the real treasure then was grain. Two such cities are mentioned in Exodus—Pithom and Rameses. The Egyptologist Naville has uncovered the city of Pithom, which was indeed built in the time of Rameses, and lies in that 'Land of Goshen' on the north-east frontier where the Children of Israel were settled. The fluctuations of the Nile could only be provided against by enormous granaries filled in good years. The possession of these granaries constituted the power of government. When a bad season came Pharaoh had the food and dealt it out to man and beast in return for plenary submission. By means of this hard leverage Egyptian civilization rose. Grim times! We may imagine these cities built by the Israelites in the capacity of state serfs as enormous food-depots upon which the administration relied to preserve the obedience of the populace and the life of the nation.

The Israelites were serviceable folk. They paid their keep, and more. Nevertheless, their ceaseless multiplication became a growing embarrassment. There was a limit to the store depots that were required, and the available labourers soon exceeded the opportunities for their useful or economic employment. The Egyptian government fell back on birth control. By various measures which are bluntly described in the book of Exodus, they sought to arrest the increase of male Israelites. Finally they determined to have the male infants killed. There was evidently at this time a strong tension between the principle of Jewish life and the ruthless force of established Egyptian civilization. It was at this moment that Moses was born.

216

The laws were hard, and pity played little part in them. But his mother loved her baby dearly, and resolved to evade the laws. With immense difficulty she concealed him till he was three months old. Then the intense will-to-live in the coming generation led her to a bold stratagem. It has its parallels in various ancient legends about great men. Sargon, the famous Sumerian King, was abandoned by his mother in a basket of reeds, and rescued and brought up by a peasant. There are similar stories about the infancies of Romulus and Cyrus. In this case the only chance for the child was that he should be planted upon the Court. Pharaoh's daughter, the Princess Royal, was accustomed to bathe in the Nile. Her routine was studied. A little ark of bulrushes floated enticingly near the bank from which she took her morning swim. Servants were sent to retrieve it. Inside this floating cradle was a perfect baby. . . 'and the babe wept!' The heart of the Princess melted and she took the little boy in her arms, and vowed he should not perish while her father's writ ran along the Nile. But a little sister of the infant Moses judiciously posted beforehand now approached. 'I know where a nurse can be found.' So the nurse was sought, and the mother came. In the wide economy of an Imperial household a niche was thus found where the baby could be reared.

The years pass. The child is a man, nurtured in the palace or its purlieus, ranking, no doubt, with the many bastards or polygamous offspring of Oriental thrones. But he is no Egyptian, no child of the sheltered progeny of the Nile valley. The wild blood of the desert, the potent blood of Beni Israel not yet mingled with the Hittite infusions, is in his veins. He walks abroad, he sees what is going on. He sees his own race exploited beyond all economic need or social justice. He sees them the drudge of Egypt, consuming their strong life and seed in the upholding of its grandeur, and even grudged the pittance which they earn. He sees them treated as a helot class; they, the free children of the wilderness who came as honoured guests and had worked every hour of their passage! Upon these general impressions he sees an Egyptian beating an Israelite; no doubt a common spectacle, an episode coming to be accepted as part of the daily social routine. But he has no doubts; not for a moment does he hesitate. He knows which side he is on, and the favours of the Court and the privileged attachments which he had with the ruling and possessing race vanish in a moment. The call of blood surges in him. He slays the Egyptian, amid the loud and continuing applause of the insurgents of the ages.

It was difficult to conceal the corpse; it was even more difficult to conceal the tale. No very lengthy interval seems to have elapsed before it was known throughout the palace that this somewhat nondescript and hitherto favoured denizen had bit the hand that fed him. How easily we can recreate their mood! The most cultured and civilized states and administration of the present day would have felt with Pharaoh that this was going altogether too far. Very likely Egyptian public opinion—and there is always public opinion where there is the slightest pretence of civilization—fixed upon this act of violence as a final proof that the weakness of the government towards these overweening strangers and intruders had reached its limit. At any rate Pharaoh—which is as good a name as any for the governing classes in any country at any time under any system—acted. He decreed death upon the murderer. We really cannot blame him; nor can we accuse the subsequent conduct of the slayer. His action also conformed to modern procedure. He fled.

In those days a little island of civilization had grown up under the peculiar physical stimulus of the Nile flood and the Nile mud with all the granary system to grip it together —a tiny island in a vast ocean of bleak and blank starvation. Few and far between were the human beings who were able to support life beyond its shores. There were, indeed, other similar islands in other parts of the world, in Mesopotamia, in Crete, in Mycenæ; but to Moses the choice of Egypt or the wilderness, all that was now open, was, in fact, virtually a choice between swift execution and the barest existence which can be conceived.

Moses fled into the Sinai Peninsula. These are the most awful deserts where human life in any form can be supported. There are others, like the vast expanses of the Sahara or the Polar ice, where human beings cannot exist at all. Still, always a very few people have been able to keep body and soul together amid the rigours of the Sinai Peninsula. There are nowadays a few hundred Bedouin inhabitants. But when an aeroplane makes a forced landing in the Sinai Peninsula the pilot nearly always perishes of thirst and starvation. In these dour recesses the fugitive Moses found a local chief and priest named Jethro. With him he took up his abode; he rendered him good service, married his daughter, Zipporah, and dwelt in extreme privation for many years. Every prophet has to come from civilization, but every prophet has to go into the wilderness. He must have a strong impression of a complex society and all that it has to give, and then he must serve periods of isolation and meditation. This is the process by which psychic dynamite is made.

Moses watched the skinny flocks which browsed upon a starveling herbage, and lived a life almost as materially restricted as theirs. He communed within himself, and then one day when the sun rode fierce in the heavens, and the dust-devils and mirages danced and flickered amid the scrub, he saw The Burning Bush. It burned, yet it was not consumed. It was a prodigy. The more it burned the less it was consumed; it seemed to renew itself from its own self-consumption. Perhaps it was not a bush at all, but his own heart that was aflame with a fire never to be quenched while the earth supports human beings.

God spoke to Moses from the Burning Bush. He said to him in effect: 'You cannot leave your fellow-countrymen in bondage. Death or freedom! Better the wilderness than slavery. You must go back and bring them out. Let them live among this thorn-scrub, or die if they cannot live. But no more let them be chained in the house of bondage.' God went a good deal further. He said from the Burning Bush, now surely inside the frame of Moses, 'I will endow you with superhuman power. There is nothing that man cannot do, if he wills it with enough resolution. Man is the epitome of the universe. All moves and exists as a result of his invincible will, which is My Will.'

Moses did not understand the bulk of this, and asked a great many questions and demanded all kinds of guarantees. God gave all the guarantees. Indeed, Moses persisted so much in his doubts and bargainings that we are told Jehovah (for that was the great new name of this God that spoke from the Burning Bush) became angry. However, in the end He made His contract with the man, and Moses got a fairly reasonable assurance in his own mind that he could work miracles. If he laid his staff upon the ground he was sure it would turn into a snake, and when he picked it up it would become a staff again. Moreover, he stipulated that he must have a spokesman. He was not himself eloquent; he could give the driving force, but he must have a competent orator, some man used to putting cases and dealing in high affairs, as his assistant. Otherwise how could he hold parley with Pharaoh and all the Ministers of the only known civilization his world could show? God met all these requests. A competent politician and trained speaker in the shape of one Aaron would be provided. Moses now remembered his kinsman Aaron, with whom he had been good friends before he had to flee from Egypt. Thereupon action! Jethro is told that his son-in-law intends to start on a great adventure. He gives his full consent. The donkey is saddled; Zipporah, the two children, and the family property are placed upon its back, and through the dust-clouds and blazing sunlight the smallest, most potent and most glorious of all the rescue forces of history starts upon its expedition.

Undue importance can easily be given to the records of the protracted duel between Moses and Pharaoh. The plagues of Egypt are famous, and most of them were the kind of plagues from which Egypt has frequently suffered—pollution of the Nile and the consequent destruction of its fish; multiplication of frogs and their invasion of the land; flies beyond all bearing; lice abounding (but some authorities say they were gnats); the death of cattle; darkness over the face of the earth such as is produced by prolonged sandstorms; the prodigy of hail in the Nile Valley; finally the death of the first-born by pestilence. The local magicians, entering fully into the spirit of the contest, kept going until the third round, measure for measure and step by step. But when the dust turned into lice they admitted with professional awe that this was 'the finger of God.'

Great interest attaches to the behaviour of Pharaoh. Across the centuries we feel the modernity of his actions. At first he was curious, and open to conviction. Quite mild plagues brought him to reason. He was ready to let the Israelites depart into the wilderness and sacrifice to their potent God. This serious concession arrested all his building plans and caused considerable derangement in the economic life of the country. It was very like a general strike. It was no doubt represented to him that the loss to the national income from this cessation of labour would be disastrous to the State. So he hardened his heart and took back in the evening what he had promised in the dawn, and in the morning what he had promised the night before. The plagues continued; the magicians dropped out. It was a dead-lift struggle between Jehovah and Pharaoh. But Jehovah did not wish to win too easily. The liberation of the Children of Israel was only a part of His high Purpose. Their liberation had to be effected in such a manner as to convince them that they were the Chosen People, with the supreme forces of the universe enlisted in their special interest, should they show themselves faithful. So Jehovah laid on his plagues on the one hand, and hardened the heart of Pharaoh on the other.

It has often happened this way in later times. How often governments and peoples plunge into struggles most reluctantly, terrified of their small beginnings, but once swimming in the torrent go on desperately with immense unsuspected reserves and force in the hopes of emerging triumphantly on the other shore. So Pharaoh and the Egyptian Government, once they had taken the plunge, got themselves into the mood that they would 'see it through'; and this perhaps 'hardened their hearts.' However, the plagues continued and one misfortune after another fell upon the agonized State, until finally a collapse occurred. Pharaoh decided to 'let the people go.'

Amid the general confusion which followed this surrender the Chosen People spoiled the Egyptians. They begged, borrowed, and stole all they could lay their hands upon, and, gathering themselves together laden with treasure, equipment, and provender, launched out from the island of civilization into the awful desert. Their best chance was to cross the isthmus which joins Africa with Asia and make for the regions we now call Palestine. But two reasons which could not be neglected weighed against this. First, the Philistines barred the road. This formidable people had already carried their military organization to a high pitch. The Israelites after 150 years of domestic servitude in Egypt were in no condition to encounter the fierce warriors of the wilds. Secondly, and concurrently, Jehovah had told Moses he must lead the liberated tribe to the neighbourhood of Mount Sinai, where other revelations of the Divine Will would be made known to them.

They marched accordingly to the northern inlet of the Red Sea. There is much dispute as to their numbers. The Bible story says they were 600,000 men, with women and children in addition. We may without impiety doubt the statistics. A clerical error may so easily have arisen. Even to-day a nought or two is sometimes misplaced. But more than two thousand years had yet to pass before the 'nought' and all its conveniences was to be at the disposal of mankind. The earlier forms of notation were more liable to error than our own. Unless the climate was very different from the present it is difficult to see how even 6,000 persons could have lived in the Sinai Peninsula without supernatural aid on a considerable and well-organized scale.

But now once again Pharaoh has changed his mind. No

doubt the resentment aroused among the Egyptians by the wholesale pillage to which they had been subjected in their hour of panic, combined with the regrets of the government at the loss of so many capable labourers and subjects, constituted a kind of situation to which very few Parliaments of the present age would be insensible. The Egyptian army was mobilized; all the chariots set out in pursuit. The fugitive tribesmen, having reached the shore of a body of water called the 'Yam Suph,' at the extreme northern end of the Gulf of Akaba, were trapped between the sea and Pharaoh's overwhelming host. Their situation was forlorn, their only resource was flight, and flight was barred by salt water.

But Jehovah did not fail. A violent eruption occurred, of which the volcanic mountains of these regions still bear the traces. The waters of the sea divided, and the Children of Israel passed dryshod across the inlet. Pharaoh and his host, hotly following them, were swallowed up by the returning waters. Thereafter, guided by a pillar of smoke by day and of fire by night, the Israelites reached the neighbourhood of Mount Sinai. Here Moses received from Jehovah the tables of those fundamental laws which were henceforward to be followed, with occasional lapses, by the highest forms of human society.

We must, at this point, examine briefly the whole question of the miracles. Everyone knows that the pollution of rivers, the flies, frogs, lice, sandstorms, and pestilence among men and cattle, are the well-known afflictions of the East. The most sceptical person can readily believe that they occurred with exceptional frequency at this juncture. The strong north wind which is said to have blown back the waters of the Red Sea may well have been assisted by a seismic and volcanic disturbance. Geologists tell us that the same fault in the earth's structure which cleft the depression of the Dead Sea in Palestine runs unbroken to the Rift Valley in what we now call the Kenya province of East Africa. The Sinai Peninsula was once volcanic, and the Bible descriptions of Mount Sinai both by day and by night are directly explicable by an eruption, which would have provided at once the pillar of cloud by daylight and of fire in the darkness. Flocks of quails frequently arrive exhausted in Egypt in their migrations, and some might well have alighted in the nick of time near the encampments of the Israelites. Renan has described the exudation by certain shrubs in the Sinai Peninsula of a white gummy substance which appears from time to time, and is undoubtedly capable of supplying a form of nourishment.

All these purely rationalistic and scientific explanations only prove the truth of the Bible story. It is silly to waste time arguing whether Jehovah broke His own natural laws to save His Chosen People or whether He merely made them work in a favourable manner. At any rate there is no doubt about one miracle. This wandering tribe, in many respects indistinguishable from numberless nomadic communities, grasped and proclaimed an idea which all the genius of Greece and all the power of Rome were incapable. There was to be only one God, a universal God, a God of nations, a just God, a God who would punish in another world a wicked man dying rich and prosperous; a God from whose service the good of the humble and of the weak and the poor was inseparable.

Books are written in many languages upon the question of how much of this was due to Moses. Devastating, inexorable modern study and criticism have proved that the Pentateuch constitutes a body of narrative and doctrine which came into being over at least the compass of several centuries. We reject, however, with scorn all those learned and laboured myths that Moses was but a legendary figure upon whom the priesthood and the people hung their essential social, moral, and religious ordinances. We believe that the most scientific view, the most up-to-date and rationalistic conception, will find its fullest satisfaction in taking the Bible story literally, and in identifying one of the greatest of human beings with the most decisive leap forward ever discernible in the human story. We remain unmoved by the tomes of Professor Gradgrind and Dr. Dryasdust. We may be sure that all these things happened just as they are set out according to Holy Writ.

We may believe that they happened to people not so very different from ourselves, and that the impressions those people received were faithfully recorded and have been transmitted across the centuries with far more accuracy than many of the telegraphed accounts we read of the goings-on of today. In the words of a forgotten work of Mr. Gladstone, we rest with assurance upon 'The impregnable rock of Holy Scripture.'

Unluckily the stresses of the Exodus, the long forty years, or whatever the period may have been which was needed in the wilderness to sharpen the Children of Israel from a domesticated race into an armed force of conquering warriors, led them to make undue claims upon Jehovah. They forgot the older tradition which the Pentateuch enshrines. They forgot the enlightened monotheism which under the heretic Pharaoh Akhnaton had left its impression upon Egypt. They appropriated Jehovah to themselves. In Renan's words, they made him revoltingly partial to the Chosen People. All Divine laws and ordinary equity were suspended or disallowed when they applied to a foreigner, especially to a foreigner whose land and property they required.

But these are the natural errors of the human heart under exceptional stresses. Many centuries were to pass before the God that spake in the Burning Bush was to manifest Himself in a new revelation, which nevertheless was the oldest of all the inspirations of the Hebrew people—as the God not only of Israel, but of all mankind who wished to serve Him; a God not only of justice, but of mercy; a God not only of self-preservation and survival, but of pity, self-sacrifice, and ineffable love.

Let the men of science and of learning expand their knowledge and probe with their researches every detail of the records which have been preserved to us from these dim ages. All they will do is to fortify the grand simplicity and essential accuracy of the recorded truths which have lighted so far the pilgrimage of man.

HOBBIES

Many remedies are suggested for the avoidance of worry and mental overstrain by persons who, over prolonged periods, have to bear exceptional responsibilities and discharge duties upon a very large scale. Some advise exercise, and others, repose. Some counsel travel, and others, retreat. Some praise solitude, and others, gaiety. No doubt all these may play their part according to the individual temperament. But the element which is constant and common in all of them is Change.

Change is the master key. A man can wear out a particular part of his mind by continually using it and tiring it, just in the same way as he can wear out the elbows of his coat. There is, however, this difference between the living cells of the brain and inanimate articles: one cannot mend the frayed elbows of a coat by rubbing the sleeves or shoulders; but the tired parts of the mind can be rested and strengthened not merely by rest, but by using other parts. It is not enough merely to switch off the lights which play upon the main and ordinary field of interest; a new field of interest must be illuminated. It is no use saying to the tired 'mental muscles' —if one may coin such an expression—'I will give you a good rest,' 'I will go for a long walk,' or 'I will lie down and think of nothing.' The mind keeps busy just the same. If it has been weighing and measuring, it goes on weighing and measuring. If it has been worrying, it goes on worrying. It is only when new cells are called into activity, when new stars become the lords of the ascendant, that relief, repose, refreshment are afforded.

A gifted American psychologist has said, 'Worry is a spasm of the emotion; the mind catches hold of something and will not let it go.' It is useless to argue with the mind in this condition. The stronger the will, the more futile the task. One can only gently insinuate something else into its convulsive grasp. And if this something else is rightly chosen, if it is really attended by the illumination of another field of interest, gradually, and often quite swiftly, the old undue grip relaxes and the process of recuperation and repair begins.

The cultivation of a hobby and new forms of interest is therefore a policy of first importance to a public man. But this is not a business that can be undertaken in a day or swiftly improvised by a mere command of the will. The growth of alternative mental interests is a long process. The seeds must be carefully chosen; they must fall on good ground; they must be sedulously tended, if the vivifying fruits are to be at hand when needed.

To be really happy and really safe, one ought to have at least two or three hobbies, and they must all be real. It is no use starting late in life to say: 'I will take an interest in this or that.' Such an attempt only aggravates the strain of mental effort. A man may acquire great knowledge of topics un-connected with his daily work, and yet hardly get any benefit or relief. It is no use doing what you like; you have got to like what you do. Broadly speaking, human beings may be divided into three classes: those who are toiled to death, those who are worried to death, and those who are bored to death. It is no use offering the manual labourer, tired out with a hard week's sweat and effort, the chance of playing a game of football or baseball on Saturday afternoon. It is no use inviting the politician or the professional or business man, who has been working or worrying about serious things for six days, to work or worry about trifling things at the week-end.

As for the unfortunate people who can command every-thing they want, who can gratify every caprice and lay their hands on almost every object of desire—for them a new pleasure, a new excitement is only an additional satiation. In vain they rush frantically round from place to place, trying to escape from avenging boredom by mere clatter and motion. For them discipline in one form or another is the most hopeful path.

It may also be said that rational, industrious, useful human beings are divided into two classes: first, those whose work is work and whose pleasure is pleasure; and secondly, those whose work and pleasure are one. Of these the former are the majority. They have their compensations. The long hours in the office or the factory bring with them as their reward, not only the means of sustenance, but a keen appetite for pleasure even in its simplest and most modest forms. But Fortune's favoured children belong to the second class. Their life is a natural harmony. For them the working hours are never long enough. Each day is a holiday, and ordinary holidays when they come are grudged as enforced interruptions in an absorbing vocation. Yet to both classes the need of an alternative outlook, of a change of atmosphere, of a diversion of effort, is essential. Indeed, it may well be that those whose work is their pleasure are those who most need the means of banishing it at intervals from their mind.

The most common form of diversion is reading. In that vast and varied field millions find their mental comfort. Nothing makes a man more reverent than a library. 'A few books,' which was Lord Morley's definition of anything under five thousand, may give a sense of comfort and even of complacency. But a day in a library, even of modest dimensions, quickly dispels these illusory sensations. As you browse about, taking down book after book from the shelves and contemplating the vast, infinitely-varied store of knowledge and wisdom which the human race has accumulated and preserved, pride, even in its most innocent forms, is chased from the heart by feelings of awe not untinged with sadness. As one surveys the mighty array of sages, saints, historians, scientists, poets and philosophers whose treasures one will never be able to admire—still less enjoy—the brief tenure of our existence here dominates mind and spirit.

Think of all the wonderful tales that have been told, and

well told, which you will never know. Think of all the searching inquiries into matters of great consequence which you will never pursue. Think of all the delighting or disturbing ideas that you will never share. Think of the mighty labours which have been accomplished for your service, but of which you will never reap the harvest. But from this melancholy there also comes a calm. The bitter sweets of a pious despair melt into an agreeable sense of compulsory resignation from which we turn with renewed zest to the lighter vanities of life.

'What shall I do with all my books?' was the question; and the answer, 'Read them,' sobered the questioner. But if you cannot read them, at any rate handle them and, as it were, fondle them. Peer into them. Let them fall open where they will. Read on from the first sentence that arrests the eye. Then turn to another. Make a voyage of discovery, taking soundings of uncharted seas. Set them back on their shelves with your own hands. Arrange them on your own plan, so that if you do not know what is in them, you at least know where they are. If they cannot be your friends, let them at any rate be your acquaintances. If they cannot enter the circle of your life, do not deny them at least a nod of recognition.

It is a mistake to read too many good books when quite young. A man once told me that he had read all the books that mattered. Cross-questioned, he appeared to have read a great many, but they seemed to have made only a slight impression. How many had he understood? How many had entered into his mental composition? How many had been hammered on the anvils of his mind and afterwards ranged in an armoury of bright weapons ready to hand?

It is a great pity to read a book too soon in life. The first impression is the one that counts; and if it is a slight one, it may be all that can be hoped for. A later and second perusal may recoil from a surface already hardened by premature contact. Young people should be careful in their reading, as old people in eating their food. They should not eat too much. They should chew it well.

Since change is an essential element in diversion of all kinds, it is naturally more restful and refreshing to read in a different language from that in which one's ordinary daily work is done. To have a second language at your disposal, even if you only know it enough to read it with pleasure, is a sensible advantage. Our educationalists are too often anxious to teach children so many different languages that they never get far enough in any one to derive any use or enjoyment from their study. The boy learns enough Latin to detest it; enough Greek to pass an examination; enough French to get from Calais to Paris; enough German to exhibit a diploma; enough Spanish or Italian to tell which is which; but not enough of any to secure the enormous boon of access to a second literature.

Choose well, choose wisely, and choose one. Concentrate upon that one. Do not be content until you find yourself reading in it with real enjoyment. The process of reading for pleasure in another language rests the mental muscles; it enlivens the mind by a different sequence and emphasis of ideas. The mere form of speech excites the activity of separate brain-cells, relieving in the most effective manner the fatigue of those in hackneyed use. One may imagine that a man who blew the trumpet for his living would be glad to play the violin for his amusement. So it is with reading in another language than your own.

But reading and book-love in all their forms suffer from one serious defect: they are too nearly akin to the ordinary daily round of the brain-worker to give that element of change and contrast essential to real relief. To restore psychic equilibrium we should call into use those parts of the mind which direct both eye and hand. Many men have found great advantage in practising a handicraft for pleasure. Joinery, chemistry, book-binding, even brick-laying—if one were interested in them and skilful at them—would give a real relief to the over-tired brain. But, best of all and easiest to procure are sketching and painting in all their forms. I consider myself very lucky that late in life I have been able to develop this new taste and pastime. Painting came to my rescue in a most trying time, and I shall venture in a concluding chapter to express the gratitude I feel.

Painting is a companion with whom one may hope to walk a great part of life's journey,

> 'Age cannot wither her nor custom stale
> Her infinite variety.'

One by one the more vigorous sports and exacting games fall away. Exceptional exertions are purchased only by a more pronounced and more prolonged fatigue. Muscles may relax, and feet and hands slow down; the nerve of youth and manhood may become less trusty. But painting is a friend who makes no undue demands, excites to no exhausting pursuits, keeps faithful pace even with feeble steps, and holds her canvas as a screen between us and the envious eyes of Time or the surly advance of Decrepitude.

Happy are the painters, for they shall not be lonely. Light and colour, peace and hope, will keep them company to the end, or almost to the end, of the day.

PAINTING AS A PASTIME

To have reached the age of forty without ever handling a brush or fiddling with a pencil, to have regarded with mature eye the painting of pictures of any kind as a mystery, to have stood agape before the chalk of the pavement artist, and then suddenly to find oneself plunged in the middle of a new and intense form of interest and action with paints and palettes and canvases, and not to be discouraged by results, is an astonishing and enriching experience. I hope it may be shared by others. I should be glad if these lines induced others to try the experiment which I have tried, and if some at least were to find themselves dowered with an absorbing new amusement delightful to themselves, and at any rate not violently harmful to man or beast.

I hope this is modest enough: because there is no subject on which I feel more humble or yet at the same time more natural. I do not presume to explain how to paint, but only how to get enjoyment. Do not turn the superior eye of critical passivity upon these efforts. Buy a paint-box and have a try. If you need something to occupy your leisure, to divert your mind from the daily round, to illuminate your holidays, do not be too ready to believe that you cannot find what you want here. Even at the advanced age of forty! It would be a sad pity to shuffle or scramble along through one's playtime with golf and bridge, pottering, loitering, shifting from one heel to the other, wondering what on earth to do—as perhaps is the fate of some unhappy beings—when all the while, if you only knew, there is close at hand a wonderful new world of thought and craft, a sunlit garden gleaming with light and colour of which you have the key in your waistcoat-pocket. Inexpensive independence, a mobile and perennial

232

pleasure apparatus, new mental food and exercise, the old harmonies and symmetries in an entirely different language, an added interest to every common scene, an occupation for every idle hour, an unceasing voyage of entrancing discovery—these are high prizes. Make quite sure they are not yours. After all, if you try, and fail, there is not much harm done. The nursery will grab what the studio has rejected. And then you can always go out and kill some animal, humiliate some rival on the links, or despoil some friend across the green table. You will not be worse off in any way. In fact you will be better off. You will know 'beyond a peradventure,' to quote a phrase disagreeably reminiscent, that that is really what you were meant to do in your hours of relaxation.

But if, on the contrary, you are inclined—late in life though it be—to reconnoitre a foreign sphere of limitless extent, then be persuaded that the first quality that is needed is Audacity. There really is no time for the deliberate approach. Two years of drawing-lessons, three years of copying woodcuts, five years of plaster casts—these are for the young. They have enough to bear. And this thorough grounding is for those who, hearing the call in the morning of their days, are able to make painting their paramount lifelong vocation. The truth and beauty of line and form which by the slightest touch or twist of the brush a real artist imparts to every feature of his design must be founded on long, hard, persevering apprenticeship and a practice so habitual that it has become instinctive. We must not be too ambitious. We cannot aspire to masterpieces. We may content ourselves with a joy ride in a paint-box. And for this Audacity is the only ticket.

I shall now relate my personal experience. When I left the Admiralty at the end of May, 1915, I still remained a member of the Cabinet and of the War Council. In this position I knew everything and could do nothing. The change from the intense executive activities of each day's work at

the Admiralty to the narrowly-measured duties of a coun-
sellor left me gasping. Like a sea-beast fished up from the
depths, or a diver too suddenly hoisted, my veins threatened
to burst from the fall in pressure. I had great anxiety and
no means of relieving it; I had vehement convictions and
small power to give effect to them. I had to watch the unhappy
casting-away of great opportunities, and the feeble execution
of plans which I had launched and in which I heartily believed. I had long hours of utterly unwonted leisure in which
to contemplate the frightful unfolding of the War. At a
moment when every fibre of my being was inflamed to action,
I was forced to remain a spectator of the tragedy, placed
cruelly in a front seat. And then it was that the Muse of
Painting came to my rescue—out of charity and out of
chivalry, because after all she had nothing to do with me—
and said, 'Are these toys any good to you? They amuse some
people.'

Some experiments one Sunday in the country with the children's paint-box led me to procure the next morning a complete outfit for painting in oils.

Having bought the colours, an easel, and a canvas, the next
step was *to begin*. But what a step to take! The palette gleamed
with beads of colour; fair and white rose the canvas; the
empty brush hung poised, heavy with destiny, irresolute in
the air. My hand seemed arrested by a silent veto. But after
all the sky on this occasion was unquestionably blue, and a
pale blue at that. There could be no doubt that blue paint
mixed with white should be put on the top part of the canvas.
One really does not need to have had an artist's training to
see that. It is a starting-point open to all. So very gingerly I
mixed a little blue paint on the palette with a very small brush,
and then with infinite precaution made a mark about as big
as a bean upon the affronted snow-white shield. It was a challenge, a deliberate challenge; but so subdued, so halting, indeed so cataleptic, that it deserved no response. At that moment the loud approaching sound of a motor-car was heard in
the drive. From this chariot there stepped swiftly and lightly

none other than the gifted wife of Sir John Lavery. 'Painting! But what are you hesitating about? Let me have a brush— the big one.' Splash into the turpentine, wallop into the blue and the white, frantic flourish on the palette—clean no longer —and then several large, fierce strokes and slashes of blue on the absolutely cowering canvas. Anyone could see that it could not hit back. No evil fate avenged the jaunty violence. The canvas grinned in helplessness before me. The spell was broken. The sickly inhibitions rolled away. I seized the largest brush and fell upon my victim with Berserk fury. I have never felt any awe of a canvas since.

Everyone knows the feelings with which one stands shivering on a spring-board, the shock when a friendly foe steals up behind and hurls you into the flood, and the ardent glow which thrills you as you emerge breathless from the plunge.

This beginning with Audacity, or being thrown into the middle of it, is already a very great part of the art of painting. But there is more in it than that.

> La peinture à l'huile
> Est bien difficile,
> Mais c'est beaucoup plus beau
> Que la peinture à l'eau.

I write no word in disparagement of water-colours. But there really is nothing like oils. You have a medium at your disposal which offers real power, if you only can find out how to use it. Moreover, it is easier to get a certain distance along the road by its means than by water-colour. First of all, you can correct mistakes much more easily. One sweep of the palette-knife 'lifts' the blood and tears of a morning from the canvas and enables a fresh start to be made; indeed the canvas is all the better for past impressions. Secondly, you can approach your problem from any direction. You need not build downwards awkwardly from white paper to your darkest dark. You may strike where you please, beginning if you will with a moderate central arrangement of middle tones, and then hurling in the extremes when the psychological moment comes.

Lastly, the pigment itself is such nice stuff to handle (if it does not retaliate). You can build it on layer after layer if you like. You can keep on experimenting. You can change your plan to meet the exigencies of time or weather. And always remember you can scrape it all away.

Just to paint is great fun. The colours are lovely to look at and delicious to squeeze out. Matching them, however crudely, with what you see is fascinating and absolutely absorbing. Try it if you have not done so—before you die. As one slowly begins to escape from the difficulties of choosing the right colours and laying them on in the right places and in the right way, wider considerations come into view. One begins to see, for instance, that painting a picture is like fighting a battle; and trying to paint a picture is, I suppose, like trying to fight a battle. It is, if anything, more exciting than fighting it successfully. But the principle is the same. It is the same kind of problem, as unfolding a long, sustained, interlocked argument. It is a proposition which, whether of few or numberless parts, is commanded by a single unity of conception. And we think—though I cannot tell—that painting a great picture must require an intellect on the grand scale. There must be that all-embracing view which presents the beginning and the end, the whole and each part, as one instantaneous impression retentively and untiringly held in the mind. When we look at the larger Turners—canvases yards wide and tall—and observe that they are all done in one piece and represent one single second of time, and that every innumerable detail, however small, however distant, however subordinate, is set forth naturally and in its true proportion and relation, without effort, without failure, we must feel in presence of an intellectual manifestation the equal in quality and intensity of the finest achievements of warlike action, of forensic argument, or of scientific or philosophical adjudication.

In all battles two things are usually required of the Commander-in-Chief: to make a good plan for his army and, secondly, to keep a strong reserve. Both these are also obligatory upon the painter. To make a plan, thorough reconnaissance of the country where the battle is to be fought is needed. Its fields, its mountains, its rivers, its bridges, its trees, its flowers, its atmosphere—all require and repay attentive observation from a special point of view. One is quite astonished to find how many things there are in the landscape, and in every object in it, one never noticed before. And this is a tremendous new pleasure and interest which invests every walk or drive with an added object. So many colours on the hillside, each different in shadow and in sunlight; such brilliant reflections in the pool, each a key lower than what they repeat; such lovely lights gilding or silvering surface or outline, all tinted exquisitely with pale colour, rose, orange, green, or violet. I found myself instinctively as I walked noting the tint and character of a leaf, the dreamy purple shades of mountains, the exquisite lacery of winter branches, the dim pale silhouettes of far horizons. And I had lived for over forty years without ever noticing any of them except in a general way, as one might look at a crowd and say, 'What a lot of people!'

I think this heightened sense of observation of Nature is one of the chief delights that have come to me through trying to paint. No doubt many people who are lovers of art have acquired it in a high degree without actually practising. But I expect that nothing will make one observe more quickly or more thoroughly than having to face the difficulty of representing the thing observed. And mind you, if you do observe accurately and with refinement, and if you do record what you have seen with tolerable correspondence, the result follows on the canvas with startling obedience. Even if only four or five main features are seized and truly recorded, these by themselves will carry a lot of ill-success or half-success. Answer five big questions out of all the hundreds in the examination paper correctly and well, and though you may not win a prize, at any rate you will not be absolutely ploughed.

But in order to make his plan, the General must not only reconnoitre the battle-ground, he must also study the achievements of the great Captains of the past. He must bring the observations he has collected in the field into comparison with the treatment of similar incidents by famous chiefs. Then the galleries of Europe take on a new—and to me at least a severely practical—interest. 'This, then, is how —— painted a cataract. Exactly, and there is that same light I noticed last week in the waterfall at ——.' And so on. You see the difficulty that baffled you yesterday; and you see how easily it has been overcome by a great or even by a skilful painter. Not only is your observation of Nature sensibly improved and developed, but you look at the masterpieces of art with an analysing and a comprehending eye.

The whole world is open with all its treasures. The simplest objects have their beauty. Every garden presents innumerable fascinating problems. Every land, every parish, has its own tale to tell. And there are many lands differing from each other in countless ways, and each presenting delicious variants of colour, light, form, and definition. Obviously, then, armed with a paint-box, one cannot be bored, one cannot be left at a loose end, one cannot 'have several days on one's hands.' Good gracious! what there is to admire and how little time there is to see it in! For the first time one begins to envy Methuselah. No doubt he made a very indifferent use of his opportunities.

But it is in the use and withholding of their reserves that the great commanders have generally excelled. After all, when once the last reserve has been thrown in, the commander's part is played. If that does not win the battle, he has nothing else to give. The event must be left to luck and to the fighting troops. But these last, in the absence of high direction, are apt to get into sad confusion, all mixed together in a nasty mess, without order or plan—and consequently without effect. Mere masses count no more. The largest brush, the brightest colours cannot even make an impression. The pictorial battlefield becomes a sea of mud mercifully veiled by the fog of war. It is evident there has been a serious defeat. Even though the General plunges in himself and emerges bespattered, as he sometimes does, he will not retrieve the day.

In painting, the reserves consist in Proportion or Relation. And it is here that the art of the painter marches along the road which is traversed by all the greatest harmonies in thought. At one side of the palette there is white, at the other black; and neither is ever used 'neat'. Between these two rigid limits all the action must lie, all the power required must be generated. Black and white themselves placed in juxtaposition make no great impression; and yet they are the most that you can do in pure contrast. It is wonderful—after one has tried and failed often—to see how easily and surely the true artist is able to produce every effect of light and shade, of sunshine and shadow, of distance or nearness, simply by expressing justly the relations between the different planes and surfaces with which he is dealing. We think that this is founded upon a sense of proportion, trained no doubt by practice, but which in its essence is a frigid manifestation of mental power and size. We think that the same mind's eye that can justly survey and appraise and prescribe beforehand the values of a truly great picture in one all-embracing regard, in one flash of simultaneous and homogeneous comprehension, would also with a certain acquaintance with the special technique be able to pronounce with sureness upon any other high activity of the human intellect. This was certainly true of the great Italians.

I have written in this way to show how varied are the delights which may be gained by those who enter hopefully and thoughtfully upon the pathway of painting; how enriched they will be in their daily vision, how fortified in their independence, how happy in their leisure. Whether you feel that your soul is pleased by the conception or contemplation of harmonies, or that your mind is stimulated by the aspect of magnificent problems, or whether you are content to find fun in trying to observe and depict the jolly things you see, the vistas of possibility are limited only by the shortness of life. Every day you may make progress. Every step may be fruitful. Yet there will stretch out before you an ever-lengthening, ever-ascending, ever-improving path. You know you will never

239

get to the end of the journey. But this, so far from discourag-
ing, only adds to the joy and glory of the climb.

Try it, then, before it is too late and before you mock at me.
Try it while there is time to overcome the preliminary difficulties. Learn enough of the language in your prime to open this
new literature to your age. Plant a garden in which you can
sit when digging days are done. It may be only a small garden,
but you will see it grow. Year by year it will bloom and ripen.
Year by year it will be better cultivated. The weeds will be
cast out. The fruit-trees will be pruned and trained. The
flowers will bloom in more beautiful combinations. There will
be sunshine there even in the winter-time, and cool shade, and
the play of shadow on the pathway in the shining days of
June.

I must say I like bright colours. I agree with Ruskin in his
denunciation of that school of painting who 'eat slate-pencil
and chalk, and assure everybody that they are nicer and purer
than strawberries and plums.' I cannot pretend to feel impar-
tial about the colours. I rejoice with the brilliant ones, and am
genuinely sorry for the poor browns. When I get to heaven I
mean to spend a considerable portion of my first million years
in painting, and so get to the bottom of the subject. But then
I shall require a still gayer palette than I get here below. I
expect orange and vermilion will be the darkest, dullest colours upon it, and beyond them there will be a whole range of
wonderful new colours which will delight the celestial eye.

Chance led me one autumn to a secluded nook on the Côte
d'Azur, between Marseilles and Toulon, and there I fell in
with one or two painters who revelled in the methods of the
modern French school. These were disciples of Cézanne. They
view Nature as a mass of shimmering light in which forms and
surfaces are comparatively unimportant, indeed, hardly visible, but which gleams and glows with beautiful harmonies
and contrasts of colour. Certainly it was of great interest to
me to come suddenly in contact with this entirely different
way of looking at things. I had hitherto painted the sea flat,
with long, smooth strokes of mixed pigment in which the tints

240

varied only by gradations. Now I must try to represent it by in-numerable small separate lozenge-shaped points and patches of colour—often pure colour—so that it looked more like a tessellated pavement than a marine picture. It sounds curious. All the same, do not be in a hurry to reject the method. Go back a few yards and survey the result. Each of these little points of colour is now playing his part in the general effect. Individually invisible, he sets up a strong radiation, of which the eye is conscious without detecting the cause. Look also at the blue of the Mediterranean. How can you depict and record it? Certainly not by any single colour that was ever manufac-tured. The only way in which that luminous intensity of blue can be simulated is by this multitude of tiny points of varied colour all in true relation to the rest of the scheme. Difficult? Fascinating!

Nature presents itself to the eye through the agency of these individual points of light, each of which sets up the vibrations peculiar to its colour. The brilliancy of a picture must there-fore depend partly upon the frequency with which these points are found on any given area of the canvas, and partly on their just relation to one another. Ruskin says in his *Elements of Drawing*, from which I have already quoted, 'You will not, in Turner's largest oil pictures, perhaps six or seven feet long by four or five high, find one spot of colour as large as a grain of wheat ungradated.' But the gradations of Turner differ from those of the modern French school by being gently and almost imperceptibly evolved one from another instead of being bod-ily and even roughly separated; and the brush of Turner fol-lowed the form of the objects he depicted, while our French friends often seem to take a pride in directly opposing it. For instance, they would prefer to paint a sea with up and down strokes rather than with horizontal; or a tree-trunk from right to left rather than up and down. This, I expect, is due to falling in love with one's theories, and making sacrifices of truth to them in order to demonstrate fidelity and admiration.

But surely we owe a debt to those who have so wonderfully vivified, brightened, and illuminated modern landscape painting. Have not Manet and Monet, Cézanne and Matisse, rendered to painting something of the same service which Keats and Shelley gave to poetry after the solemn and ceremonious literary perfections of the eighteenth century? They have brought back to the pictorial art a new draught of *joie de vivre*; and the beauty of their work is instinct with gaiety, and floats in sparkling air.

I do not expect these masters would particularly appreciate my defence, but I must avow an increasing attraction to their work. Lucid and exact expression is one of the characteristics of the French mind. The French language has been made the instrument of the admirable gift. Frenchmen talk and write just as well about painting as they have done about love, about war, about diplomacy, or cooking. Their terminology is precise and complete. They are therefore admirably equipped to be teachers in the theory of any of these arts. Their critical faculty is so powerfully developed that it is perhaps some restraint upon achievement. But it is a wonderful corrective to others as well as to themselves.

My French friend, for instance, after looking at some of my daubs, took me round the galleries of Paris, pausing here and there. Wherever he paused, I found myself before a picture which I particularly admired. He then explained that it was quite easy to tell, from the kind of things I had been trying to do, what were the things I liked. Never having taken any interest in pictures till I tried to paint, I had no preconceived opinions. I just felt, for reasons I could not fathom, that I liked some much more than others. I was astonished that anyone else should, on the most cursory observation of my work, be able so surely to divine a taste which I had never consciously formed. My friend said that it is not a bad thing to know nothing at all about pictures, but to have a matured mind trained in other things and a new strong interest for painting. The elements are there from which a true taste in art can be formed with time and guidance, and there are no obstacles or imperfect conceptions in the way. I hope this is true. Certainly the last part is true.

Once you begin to study it, all Nature is equally interesting and equally charged with beauty. I was shown a picture by Cézanne of a blank wall of a house, which he had made instinct with the most delicate lights and colours. Now I often amuse myself when I am looking at a wall or a flat surface of any kind by trying to distinguish all the different colours and tints which can be discerned upon it, and considering whether these arise from reflections or from natural hue. You would be astonished the first time you tried this to see how many and what beautiful colours there are even in the most commonplace objects, and the more carefully and frequently you look the more variations do you perceive.

But these are no reasons for limiting oneself to the plainest and most ordinary objects and scenes. Mere prettiness of scene, to be sure, is not needed for a beautiful picture. In fact, artificially-made pretty places are very often a hindrance to a good picture. Nature will hardly stand a double process of beautification: one layer of idealism on top of another is too much of a good thing. But a vivid scene, a brilliant atmosphere, novel and charming lights, impressive contrasts, if they strike the eye all at once, arouse an interest and an ardour which will certainly be reflected in the work which you try to do, and will make it seem easier.

It would be interesting if some real authority investigated carefully the part which memory plays in painting. We look at the object with an intent regard, then at the palette, and thirdly at the canvas. The canvas receives a message dispatched usually a few seconds before from the natural object. But it has come through a post-office *en route*. It has been transmitted in code. It has been turned from light into paint. It reaches the canvas a cryptogram. Not until it has been placed in its correct relation to everything else that is on the canvas can it be deciphered, is its meaning apparent, is it translated once again from mere pigment into light. And the light this time is not of Nature but of Art. The whole of this considerable process is carried through on the wings or the wheels of memory. In most cases we think it is the wings—airy and quick like a butterfly from flower to flower. But all heavy traffic and all that has to go a long journey must travel on wheels.

In painting in the open air the sequence of actions is so rapid that the process of translation into and out of pigment may seem to be unconscious. But all the greatest landscapes have been painted indoors, and often long after the first impressions were gathered. In a dim cellar the Dutch or Italian master recreated the gleaming ice of a Netherlands carnival or the lustrous sunshine of Venice or the Campagna. Here, then, is required a formidable memory of the visual kind. Not only do we develop our powers of observation, but also those of carrying the record—of carrying it through an extraneous medium and of reproducing it, hours, days, or even months after the scene has vanished or the sunlight died.

I was told by a friend that when Whistler guided a school in Paris he made his pupils observe their model on the ground floor, and then run upstairs and paint their picture piece by piece on the floor above. As they became more proficient he put their easels up a storey higher, till at last the *élite* were scampering with their decision up six flights into the attic—praying it would not evaporate on the way. This is, perhaps, only a tale. But it shows effectively of what enormous importance a trained, accurate, retentive memory must be to an artist; and conversely what a useful exercise painting may be for the development of an accurate and retentive memory.

There is no better exercise for the would-be artist than to study and devour a picture, and then, without looking at it again, to attempt the next day to reproduce it. Nothing can more exactly measure the progress both of observation and memory. It is still harder to compose out of many separate, well-retained impressions, aided though they be by sketches and colour notes, a new complete conception. But this is the only way in which great landscapes have been painted—or can be painted. The size of the canvas alone precludes its being handled out of doors. The fleeting light imposes a rigid time-limit. The same light never returns. One cannot go back day after day without the picture getting stale. The painter must choose between a rapid impression, fresh and warm and living, but probably deserving only of a short life, and the cold, profound, intense effort of memory, knowledge, and willpower, prolonged perhaps for weeks, from which a masterpiece can alone result. It is much better not to fret too much about the latter. Leave to the masters of art trained by a lifetime of devotion the wonderful process of picture-building and picture-creation. Go out into the sunlight and be happy with what you see.

Painting is complete as a distraction. I know of nothing which, without exhausting the body, more entirely absorbs the mind. Whatever the worries of the hour or the threats of the future, once the picture has begun to flow along, there is no room for them in the mental screen. They pass out into shadow and darkness. All one's mental light, such as it is, becomes concentrated on the task. Time stands respectfully aside, and it is only after many hesitations that luncheon knocks gruffly at the door. When I have had to stand up on parade, or even, I regret to say, in church, for half an hour at a time, I have always felt that the erect position is not natural to man, has only been painfully acquired, and is only with fatigue and difficulty maintained. But no one who is fond of painting finds the slightest inconvenience, as long as the interest holds, in standing to paint for three or four hours at a stretch.

Lastly, let me say a word on painting as a spur to travel. There is really nothing like it. Every day and all day is provided with its expedition and its occupation—cheap, attainable, innocent, absorbing, recuperative. The vain racket of the tourist gives place to the calm enjoyment of the philosopher, intensified by an enthralling sense of action and endeavour. Every country where the sun shines and every district in it has a theme of its own. The lights, the atmosphere, the aspect, the spirit, are all different; but each has its native charm. Even if you are only a poor painter you can feel the influence of the scene, guiding your brush, selecting the tubes you squeeze on to the palette. Even if you cannot portray it as you see it, you feel it, you know it, and you admire it for ever. When people rush about Europe in the train from one glittering centre of work or pleasure to another, passing—at enormous expense—through a series of mammoth hotels and blatant carnivals, they little know what they are missing, and how cheaply priceless things can be obtained. The painter wanders and loiters contentedly from place to place, always on the look out for some brilliant butterfly of a picture which can be caught and set up and carried safely home.

Now I am learning to like painting even on dull days. But in my hot youth I demanded sunshine. Sir William Orpen advised me to visit Avignon on account of its wonderful light, and certainly there is no more delightful centre for a would-be painter's activities: then Egypt, fierce and brilliant, presenting in infinite variety the single triplex theme of the Nile, the desert, and the sun; or Palestine, a land of rare beauty—the beauty of the turquoise and the opal—which well deserves the attention of some real artist, and has never been portrayed to the extent that is its due. And what of India? Who has ever interpreted its lurid splendours? But after all, if only the sun will shine, one does not need to go beyond one's own country. There is nothing more intense than the burnished steel and gold of a Highland stream; and at the beginning and close of almost every day the Thames displays to the citizens of London glories and delights which one must travel far to rival.